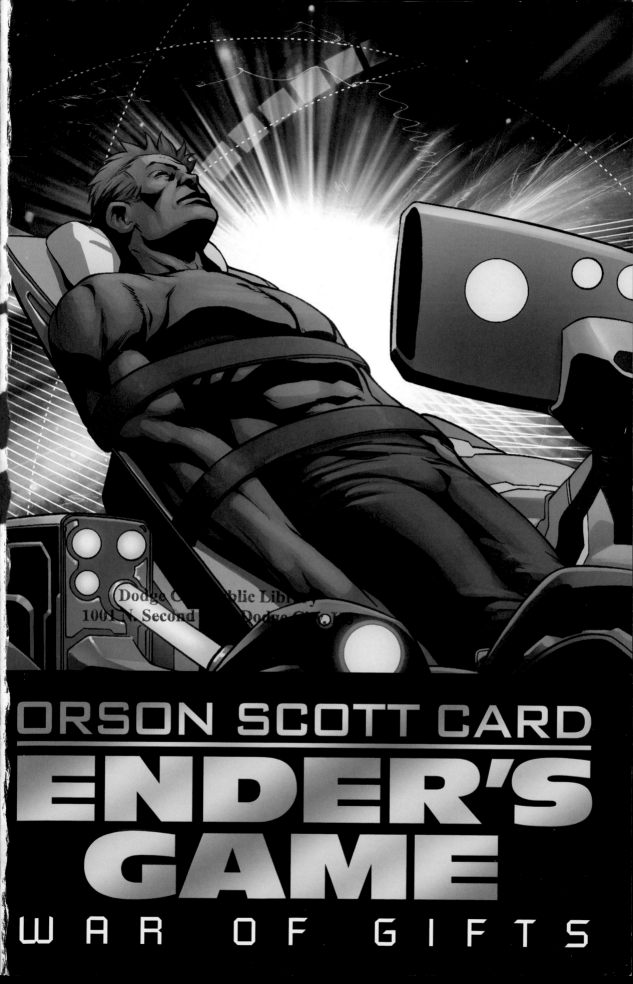

ORSON SCOTT CARD

ENDER'S GAME

WAR OF GIFTS

ORSON SCOTT CARD
ENDER'S GAME
WAR OF GIFTS

Creative Director & Executive Director: **ORSON SCOTT CARD**
Script: **JAKE BLACK** (*Recruiting Valentine* & *War of Gifts*)
& AARON JOHNSON (*Mazer in Prison* & *League War*)
Art: **TIMOTHY GREEN II** • Color Art: **EDWARD BOLA**
Pencils, *Mazer in Prison*: **POP MHAN** • Inks, *Mazer in Prison*: **NORMAN LEE**
Color Art, *Mazer in Prison*: **JIM CHARALAMPIDIS**
Cover Art: **TIMOTHY GREEN II** (*Recruiting Valentine* & *War of Gifts*) and
PASQUAL FERRY & FRANK D'ARMATA (*Mazer in Prison* & *League War*)
Letterer: **CORY PETIT**

Editor: **JORDAN D. WHITE** • Consulting Editor: **NICK LOWE**
Senior Editor: **MARK PANICCIA** • Vice President of Creative: **TOM MARVELLI**
Senior Vice President of Sales: **DAVID GABRIEL**
Senior Vice President of Strategic Development: **RUWAN JAYATILLEKE**

Special thanks to
KRISTINE CARD, KATHLEEN BELLAMY,
DARIAN ROBBINS, ANDREW BAUGHAN,
RALPH MACCHIO, LAUREN SANKOVITCH,
JIM NAUSEDAS, JIM MCCANN,
ARUNE SINGH & JEFF SUTER.

Senior Editor, Special Projects:
JEFF YOUNGQUIST
Senior Vice President of Sales:
DAVID GABRIEL
Book Designer:
RODOLFO MURAGUCHI

Collection Editor: **JENNIFER GRÜNWALD**
Assistant Editor: **ALEX STARBUCK**
Associate Editor: **JOHN DENNING**
Editor, Special Projects: **MARK D. BEAZLEY**

Editor in Chief: **JOE QUESADA**
Publisher: **DAN BUCKLEY**
Executive Producer:
ALAN FINE

ENDER'S GAME: WAR OF GIFTS. Contains material originally published in magazine form as ENDER'S GAME: RECRUITING VALENTINE, WAR OF GIFTS, MAZER IN PRISON and THE LEAGUE WAR. First printing 2010.
ISBN# 978-0-7851-3590-6. Published by MARVEL WORLDWIDE, INC., a subsidiary of MARVEL ENTERTAINMENT, LLC. OFFICE OF PUBLICATION: 417 5th Avenue, New York, NY 10016. Copyright © 2009 and 2010
Orson Scott Card. All rights reserved. $24.99. per copy in the U.S. (GST #R127032852); Canadian Agreement #40668537. All characters featured in this issue and the distinctive names and likenesses thereof, and all
related indicia are trademarks of Orson Scott Card. No similarity between any of the names, characters, persons, and/or institutions in this magazine with those of any living or dead person or institution is intended,
and any such similarity which may exist is purely coincidental. Marvel and its logos are TM & © Marvel Characters, Inc. **Printed in the U.S.A.** ALAN FINE, EVP - Office of the President, Marvel Worldwide, Inc. and
EVP & CMO Marvel Characters B.V.; DAN BUCKLEY, Chief Executive Officer and Publisher - Print, Animation & Digital Media; JIM SOKOLOWSKI, Chief Operating Officer; DAVID GABRIEL, SVP of Publishing Sales &
Circulation; DAVID BOGART, SVP of Business Affairs & Talent Management; MICHAEL PASCIULLO, VP Merchandising & Communications; JIM O'KEEFE, VP of Operations & Logistics; DAN CARR, Executive Director of
Publishing Technology; JUSTIN F. GABRIE, Director of Publishing & Editorial Operations; SUSAN CRESPI, Editorial Operations Manager; ALEX MORALES, Publishing Operations Manager; STAN LEE, Chairman Emeritus.
For information regarding advertising in Marvel Comics or on Marvel.com, please contact Ron Stern, VP of Business Development, at rstern@marvel.com. For Marvel subscription inquiries, please call 800-217-9158.
Manufactured between 4/19/10 and 5/19/10 by R.R. DONNELLEY, INC., SALEM, VA, USA.

10 9 8 7 6 5 4 3 2 1

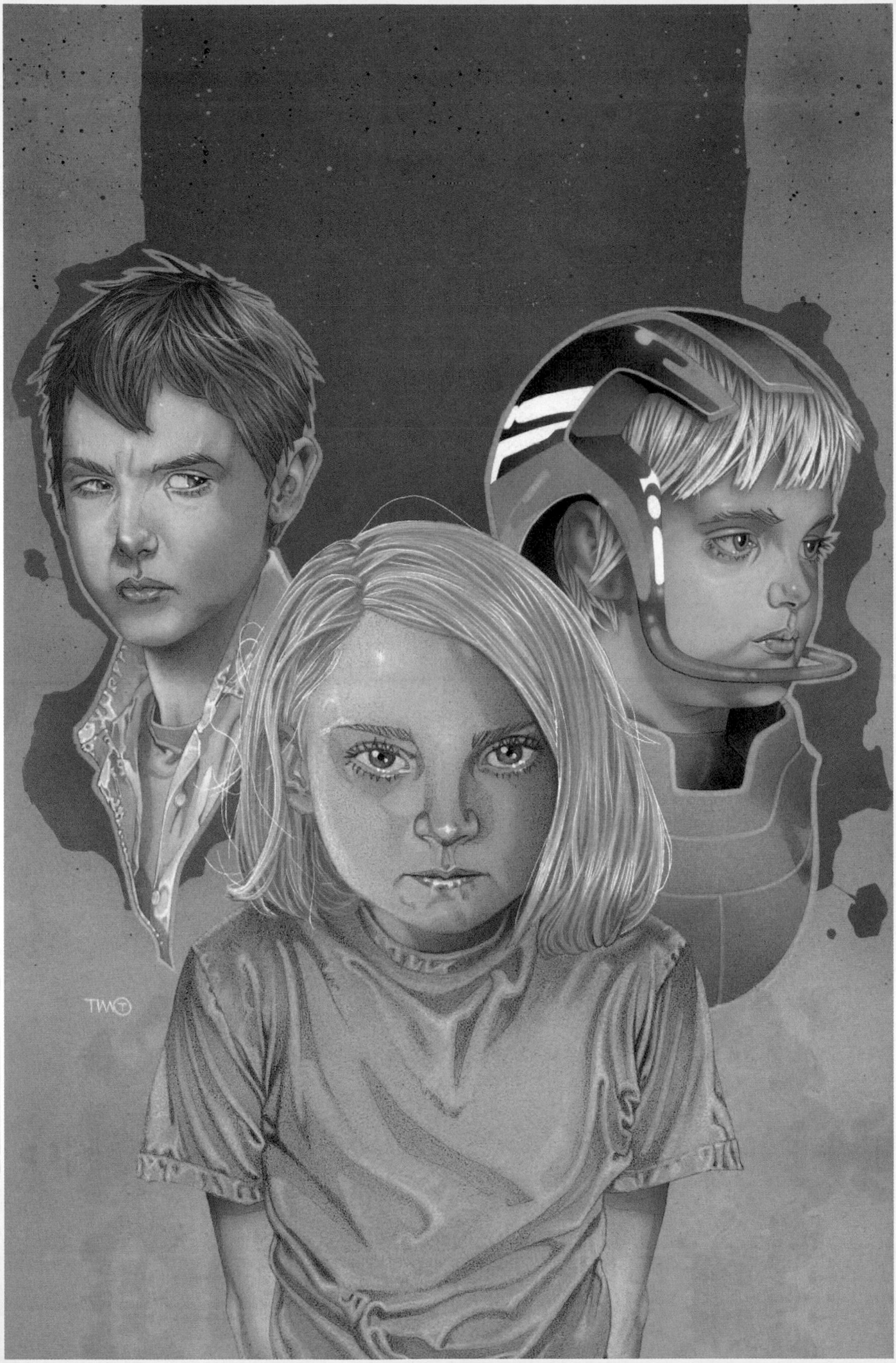

RECRUITING VALENTINE

TO: Wiggin, John Paul; Wiggin, Theresa Brown
FROM: Deming, R.S.
SUBJECT: Valentine's Application

Mr. and Mrs. Wiggin,

We have reviewed your daughter Valentine's application to study at Western Guilford Middle School, and are glad to accept her as one of our new students this fall.

As you know, Western Guilford is not only one of the most prestigious places of learning in Greensboro, North Carolina, it is also recognized nationwide for its faculty mentoring programs and student success rates. Valentine will find our classes and teachers to be superior to any she has experienced before.

Thanks to close working relationships with the Hegemony and International Fleet, our students are uniquely prepared to tackle the challenges in our ever-changing world.

We look forward to receiving Valentine this fall.

Sincerely,

R.S. Deming
Director of Admissions,
Western Guilford Middle School

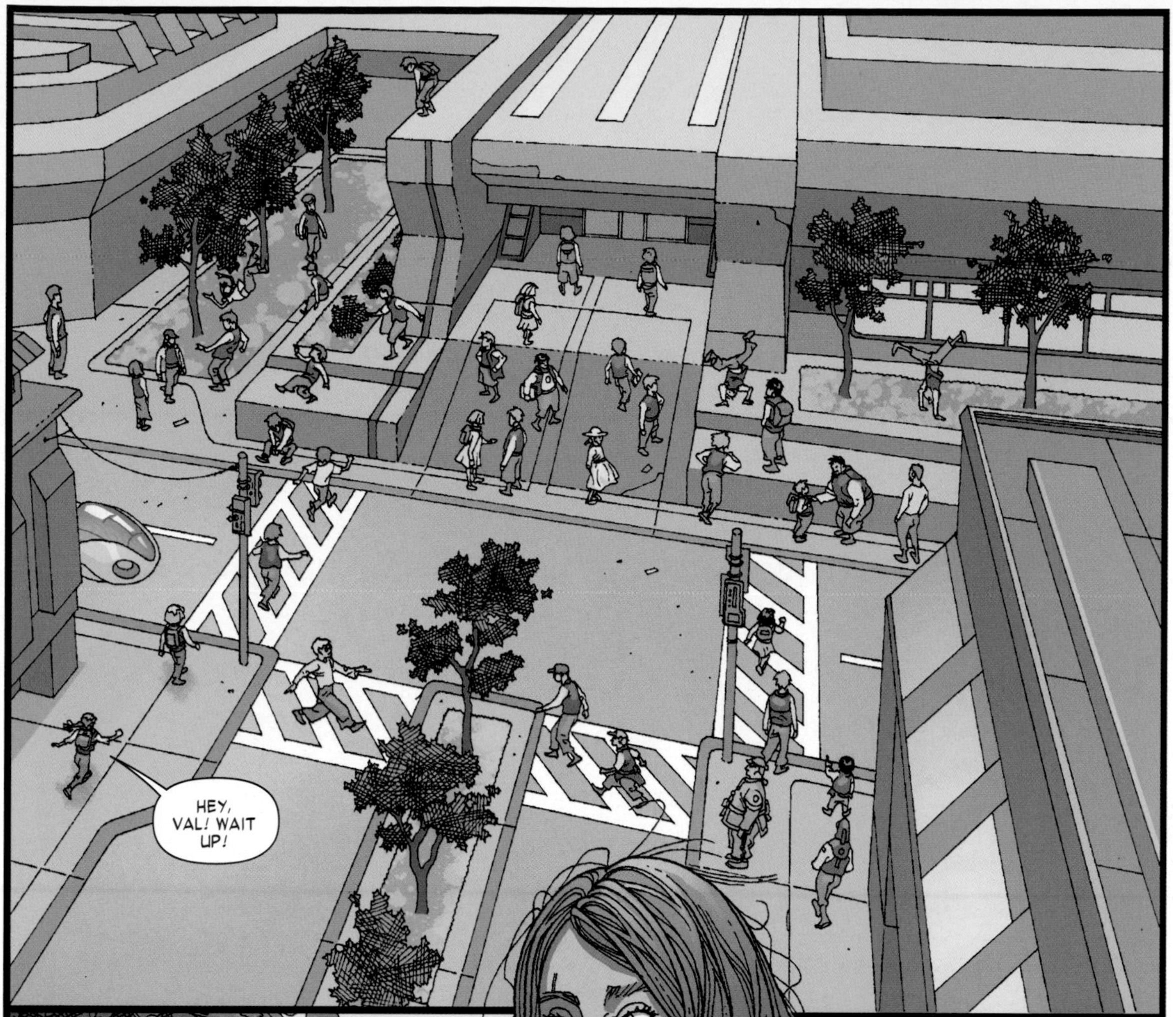
HEY, VAL! WAIT UP!

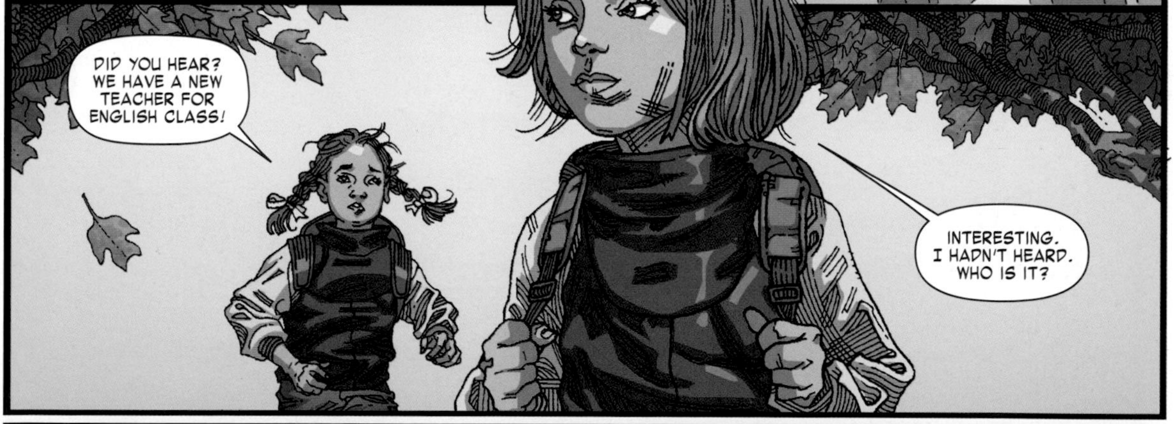
DID YOU HEAR? WE HAVE A NEW TEACHER FOR ENGLISH CLASS!
INTERESTING. I HADN'T HEARD. WHO IS IT?

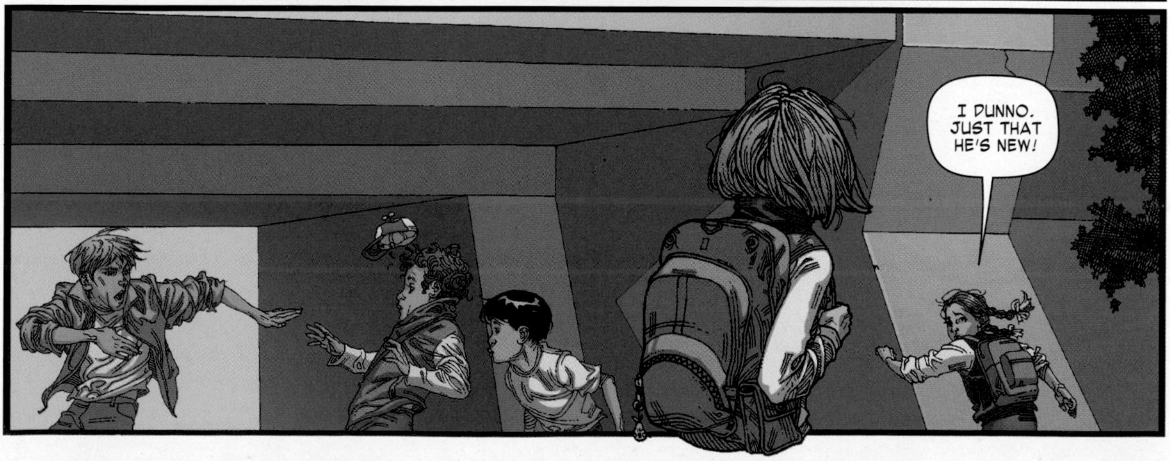
I DUNNO. JUST THAT HE'S NEW!

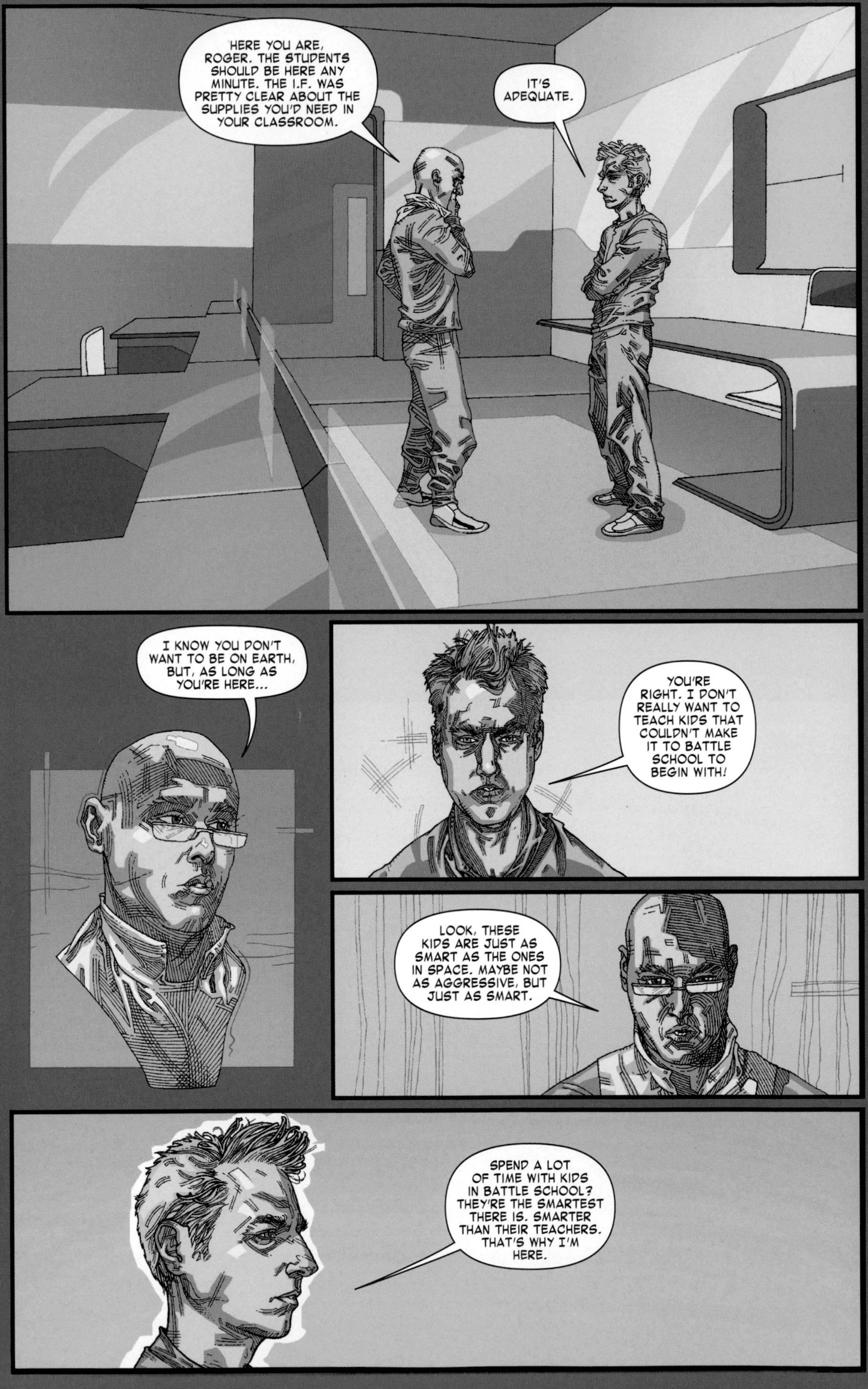
HERE YOU ARE, ROGER. THE STUDENTS SHOULD BE HERE ANY MINUTE. THE I.F. WAS PRETTY CLEAR ABOUT THE SUPPLIES YOU'D NEED IN YOUR CLASSROOM.
IT'S ADEQUATE.
I KNOW YOU DON'T WANT TO BE ON EARTH, BUT, AS LONG AS YOU'RE HERE...
YOU'RE RIGHT. I DON'T REALLY WANT TO TEACH KIDS THAT COULDN'T MAKE IT TO BATTLE SCHOOL TO BEGIN WITH!
LOOK, THESE KIDS ARE JUST AS SMART AS THE ONES IN SPACE. MAYBE NOT AS AGGRESSIVE, BUT JUST AS SMART.
SPEND A LOT OF TIME WITH KIDS IN BATTLE SCHOOL? THEY'RE THE SMARTEST THERE IS. SMARTER THAN THEIR TEACHERS. THAT'S WHY I'M HERE.

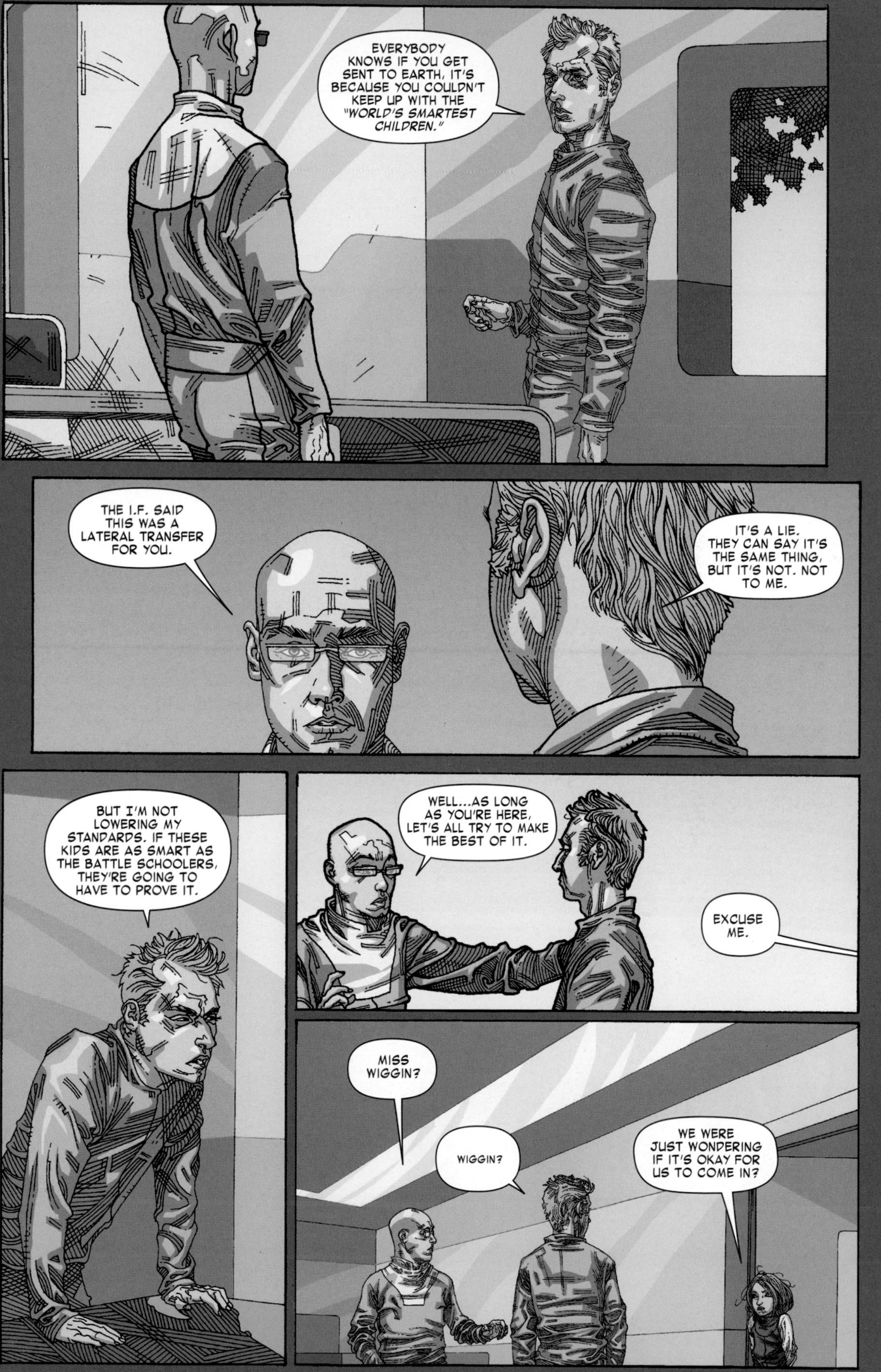
EVERYBODY KNOWS IF YOU GET SENT TO EARTH, IT'S BECAUSE YOU COULDN'T KEEP UP WITH THE "WORLD'S SMARTEST CHILDREN."
THE I.F. SAID THIS WAS A LATERAL TRANSFER FOR YOU.
IT'S A LIE. THEY CAN SAY IT'S THE SAME THING, BUT IT'S NOT. NOT TO ME.
BUT I'M NOT LOWERING MY STANDARDS. IF THESE KIDS ARE AS SMART AS THE BATTLE SCHOOLERS, THEY'RE GOING TO HAVE TO PROVE IT.
WELL...AS LONG AS YOU'RE HERE, LET'S ALL TRY TO MAKE THE BEST OF IT.
EXCUSE ME.
MISS WIGGIN?
WIGGIN?
WE WERE JUST WONDERING IF IT'S OKAY FOR US TO COME IN?

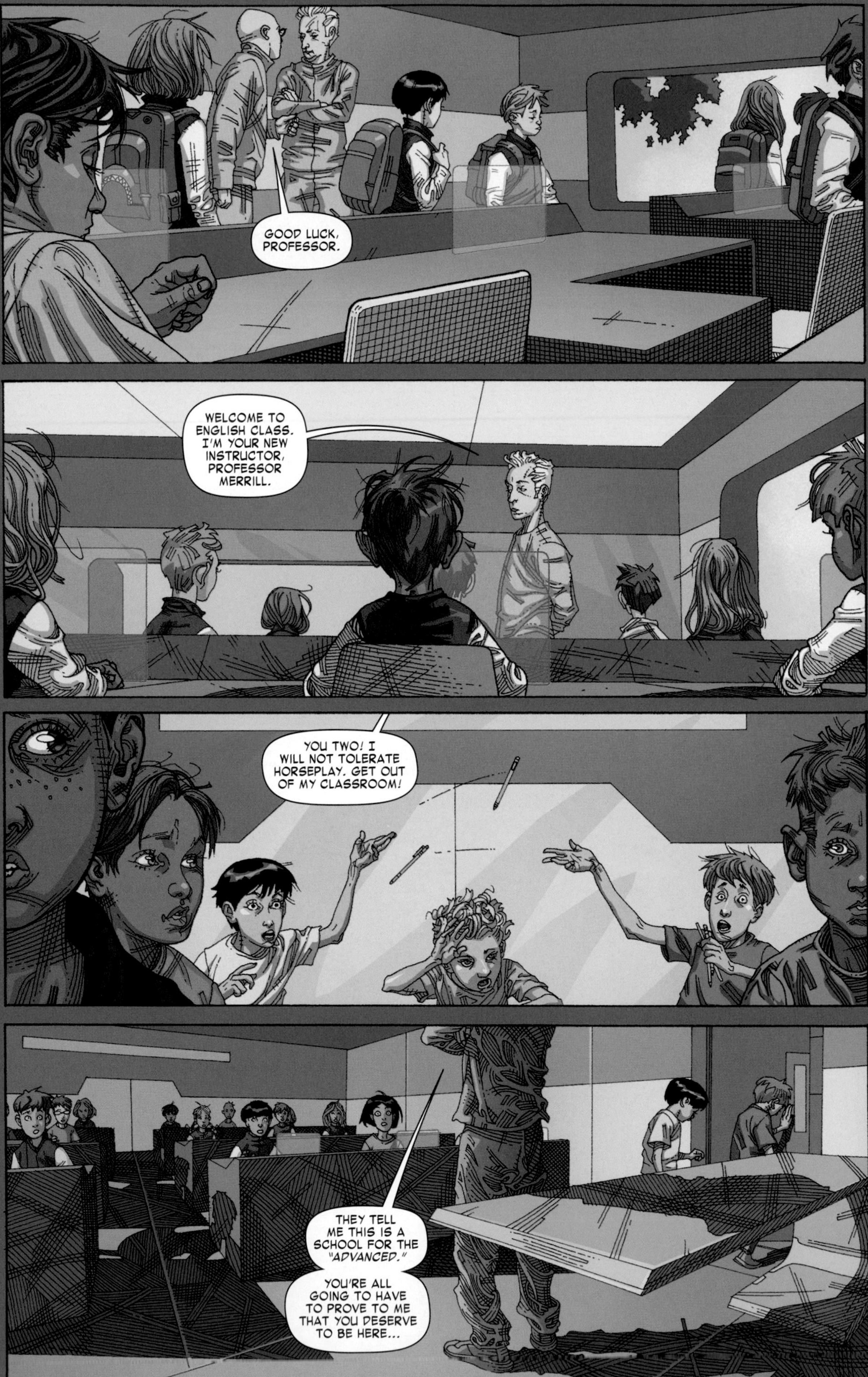
GOOD LUCK, PROFESSOR.
WELCOME TO ENGLISH CLASS. I'M YOUR NEW INSTRUCTOR, PROFESSOR MERRILL.
YOU TWO! I WILL NOT TOLERATE HORSEPLAY. GET OUT OF MY CLASSROOM!
THEY TELL ME THIS IS A SCHOOL FOR THE "ADVANCED."
YOU'RE ALL GOING TO HAVE TO PROVE TO ME THAT YOU DESERVE TO BE HERE...

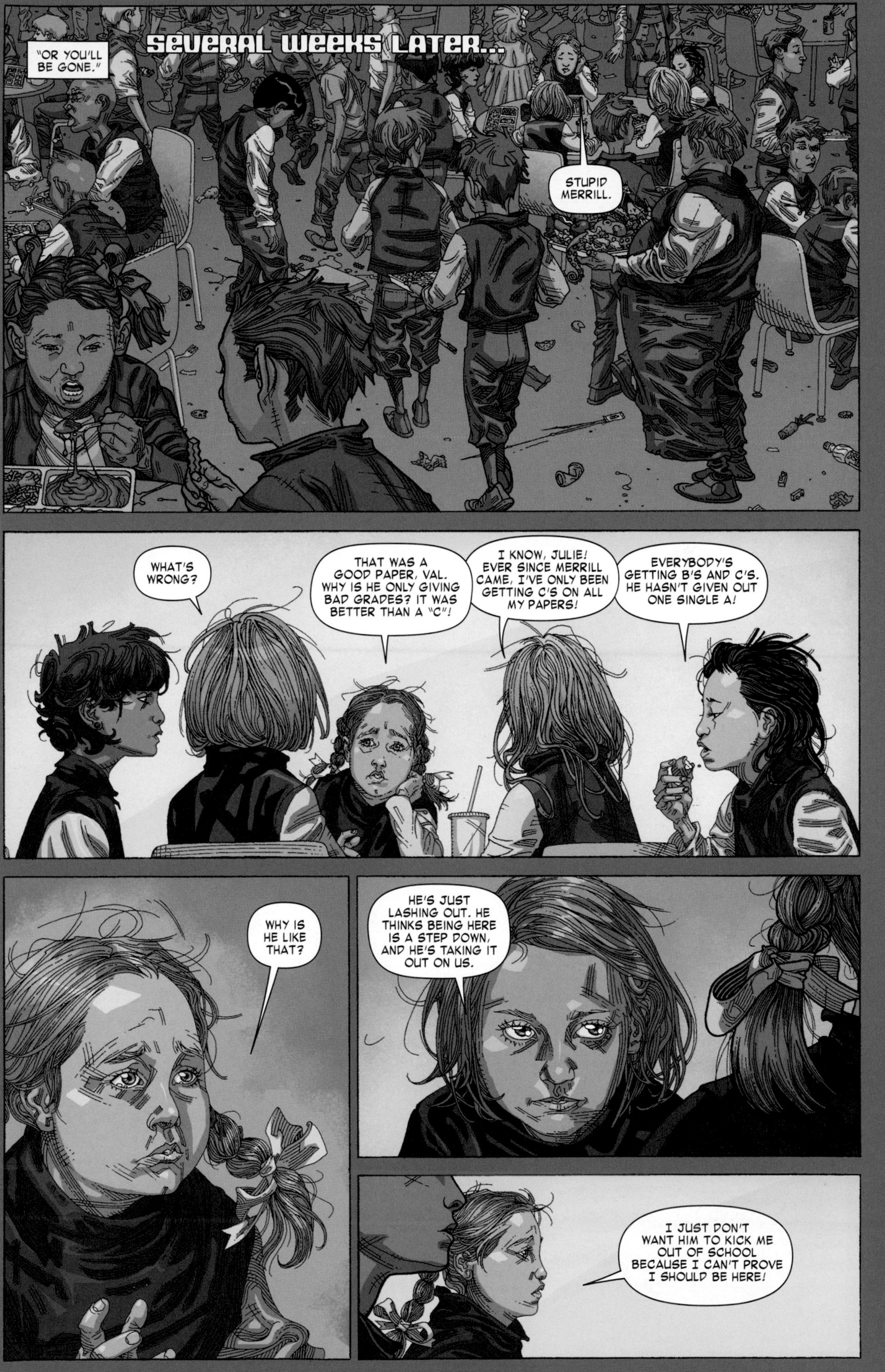
"OR YOU'LL BE GONE."
SEVERAL WEEKS LATER...
STUPID MERRILL.
WHAT'S WRONG?
THAT WAS A GOOD PAPER, VAL. WHY IS HE ONLY GIVING BAD GRADES? IT WAS BETTER THAN A "C"!
I KNOW, JULIE! EVER SINCE MERRILL CAME, I'VE ONLY BEEN GETTING C'S ON ALL MY PAPERS!
EVERYBODY'S GETTING B'S AND C'S. HE HASN'T GIVEN OUT ONE SINGLE A!
WHY IS HE LIKE THAT?
HE'S JUST LASHING OUT. HE THINKS BEING HERE IS A STEP DOWN, AND HE'S TAKING IT OUT ON US.
I JUST DON'T WANT HIM TO KICK ME OUT OF SCHOOL BECAUSE I CAN'T PROVE I SHOULD BE HERE!

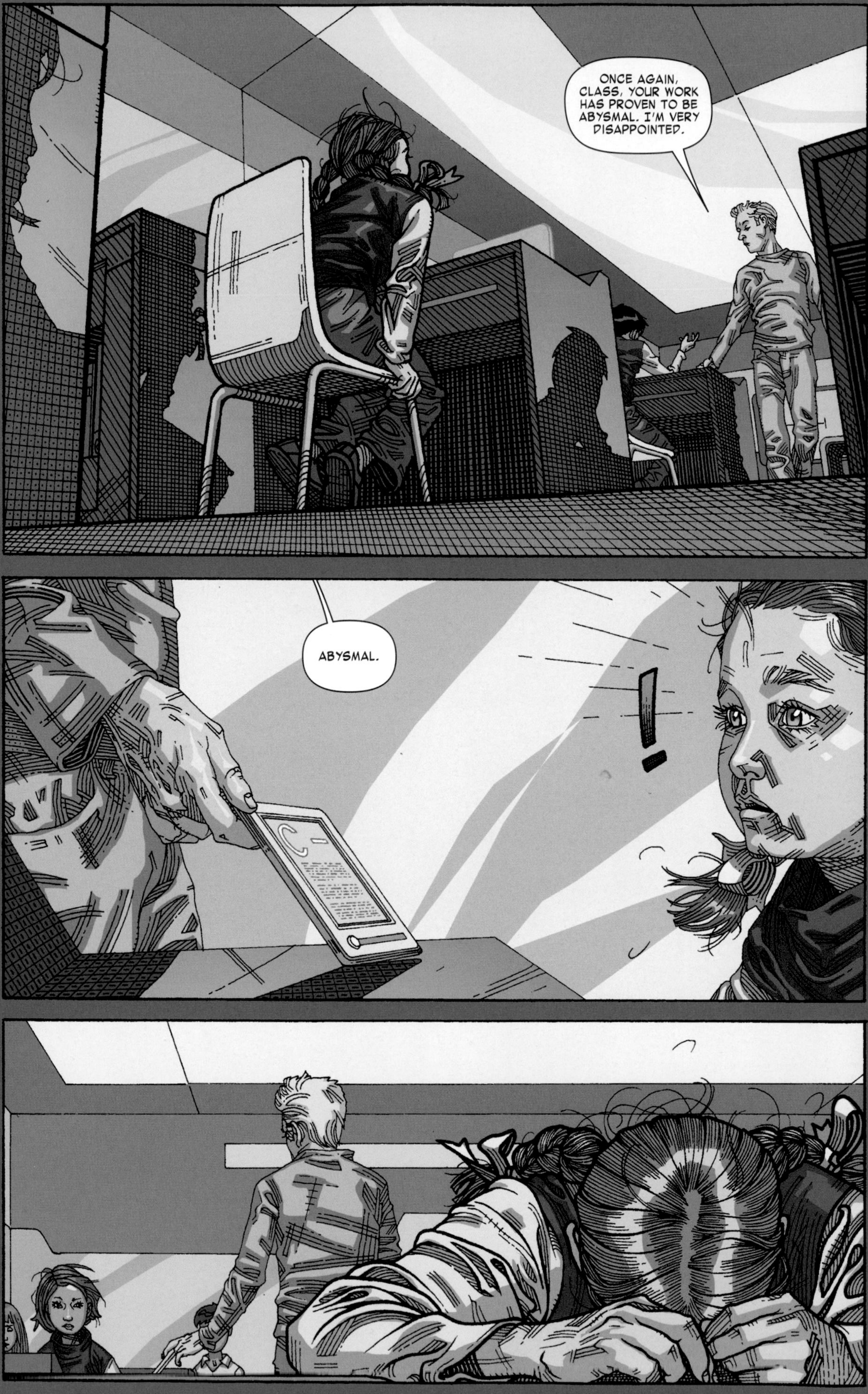
ONCE AGAIN, CLASS, YOUR WORK HAS PROVEN TO BE ABYSMAL. I'M VERY DISAPPOINTED.
ABYSMAL.
!
C-

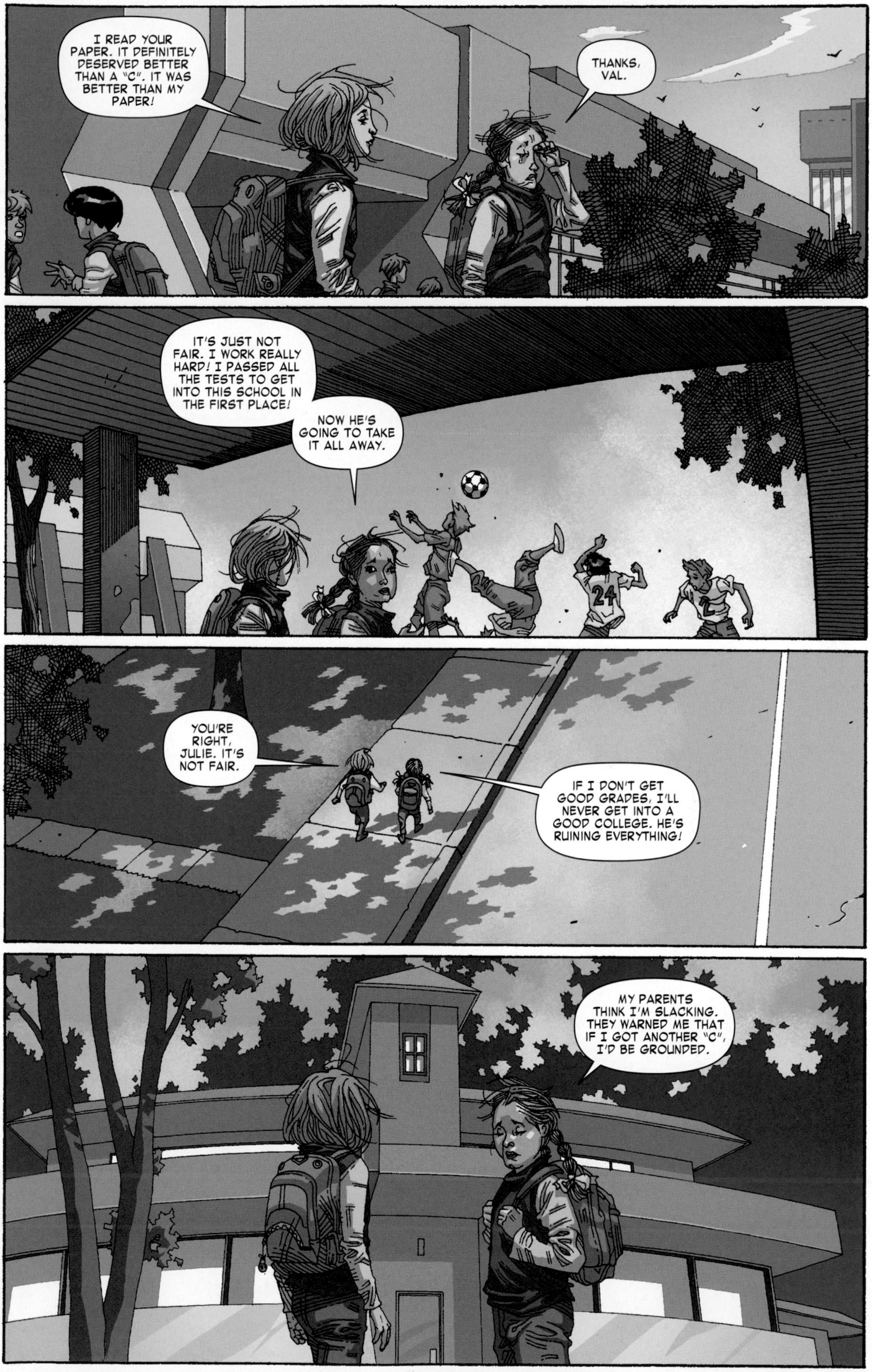
I READ YOUR PAPER. IT DEFINITELY DESERVED BETTER THAN A "C". IT WAS BETTER THAN MY PAPER!
THANKS, VAL.
IT'S JUST NOT FAIR. I WORK REALLY HARD! I PASSED ALL THE TESTS TO GET INTO THIS SCHOOL IN THE FIRST PLACE!
NOW HE'S GOING TO TAKE IT ALL AWAY.
24
YOU'RE RIGHT, JULIE. IT'S NOT FAIR.
IF I DON'T GET GOOD GRADES, I'LL NEVER GET INTO A GOOD COLLEGE. HE'S RUINING EVERYTHING!
MY PARENTS THINK I'M SLACKING. THEY WARNED ME THAT IF I GOT ANOTHER "C", I'D BE GROUNDED.

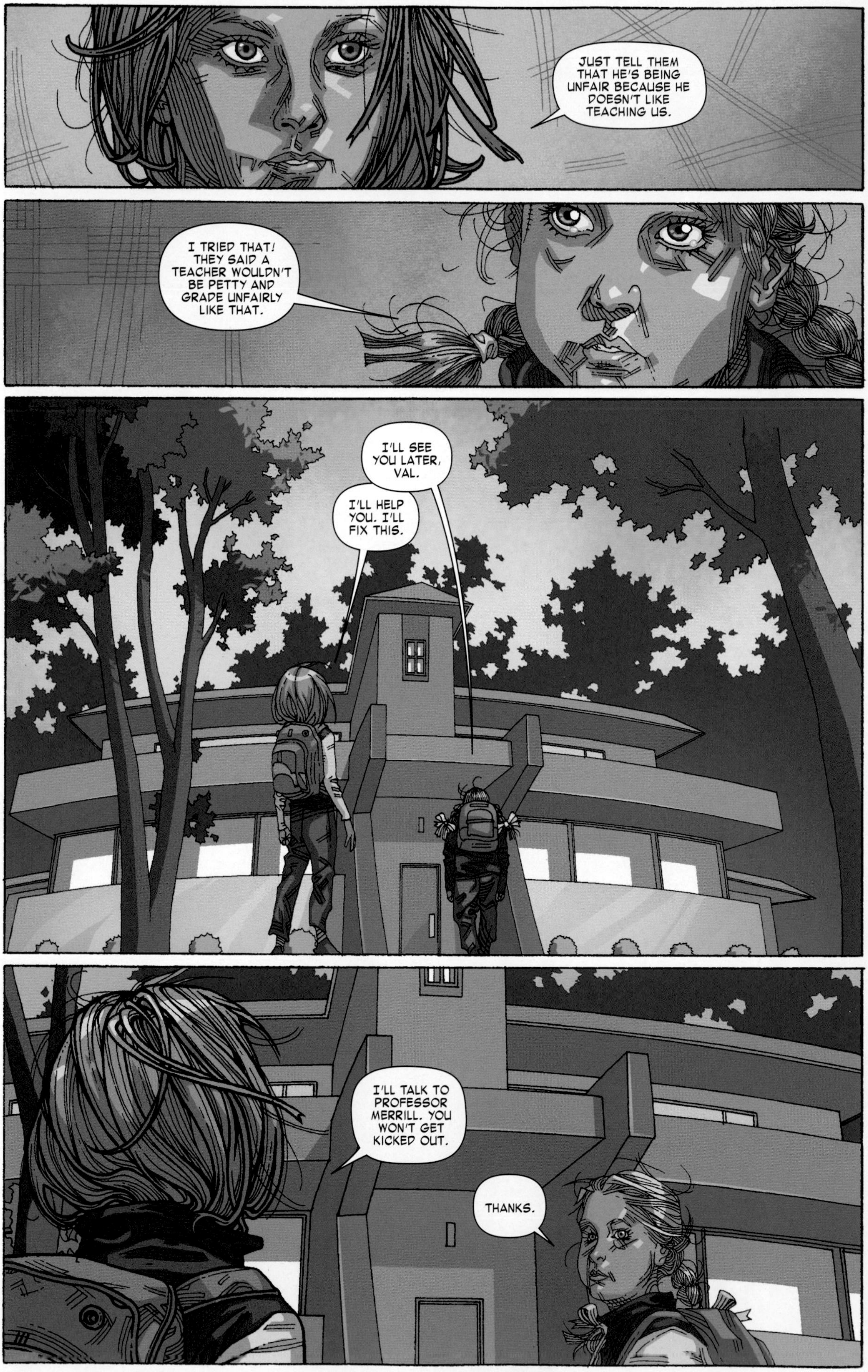
JUST TELL THEM THAT HE'S BEING UNFAIR BECAUSE HE DOESN'T LIKE TEACHING US.
I TRIED THAT! THEY SAID A TEACHER WOULDN'T BE PETTY AND GRADE UNFAIRLY LIKE THAT.
I'LL SEE YOU LATER, VAL.
I'LL HELP YOU. I'LL FIX THIS.
I'LL TALK TO PROFESSOR MERRILL. YOU WON'T GET KICKED OUT.
THANKS.

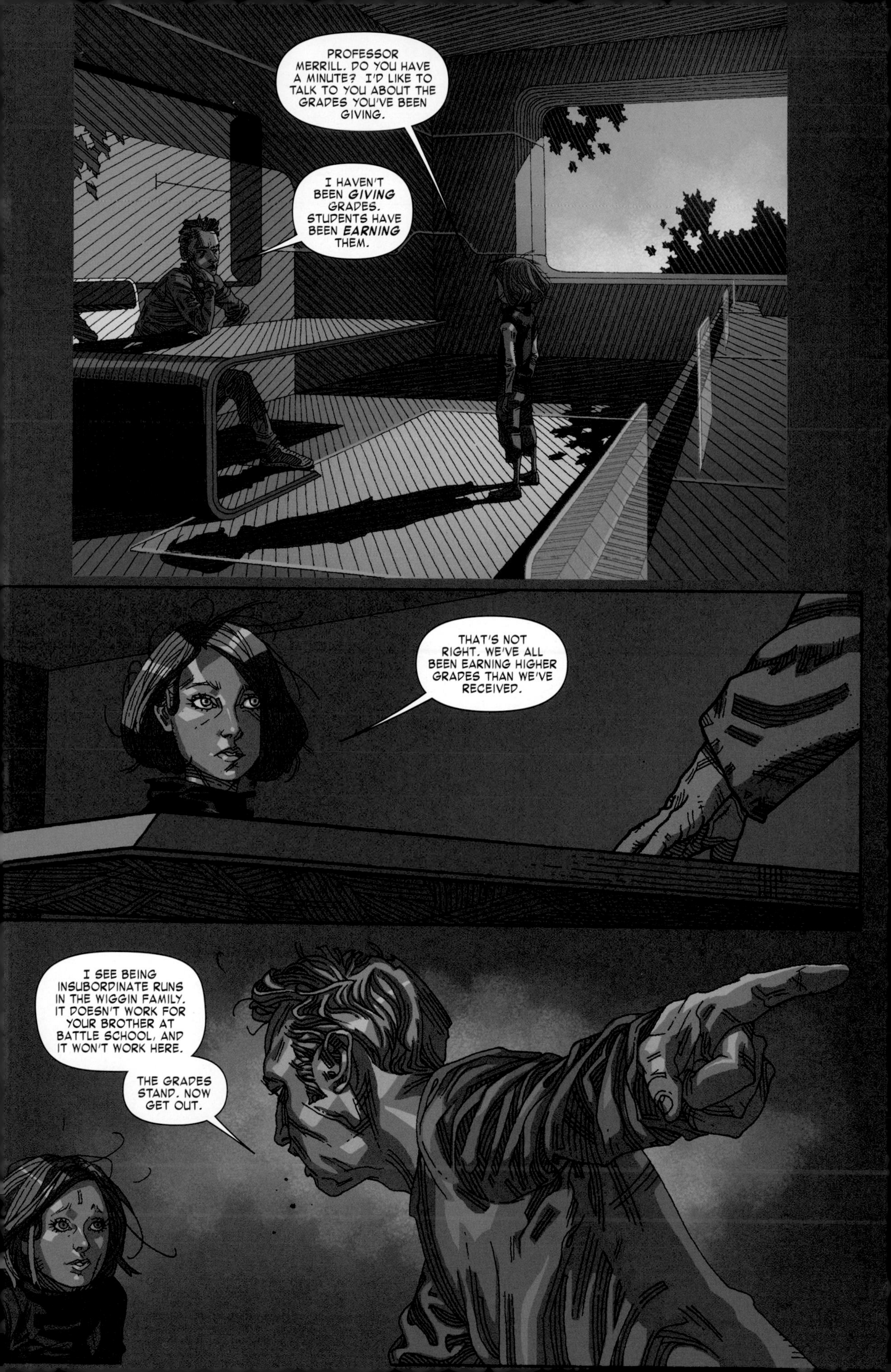
PROFESSOR MERRILL. DO YOU HAVE A MINUTE? I'D LIKE TO TALK TO YOU ABOUT THE GRADES YOU'VE BEEN GIVING.
I HAVEN'T BEEN *GIVING* GRADES. STUDENTS HAVE BEEN *EARNING* THEM.
THAT'S NOT RIGHT. WE'VE ALL BEEN EARNING HIGHER GRADES THAN WE'VE RECEIVED.
I SEE BEING INSUBORDINATE RUNS IN THE WIGGIN FAMILY. IT DOESN'T WORK FOR YOUR BROTHER AT BATTLE SCHOOL, AND IT WON'T WORK HERE.
THE GRADES STAND. NOW GET OUT.

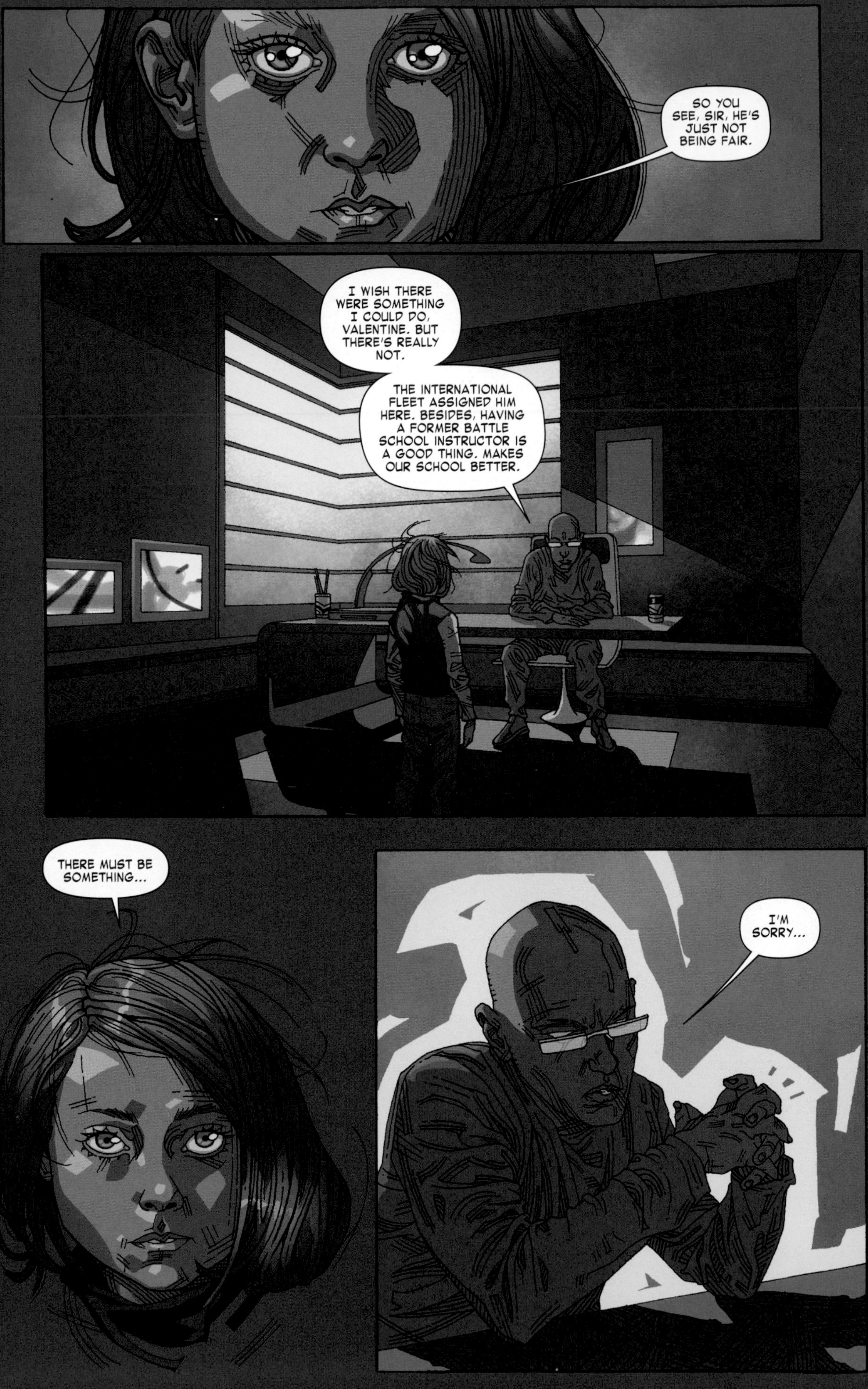
SO YOU SEE, SIR, HE'S JUST NOT BEING FAIR.
I WISH THERE WERE SOMETHING I COULD DO, VALENTINE. BUT THERE'S REALLY NOT.
THE INTERNATIONAL FLEET ASSIGNED HIM HERE. BESIDES, HAVING A FORMER BATTLE SCHOOL INSTRUCTOR IS A GOOD THING. MAKES OUR SCHOOL BETTER.
THERE MUST BE SOMETHING...
I'M SORRY...

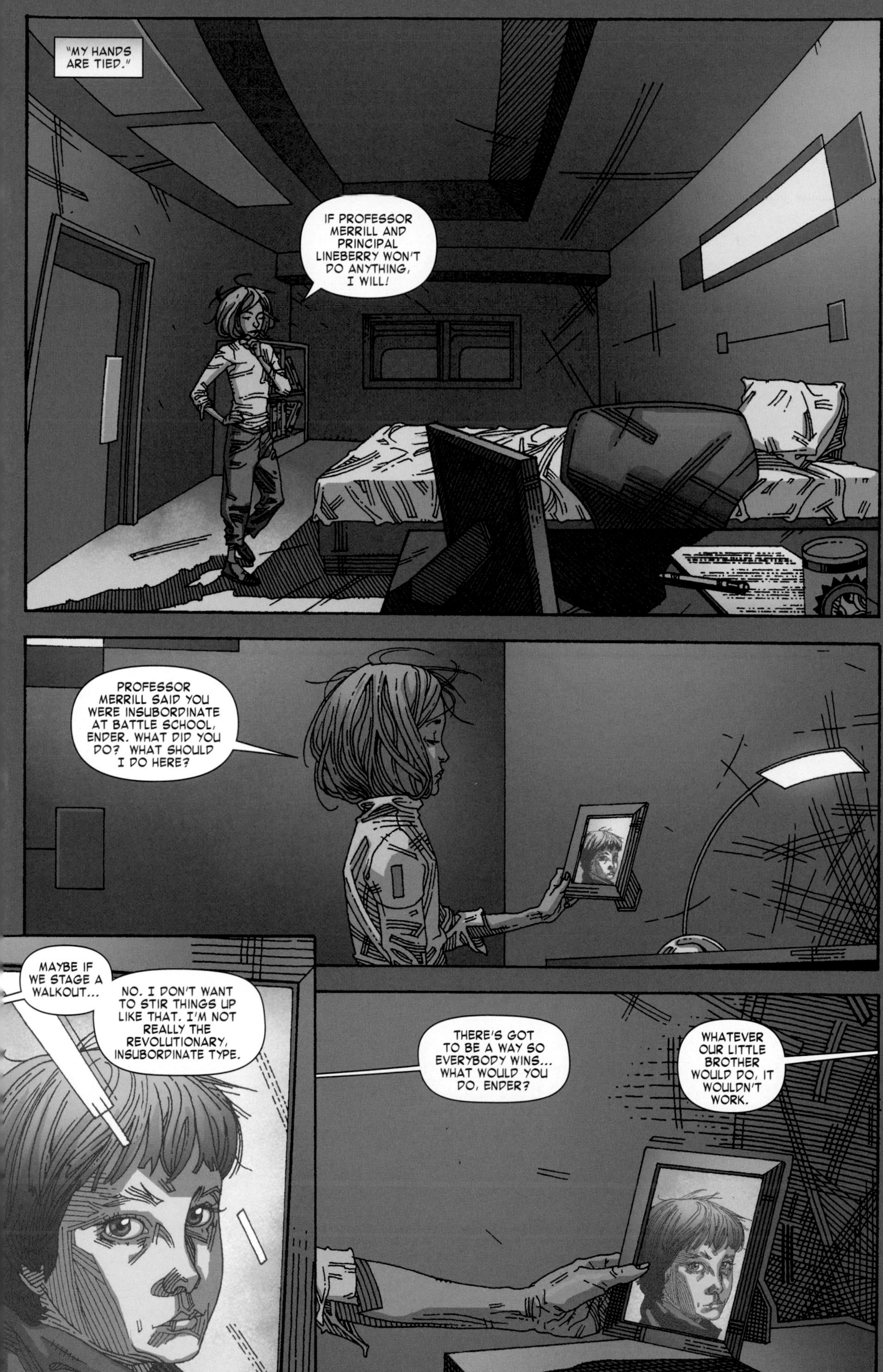
"MY HANDS ARE TIED."
IF PROFESSOR MERRILL AND PRINCIPAL LINEBERRY WON'T DO ANYTHING, I WILL!
PROFESSOR MERRILL SAID YOU WERE INSUBORDINATE AT BATTLE SCHOOL, ENDER. WHAT DID YOU DO? WHAT SHOULD I DO HERE?
MAYBE IF WE STAGE A WALKOUT...
NO. I DON'T WANT TO STIR THINGS UP LIKE THAT. I'M NOT REALLY THE REVOLUTIONARY, INSUBORDINATE TYPE.
THERE'S GOT TO BE A WAY SO EVERYBODY WINS... WHAT WOULD YOU DO, ENDER?
WHATEVER OUR LITTLE BROTHER WOULD DO, IT WOULDN'T WORK.

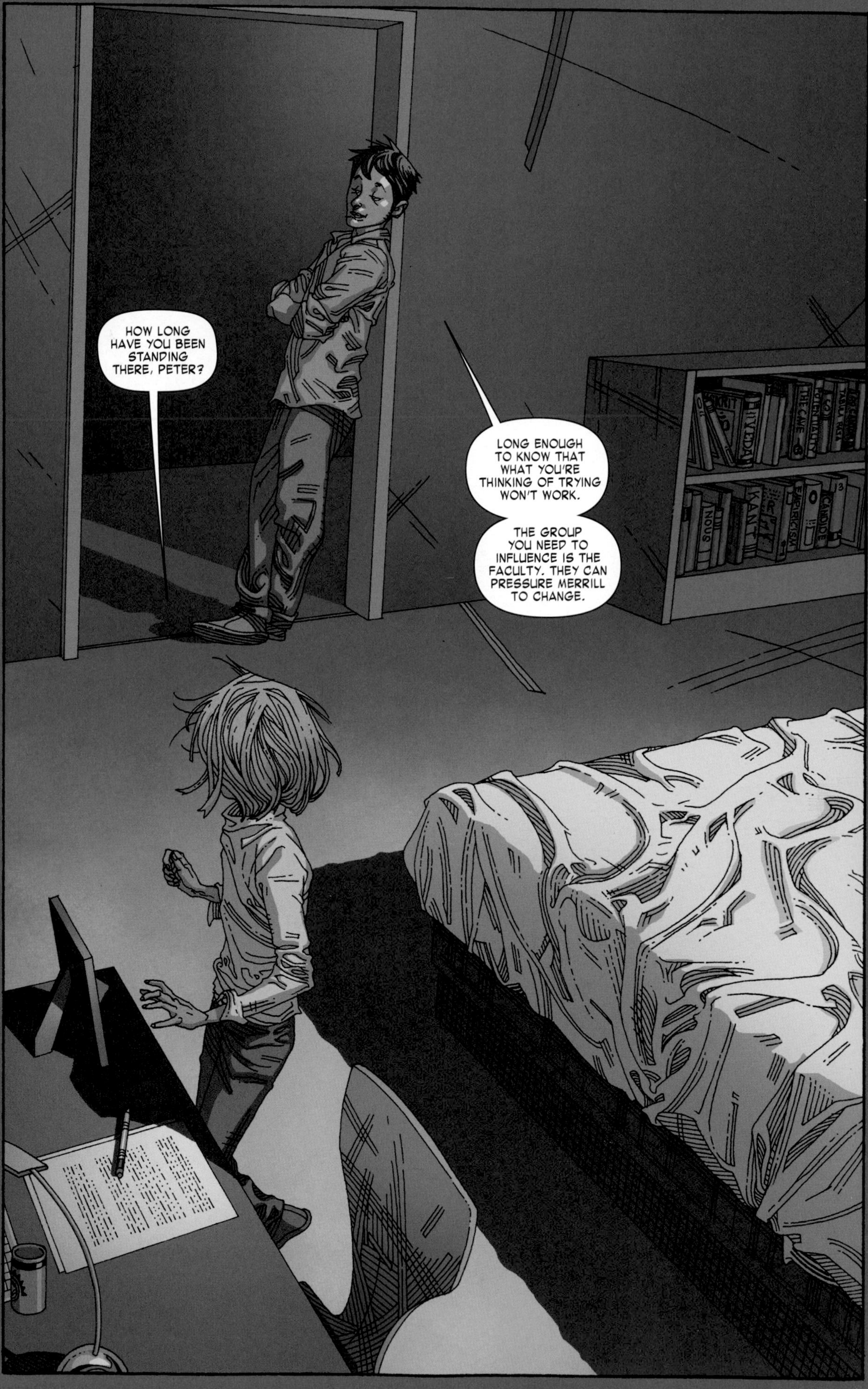
HOW LONG HAVE YOU BEEN STANDING THERE, PETER?
LONG ENOUGH TO KNOW THAT WHAT YOU'RE THINKING OF TRYING WON'T WORK.
THE GROUP YOU NEED TO INFLUENCE IS THE FACULTY. THEY CAN PRESSURE MERRILL TO CHANGE.

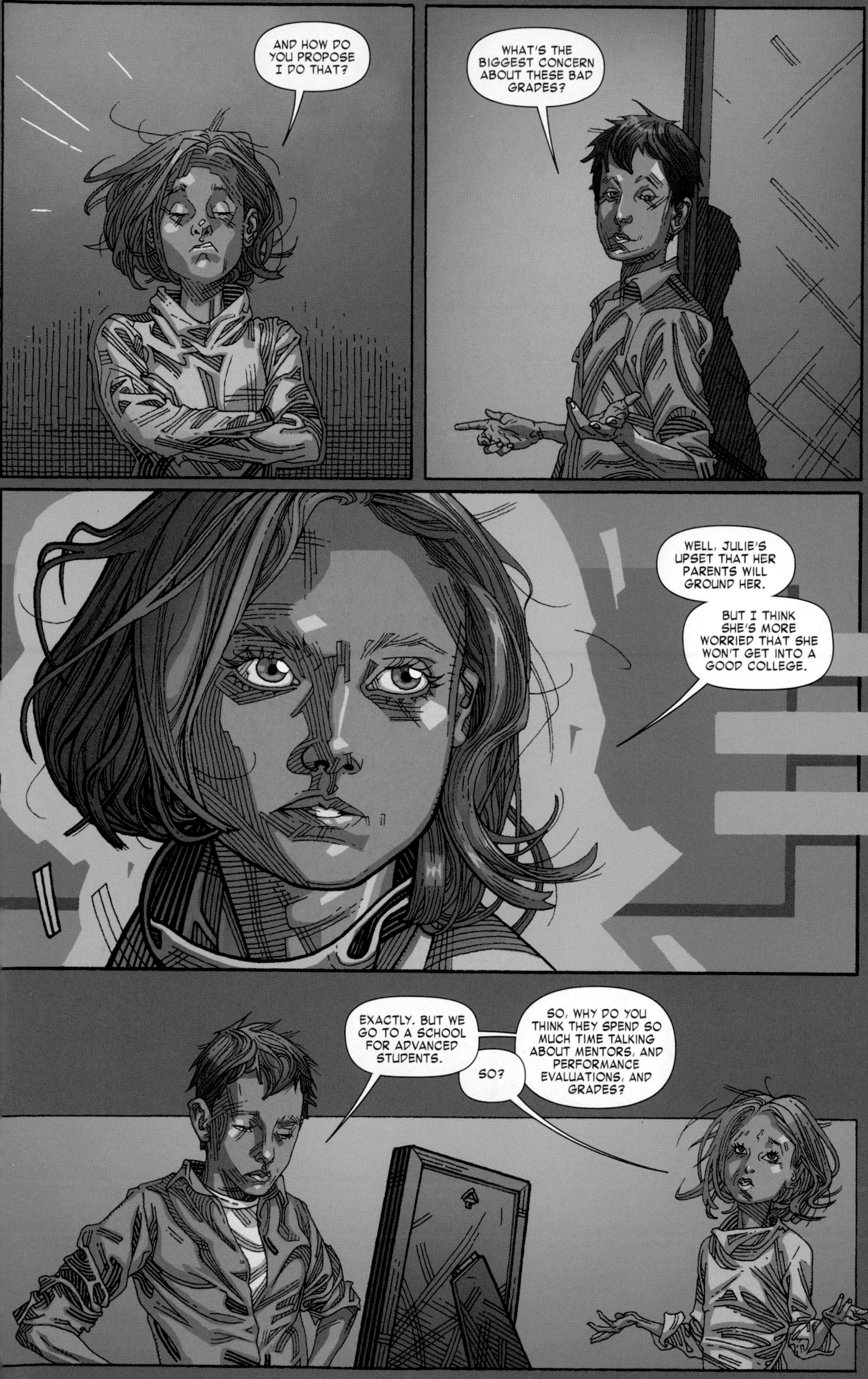
AND HOW DO YOU PROPOSE I DO THAT?
WHAT'S THE BIGGEST CONCERN ABOUT THESE BAD GRADES?
WELL, JULIE'S UPSET THAT HER PARENTS WILL GROUND HER.
BUT I THINK SHE'S MORE WORRIED THAT SHE WON'T GET INTO A GOOD COLLEGE.
EXACTLY. BUT WE GO TO A SCHOOL FOR ADVANCED STUDENTS.
SO?
SO, WHY DO YOU THINK THEY SPEND SO MUCH TIME TALKING ABOUT MENTORS, AND PERFORMANCE EVALUATIONS, AND GRADES?

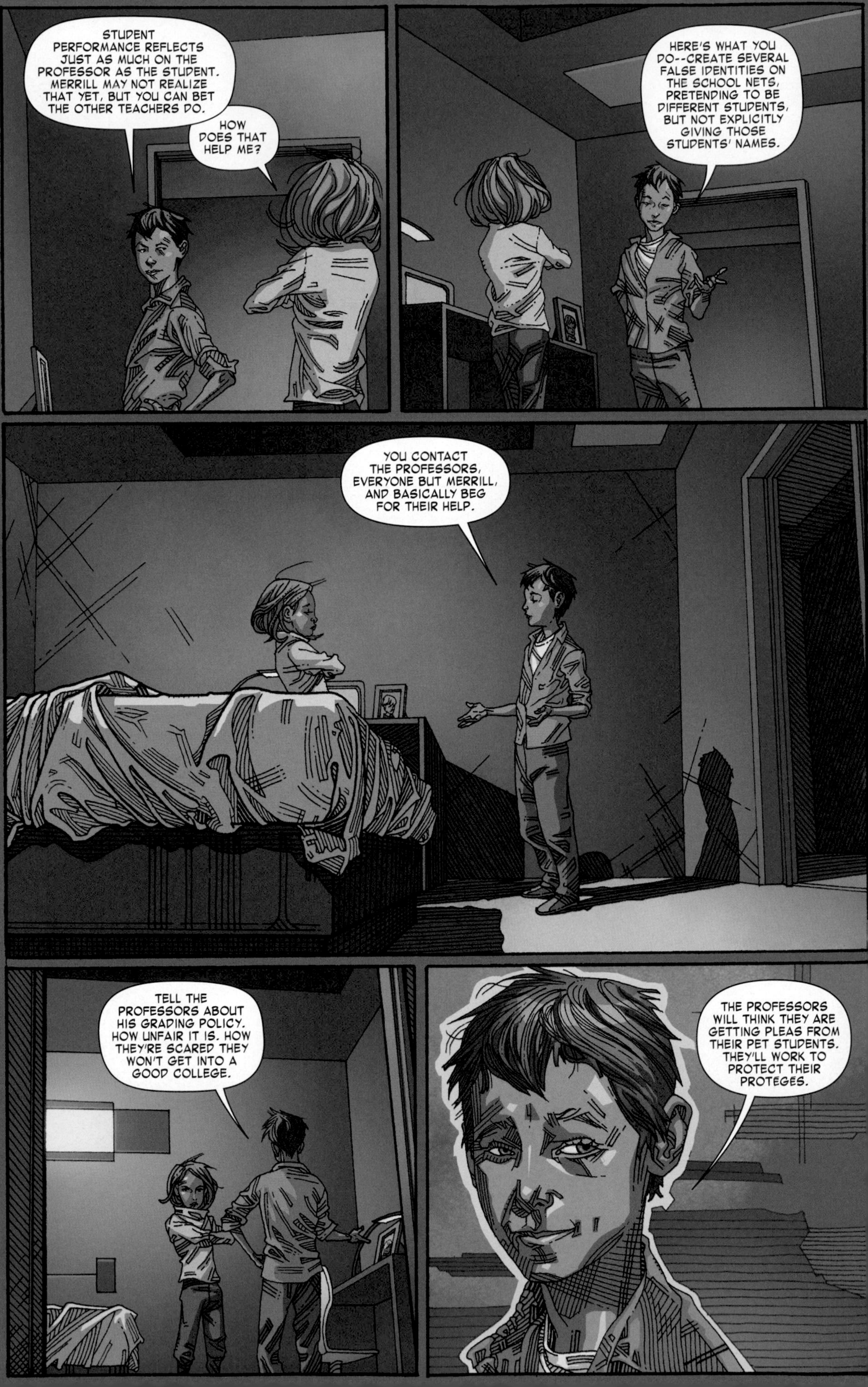
STUDENT PERFORMANCE REFLECTS JUST AS MUCH ON THE PROFESSOR AS THE STUDENT. MERRILL MAY NOT REALIZE THAT YET, BUT YOU CAN BET THE OTHER TEACHERS DO.
HOW DOES THAT HELP ME?
HERE'S WHAT YOU DO--CREATE SEVERAL FALSE IDENTITIES ON THE SCHOOL NETS, PRETENDING TO BE DIFFERENT STUDENTS, BUT NOT EXPLICITLY GIVING THOSE STUDENTS' NAMES.
YOU CONTACT THE PROFESSORS, EVERYONE BUT MERRILL, AND BASICALLY BEG FOR THEIR HELP.
TELL THE PROFESSORS ABOUT HIS GRADING POLICY. HOW UNFAIR IT IS. HOW THEY'RE SCARED THEY WON'T GET INTO A GOOD COLLEGE.
THE PROFESSORS WILL THINK THEY ARE GETTING PLEAS FROM THEIR PET STUDENTS. THEY'LL WORK TO PROTECT THEIR PROTEGES.

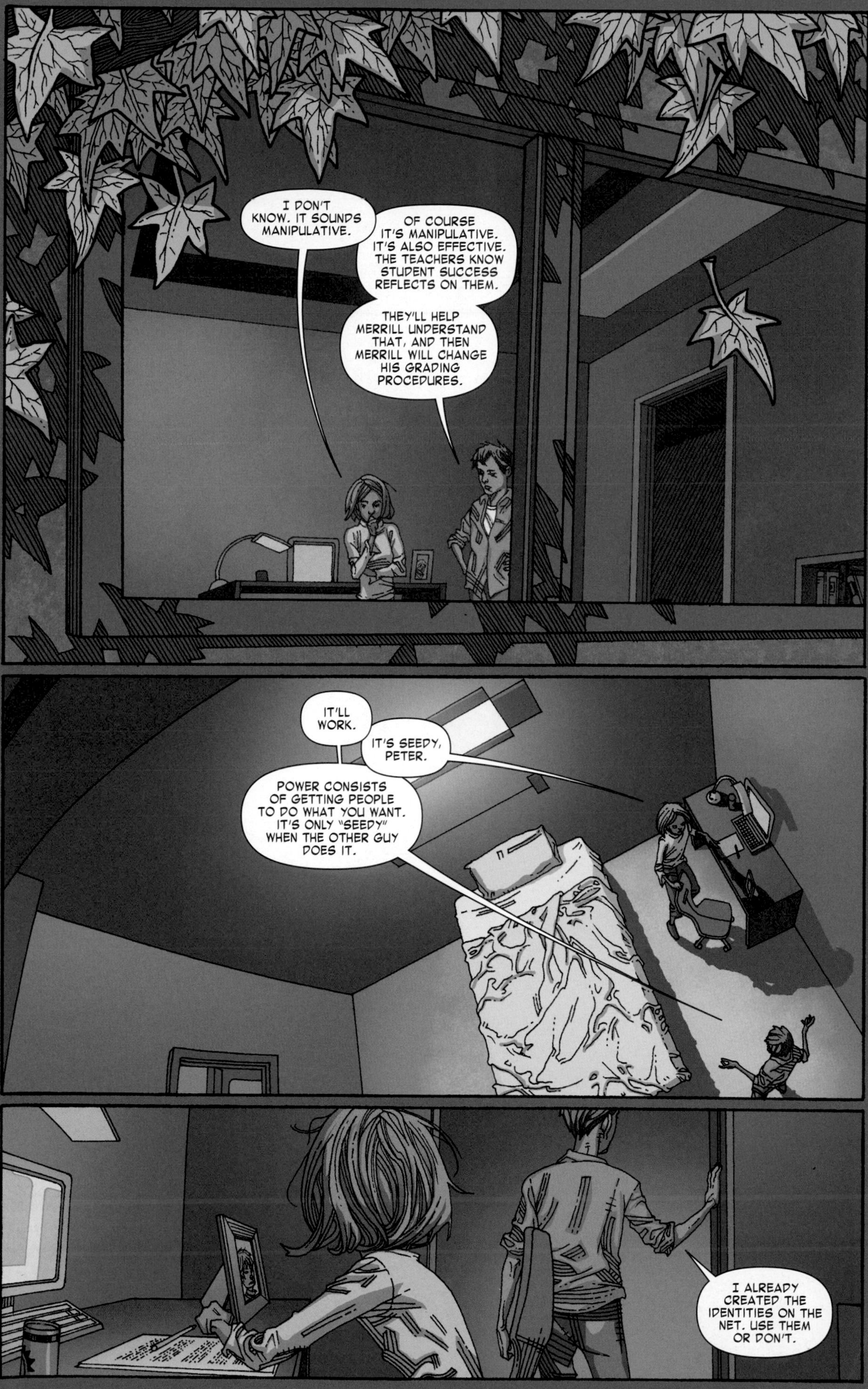
I DON'T KNOW. IT SOUNDS MANIPULATIVE.
OF COURSE IT'S MANIPULATIVE. IT'S ALSO EFFECTIVE. THE TEACHERS KNOW STUDENT SUCCESS REFLECTS ON THEM.
THEY'LL HELP MERRILL UNDERSTAND THAT, AND THEN MERRILL WILL CHANGE HIS GRADING PROCEDURES.
IT'LL WORK.
IT'S SEEDY, PETER.
POWER CONSISTS OF GETTING PEOPLE TO DO WHAT YOU WANT. IT'S ONLY "SEEDY" WHEN THE OTHER GUY DOES IT.
I ALREADY CREATED THE IDENTITIES ON THE NET. USE THEM OR DON'T.

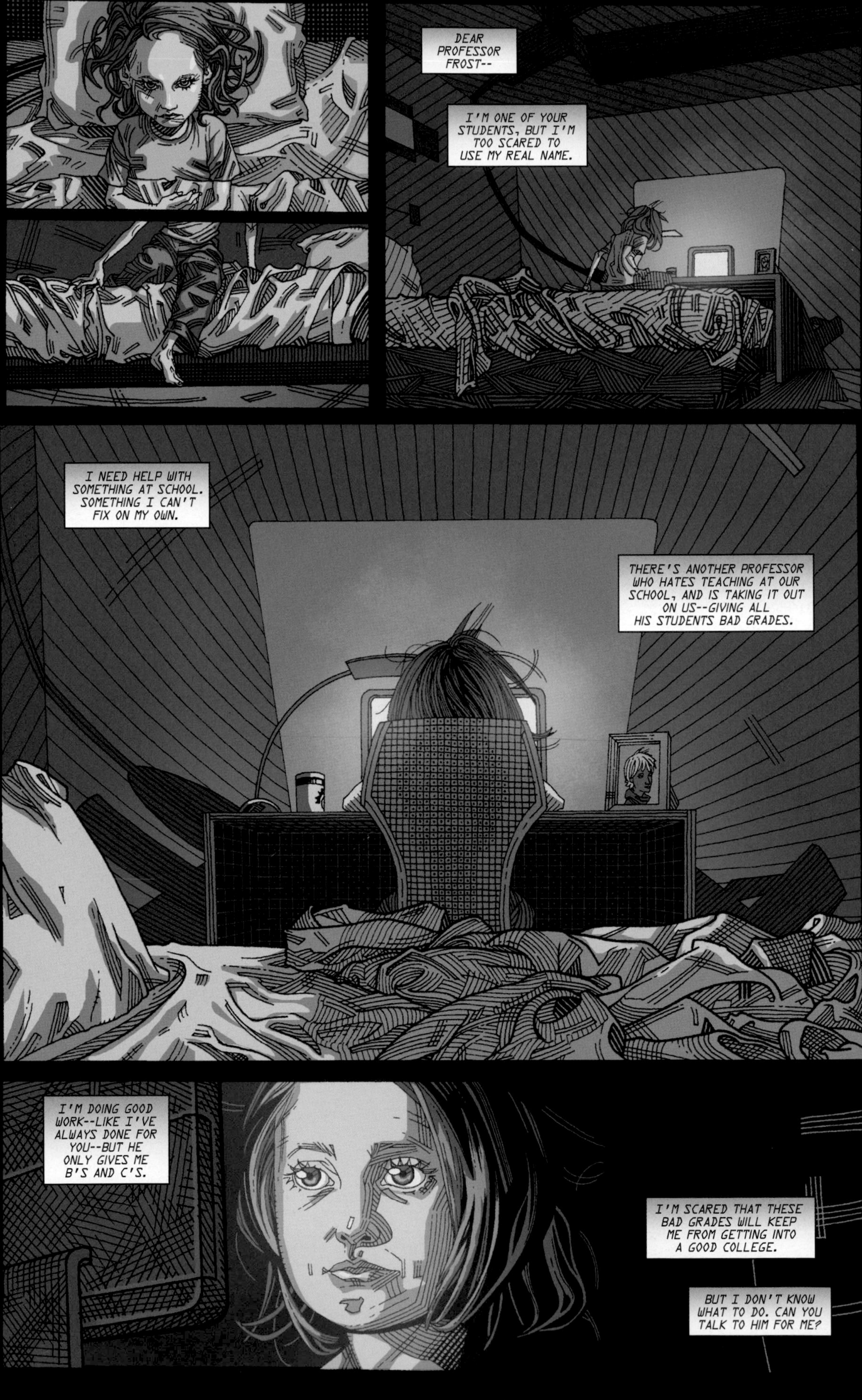
DEAR PROFESSOR FROST--
I'M ONE OF YOUR STUDENTS, BUT I'M TOO SCARED TO USE MY REAL NAME.
I NEED HELP WITH SOMETHING AT SCHOOL. SOMETHING I CAN'T FIX ON MY OWN.
THERE'S ANOTHER PROFESSOR WHO HATES TEACHING AT OUR SCHOOL, AND IS TAKING IT OUT ON US--GIVING ALL HIS STUDENTS BAD GRADES.
I'M DOING GOOD WORK--LIKE I'VE ALWAYS DONE FOR YOU--BUT HE ONLY GIVES ME B'S AND C'S.
I'M SCARED THAT THESE BAD GRADES WILL KEEP ME FROM GETTING INTO A GOOD COLLEGE.
BUT I DON'T KNOW WHAT TO DO. CAN YOU TALK TO HIM FOR ME?

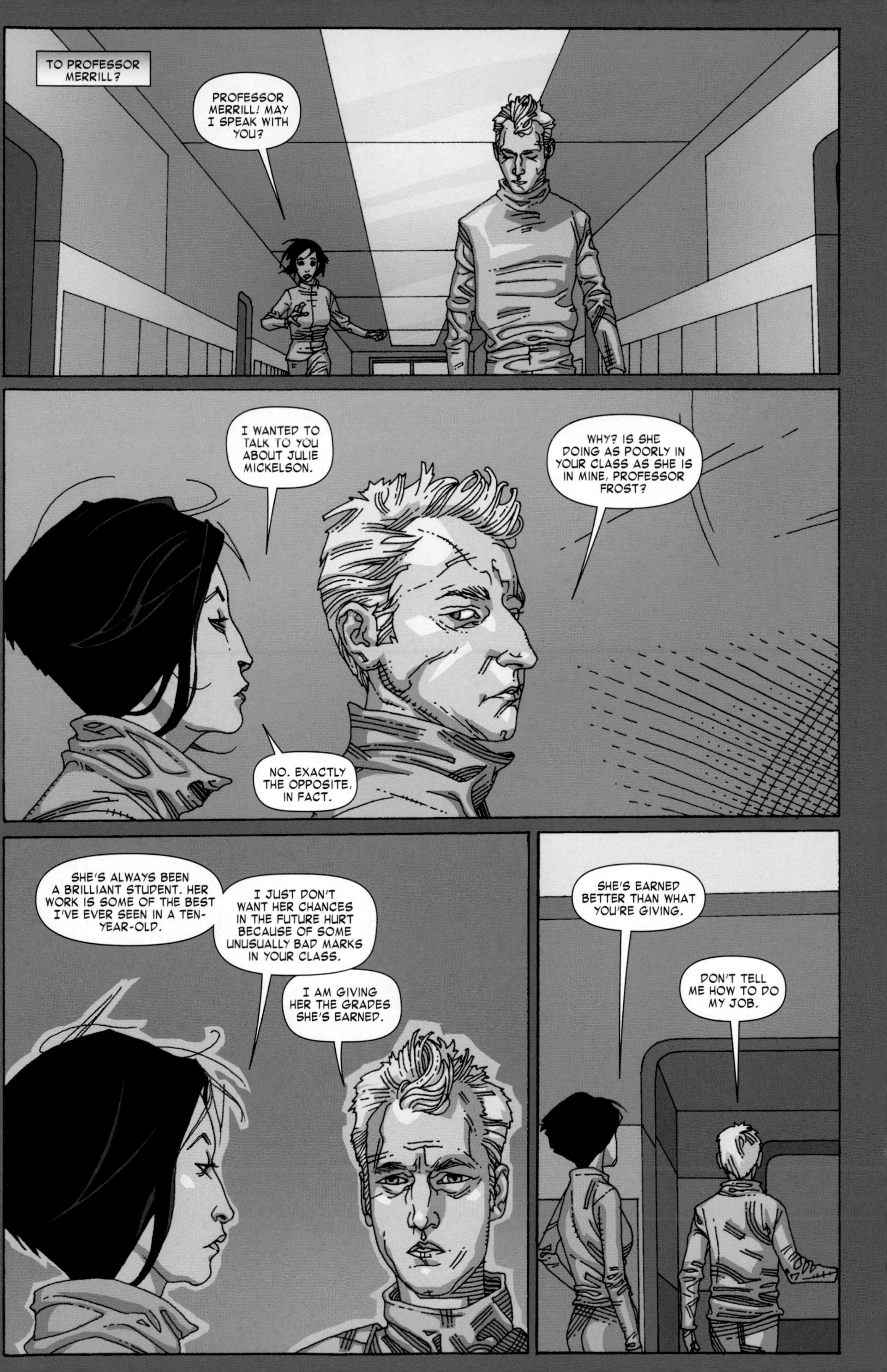
TO PROFESSOR MERRILL?
PROFESSOR MERRILL! MAY I SPEAK WITH YOU?
I WANTED TO TALK TO YOU ABOUT JULIE MICKELSON.
WHY? IS SHE DOING AS POORLY IN YOUR CLASS AS SHE IS IN MINE, PROFESSOR FROST?
NO. EXACTLY THE OPPOSITE, IN FACT.
SHE'S ALWAYS BEEN A BRILLIANT STUDENT. HER WORK IS SOME OF THE BEST I'VE EVER SEEN IN A TEN-YEAR-OLD.
I JUST DON'T WANT HER CHANCES IN THE FUTURE HURT BECAUSE OF SOME UNUSUALLY BAD MARKS IN YOUR CLASS.
I AM GIVING HER THE GRADES SHE'S EARNED.
SHE'S EARNED BETTER THAN WHAT YOU'RE GIVING.
DON'T TELL ME HOW TO DO MY JOB.

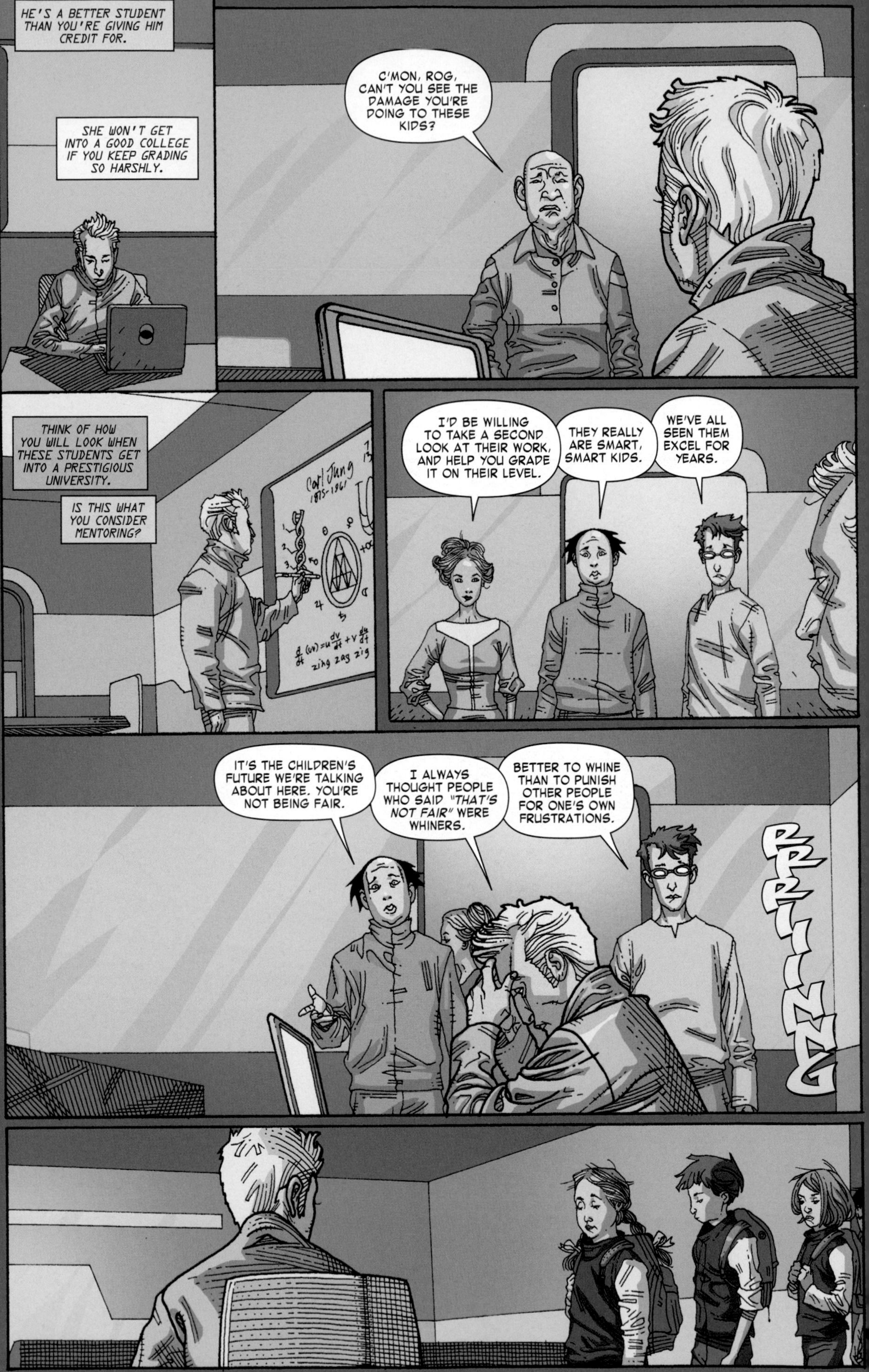
HE'S A BETTER STUDENT THAN YOU'RE GIVING HIM CREDIT FOR.
SHE WON'T GET INTO A GOOD COLLEGE IF YOU KEEP GRADING SO HARSHLY.
C'MON, ROG, CAN'T YOU SEE THE DAMAGE YOU'RE DOING TO THESE KIDS?
THINK OF HOW YOU WILL LOOK WHEN THESE STUDENTS GET INTO A PRESTIGIOUS UNIVERSITY.
IS THIS WHAT YOU CONSIDER MENTORING?
Carl Jung 1875-1961
zing zag zig
I'D BE WILLING TO TAKE A SECOND LOOK AT THEIR WORK, AND HELP YOU GRADE IT ON THEIR LEVEL.
THEY REALLY ARE SMART, SMART KIDS.
WE'VE ALL SEEN THEM EXCEL FOR YEARS.
IT'S THE CHILDREN'S FUTURE WE'RE TALKING ABOUT HERE. YOU'RE NOT BEING FAIR.
I ALWAYS THOUGHT PEOPLE WHO SAID "THAT'S NOT FAIR" WERE WHINERS.
BETTER TO WHINE THAN TO PUNISH OTHER PEOPLE FOR ONE'S OWN FRUSTRATIONS.
RRRIIING

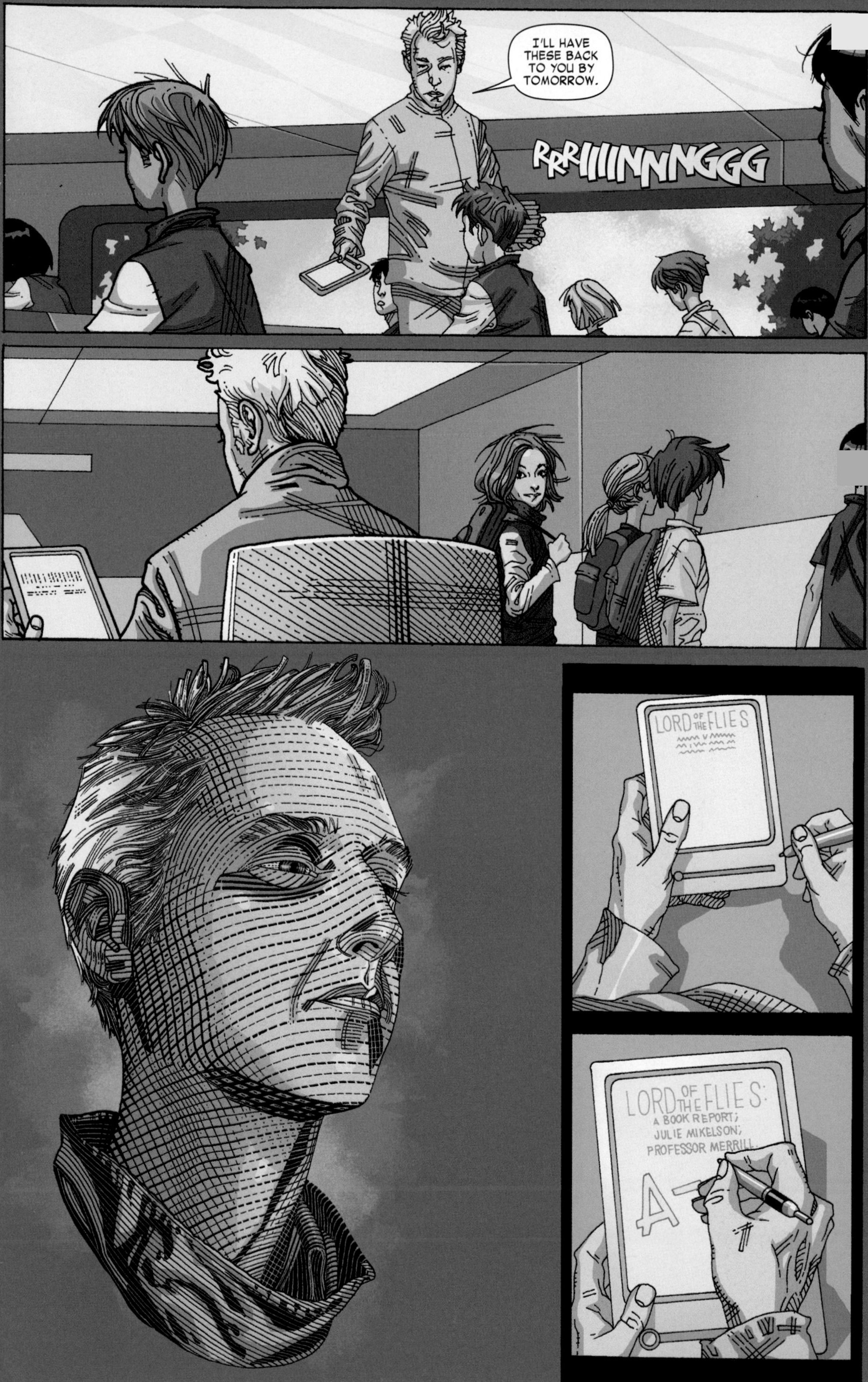
I'LL HAVE THESE BACK TO YOU BY TOMORROW.
RRRIIIIINNNNGGG
LORD OF THE FLIES
LORD OF THE FLIES:
A BOOK REPORT;
JULIE MIKELSON;
PROFESSOR MERRILL
A-

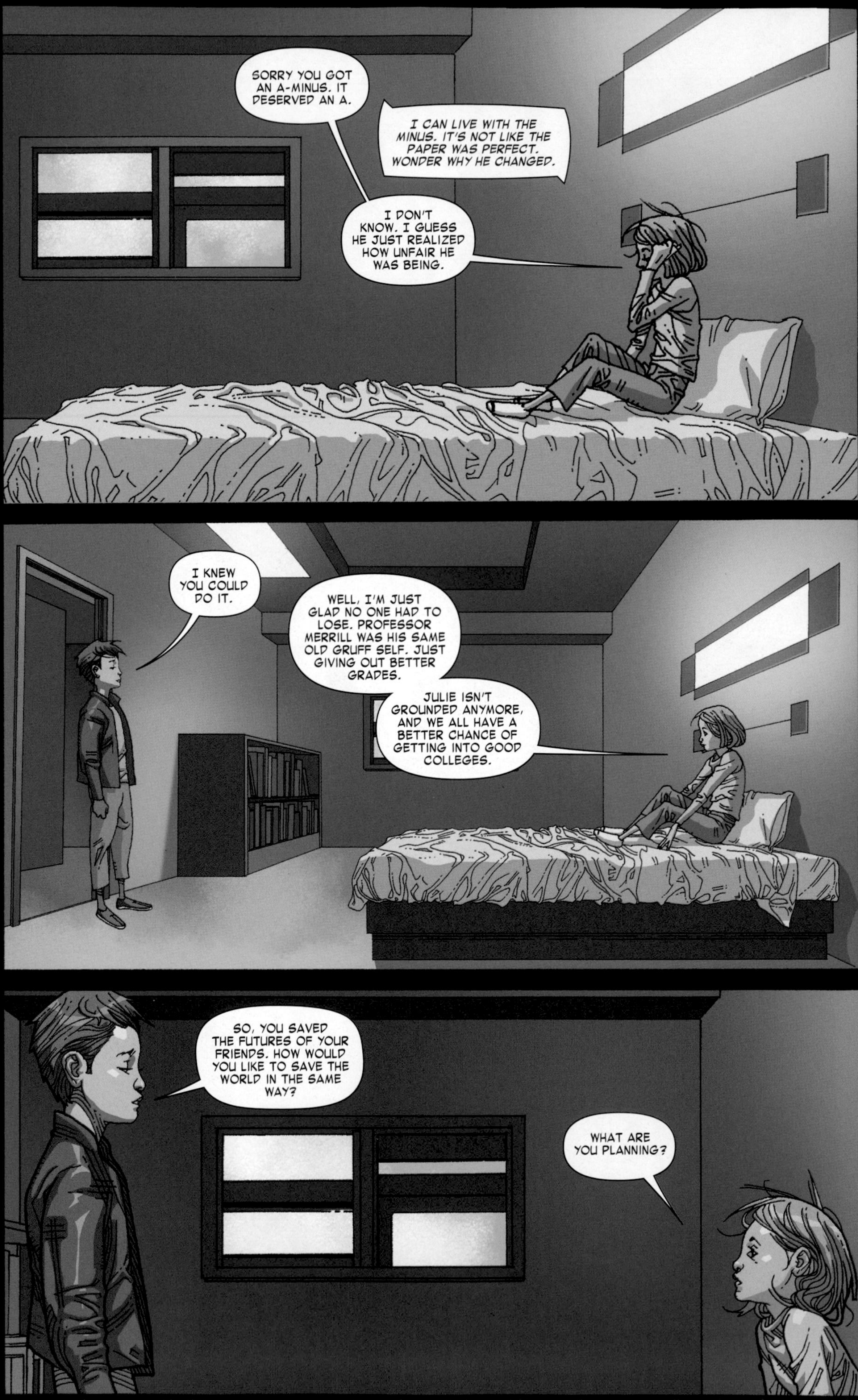
SORRY YOU GOT AN A-MINUS. IT DESERVED AN A.
I CAN LIVE WITH THE MINUS. IT'S NOT LIKE THE PAPER WAS PERFECT. WONDER WHY HE CHANGED.
I DON'T KNOW. I GUESS HE JUST REALIZED HOW UNFAIR HE WAS BEING.
I KNEW YOU COULD DO IT.
WELL, I'M JUST GLAD NO ONE HAD TO LOSE. PROFESSOR MERRILL WAS HIS SAME OLD GRUFF SELF. JUST GIVING OUT BETTER GRADES.
JULIE ISN'T GROUNDED ANYMORE, AND WE ALL HAVE A BETTER CHANCE OF GETTING INTO GOOD COLLEGES.
SO, YOU SAVED THE FUTURES OF YOUR FRIENDS. HOW WOULD YOU LIKE TO SAVE THE WORLD IN THE SAME WAY?
WHAT ARE YOU PLANNING?

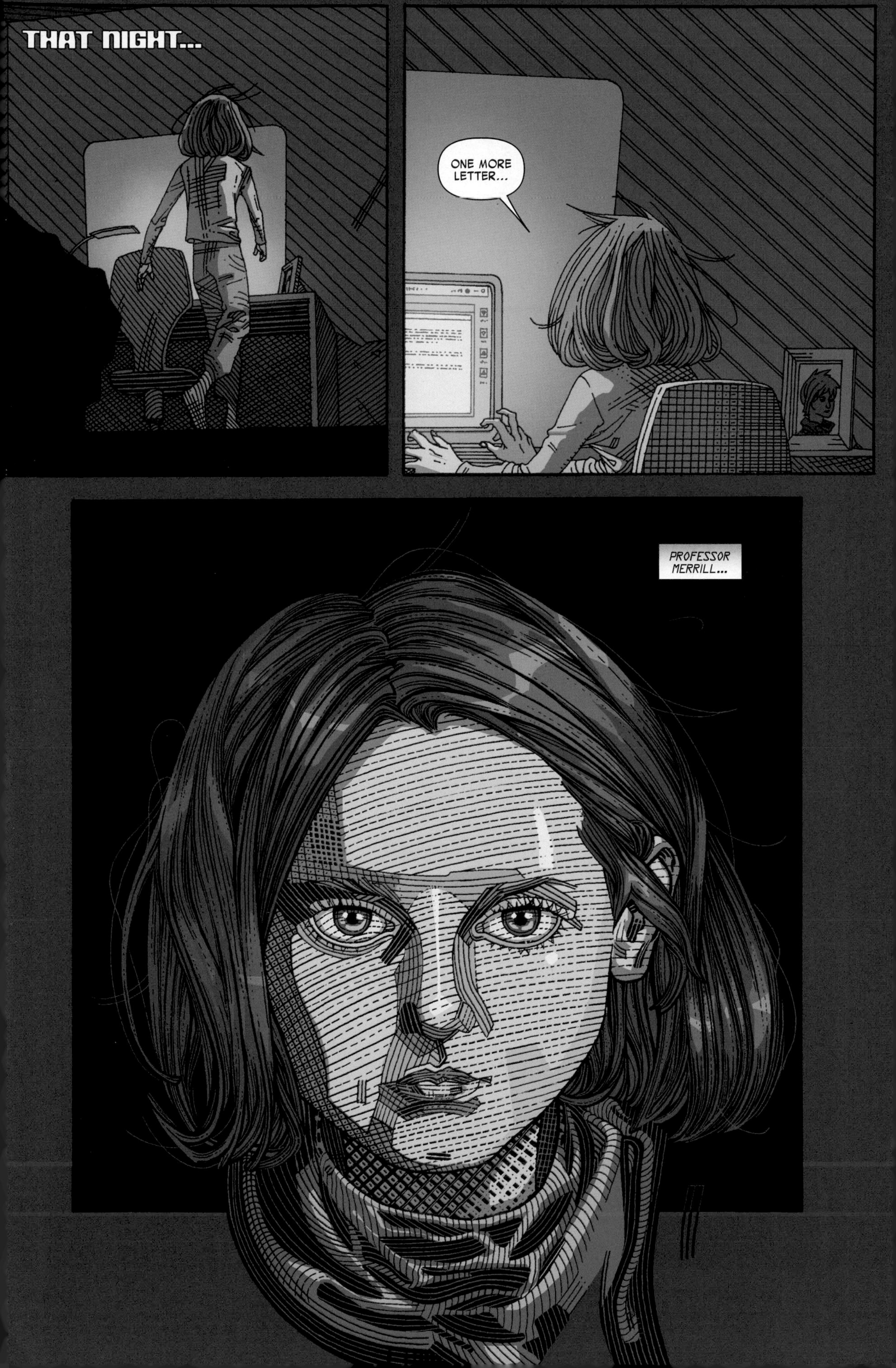
THAT NIGHT...
ONE MORE LETTER...
PROFESSOR MERRILL...

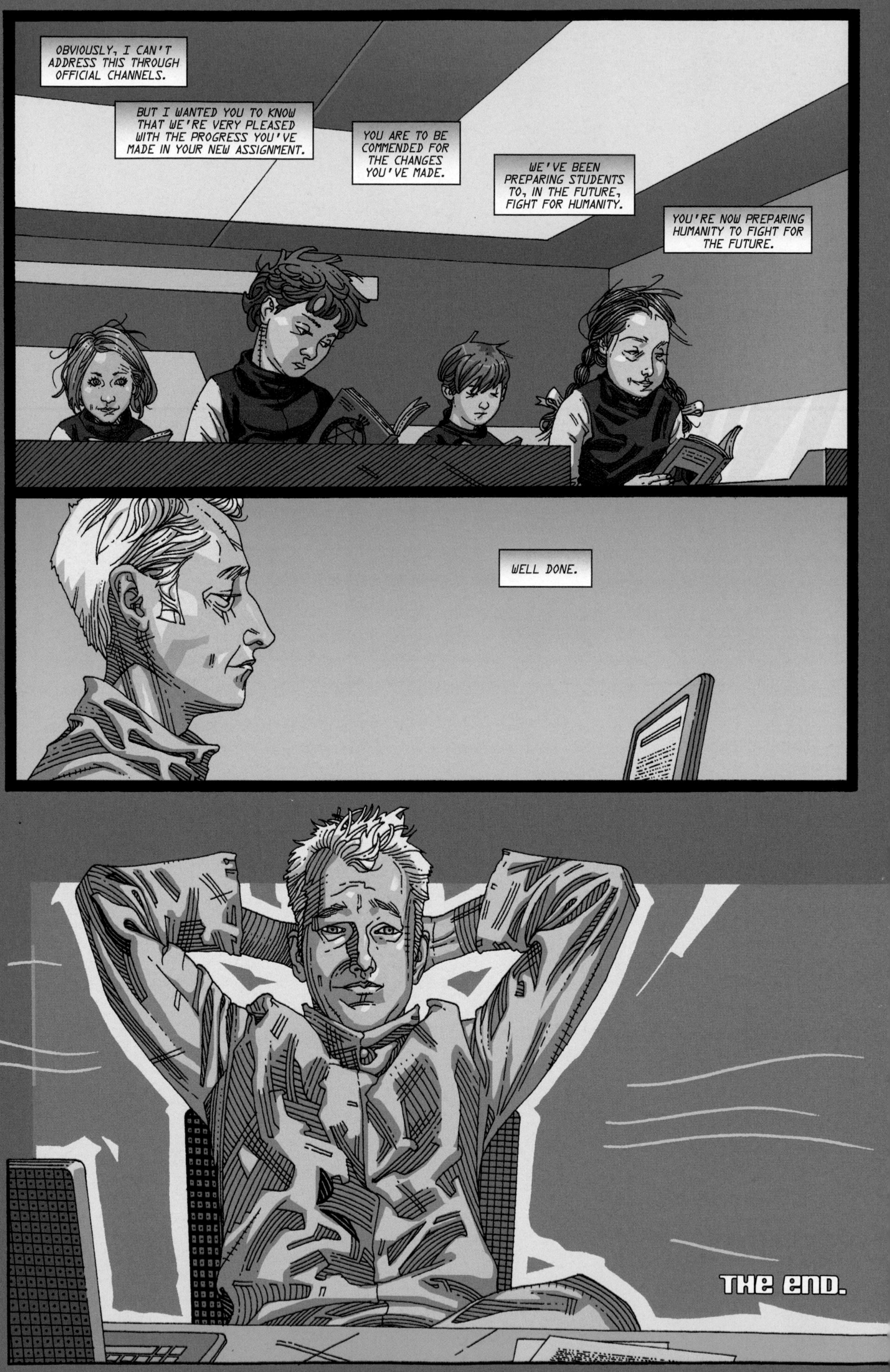
OBVIOUSLY, I CAN'T ADDRESS THIS THROUGH OFFICIAL CHANNELS.
BUT I WANTED YOU TO KNOW THAT WE'RE VERY PLEASED WITH THE PROGRESS YOU'VE MADE IN YOUR NEW ASSIGNMENT.
YOU ARE TO BE COMMENDED FOR THE CHANGES YOU'VE MADE.
WE'VE BEEN PREPARING STUDENTS TO, IN THE FUTURE, FIGHT FOR HUMANITY.
YOU'RE NOW PREPARING HUMANITY TO FIGHT FOR THE FUTURE.
WELL DONE.
THE END.

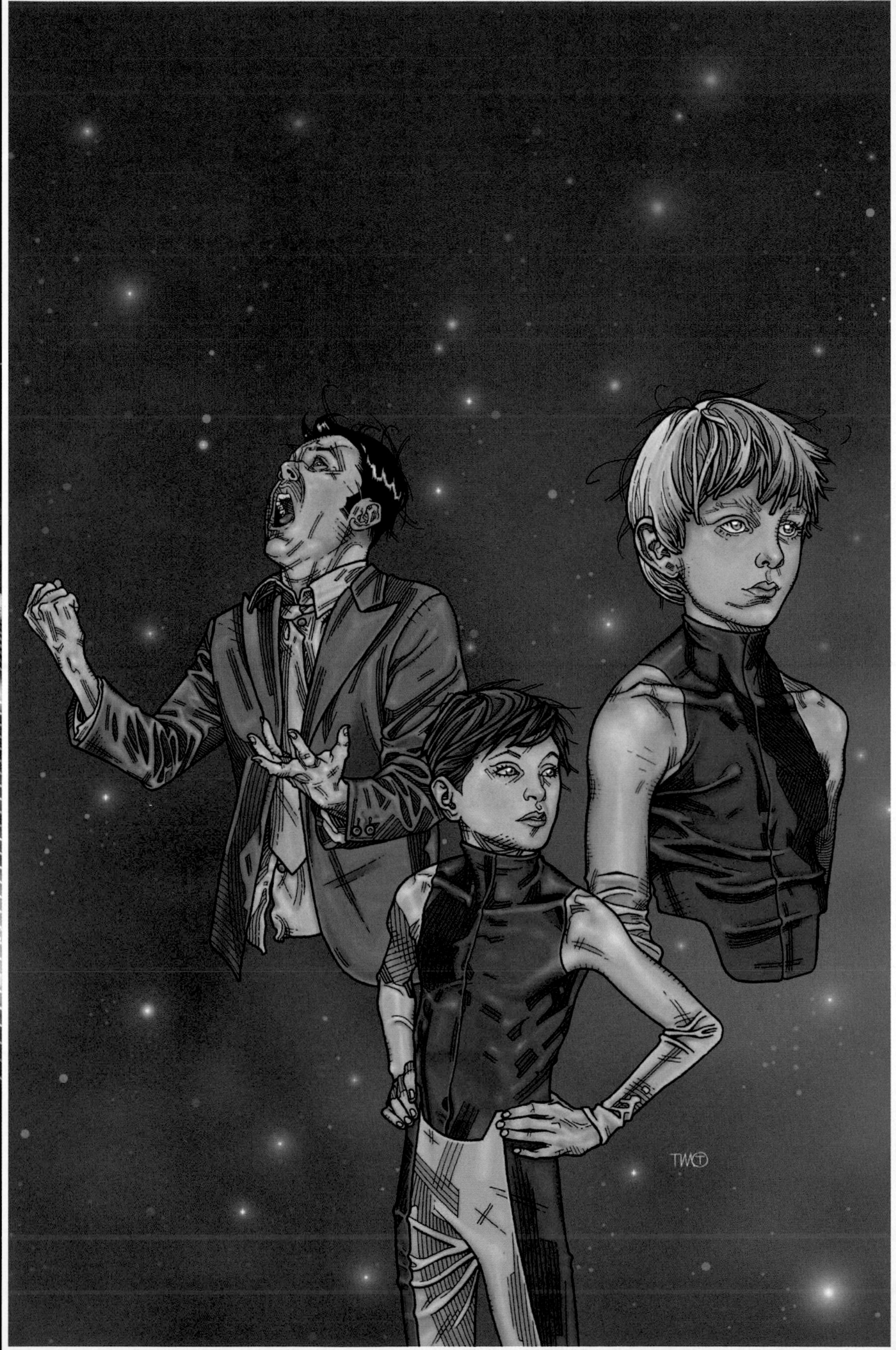
TWC

WAR OF GIFTS

ATTENTION: NEW LAUNCH GROUP MEMBERS

Welcome to the International Fleet. Because of your exceptional talents and skills, you have been selected to attend Battle School. Here you will receive the training that will make you an invaluable member of the International Fleet over the course of your life.

As you begin your period of study and training at Battle School, there are a few rules of which you must be aware:

*You will be assigned to an army led by a Commander. Your commander will help you understand the rules of the Battle Room, thus helping you advance here at Battle School.

*Lights out is at 2200 hours for new launch groups.

*You will eat, study, and spend almost all of your time with your army. Socializing with students outside of your army is allowed, but discouraged.

*Grievances must be submitted first to your Commander. If you are not satisfied with his response, then you may bring grievances to a Battle School counselor.

*To maintain order and equality in Battle School, all religious observances are strictly prohibited.

*Regulation uniforms and flash suits are the only clothing permitted.

*Physical violence between students, except in clear self-defense, is grounds for removal from Battle School.

Again, we welcome you to Battle School. We wish you the greatest achievement during your time here. You stand as one selected to help protect the human race from annihilation by the Formics. Your success here may mean the very survival of humanity.

Sincerely,

Matthew London
Associate Under-director of Admissions
International Fleet Battle School

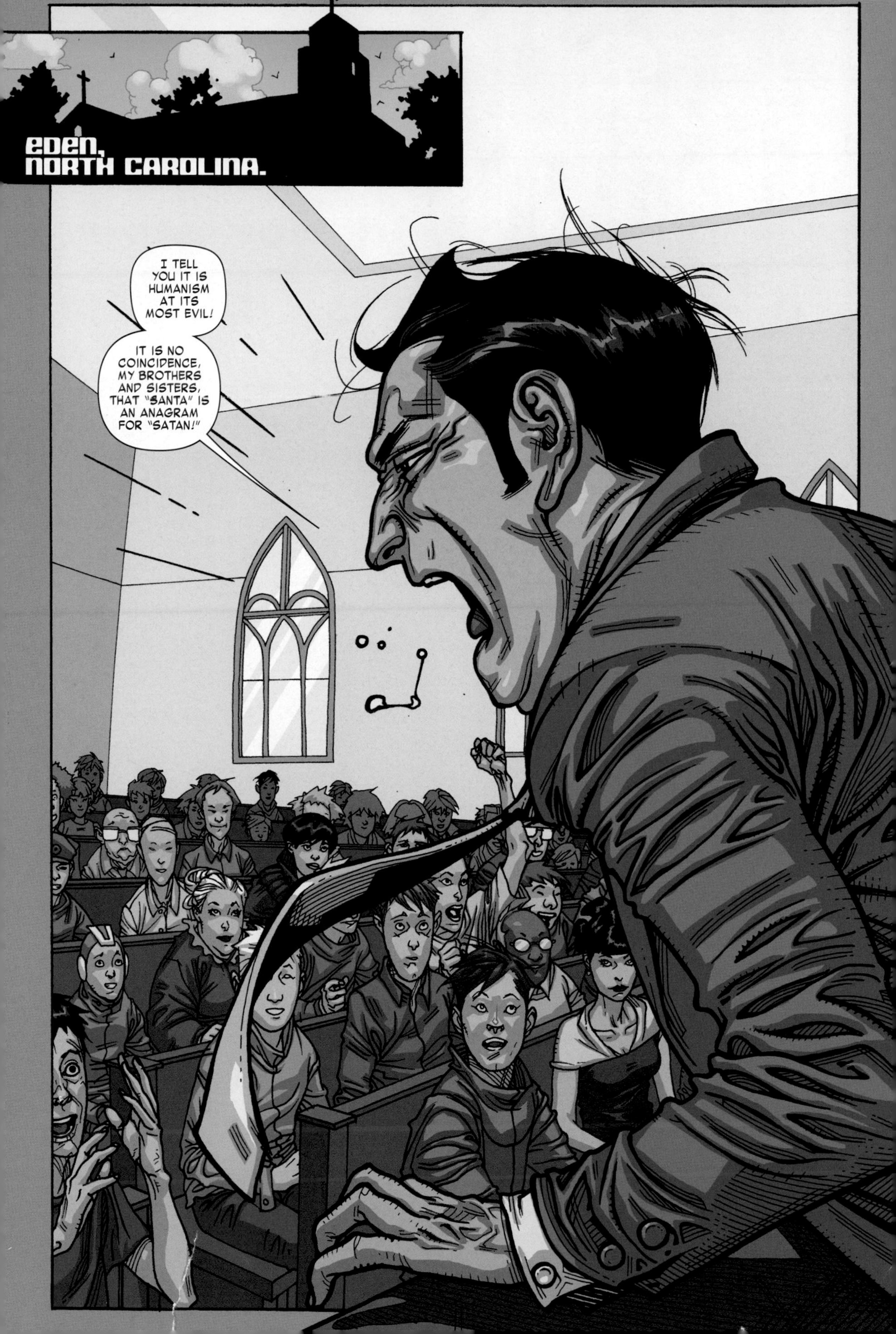
EDEN, NORTH CAROLINA.
I TELL YOU IT IS HUMANISM AT ITS MOST EVIL!
IT IS NO COINCIDENCE, MY BROTHERS AND SISTERS, THAT "SANTA" IS AN ANAGRAM FOR "SATAN!"

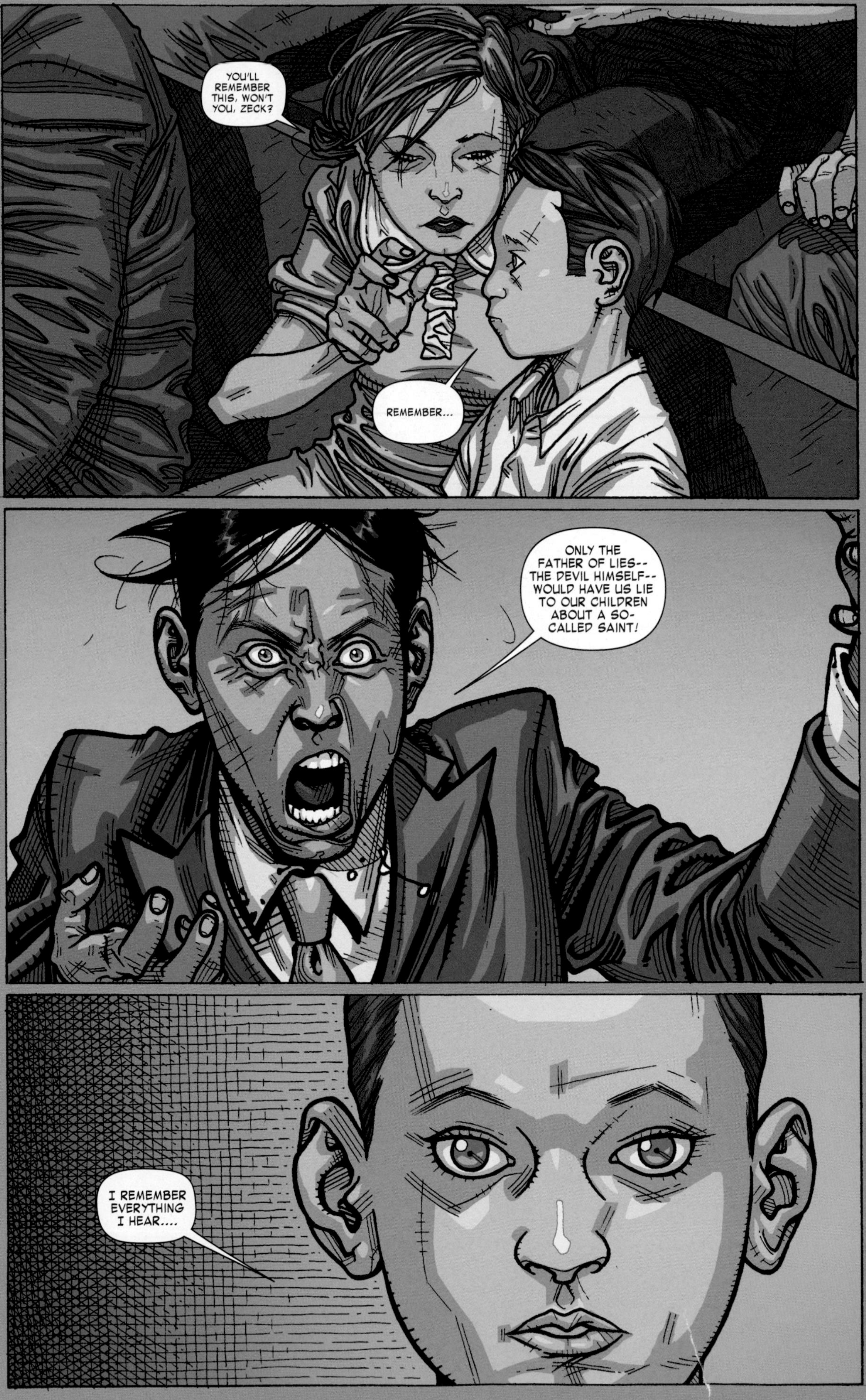
YOU'LL REMEMBER THIS, WON'T YOU, ZECK?
REMEMBER...
ONLY THE FATHER OF LIES-- THE DEVIL HIMSELF-- WOULD HAVE US LIE TO OUR CHILDREN ABOUT A SO-CALLED SAINT!
I REMEMBER EVERYTHING I HEAR....

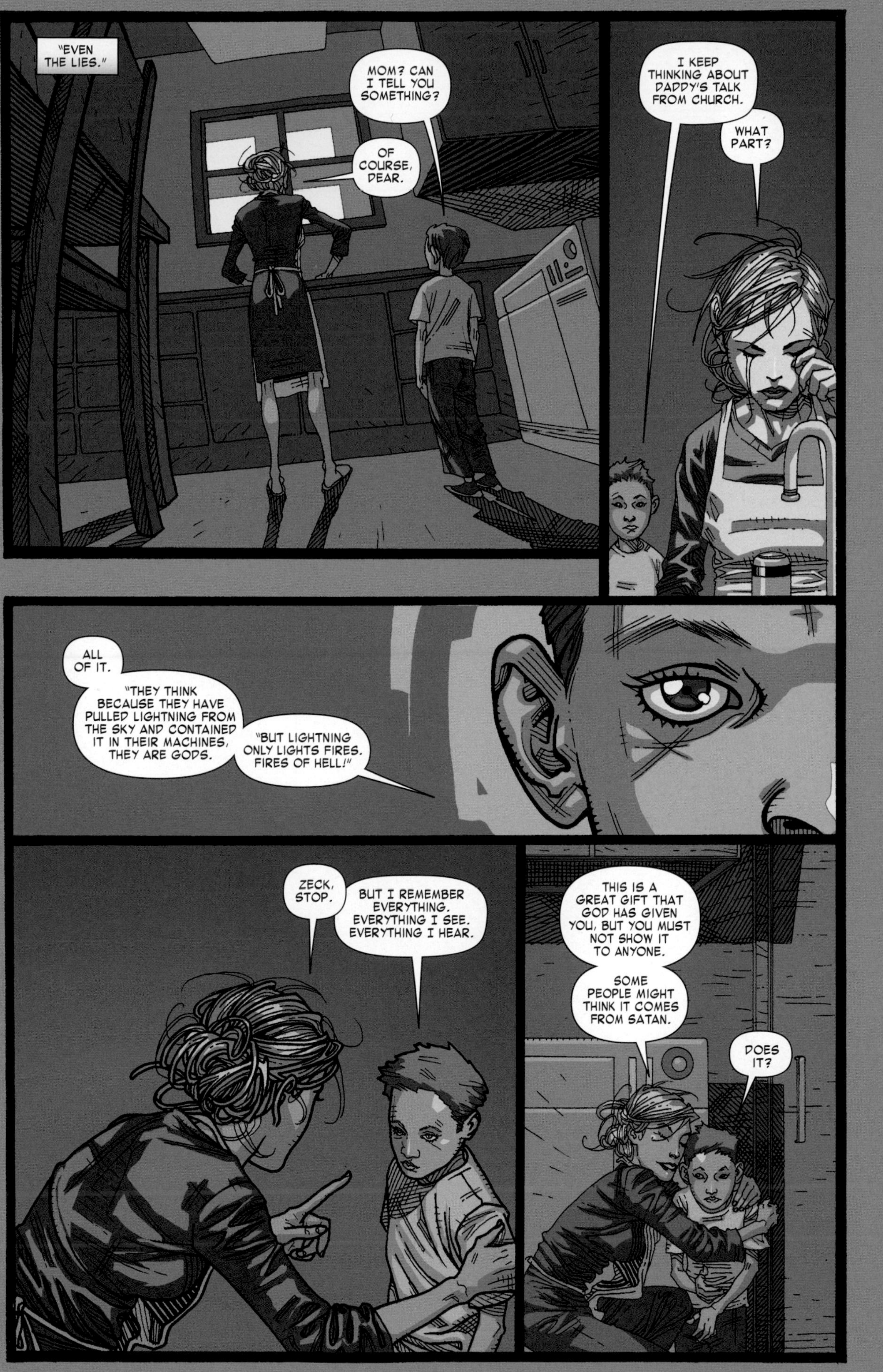
"EVEN THE LIES."
MOM? CAN I TELL YOU SOMETHING?
OF COURSE, DEAR.
I KEEP THINKING ABOUT DADDY'S TALK FROM CHURCH.
WHAT PART?
ALL OF IT.
"THEY THINK BECAUSE THEY HAVE PULLED LIGHTNING FROM THE SKY AND CONTAINED IT IN THEIR MACHINES, THEY ARE GODS.
"BUT LIGHTNING ONLY LIGHTS FIRES. FIRES OF HELL!"
ZECK, STOP.
BUT I REMEMBER EVERYTHING. EVERYTHING I SEE. EVERYTHING I HEAR.
THIS IS A GREAT GIFT THAT GOD HAS GIVEN YOU, BUT YOU MUST NOT SHOW IT TO ANYONE.
SOME PEOPLE MIGHT THINK IT COMES FROM SATAN.
DOES IT?

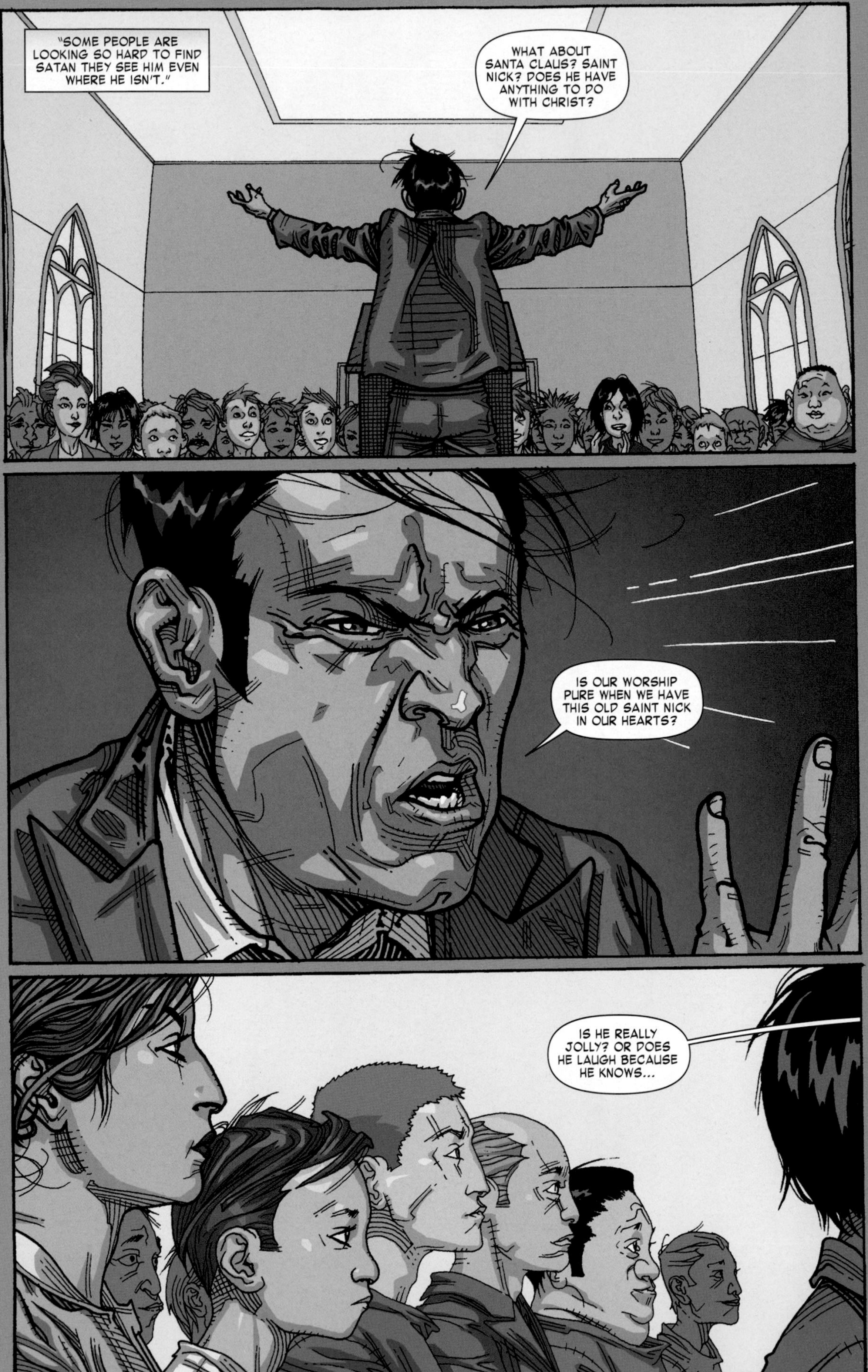
"SOME PEOPLE ARE LOOKING SO HARD TO FIND SATAN THEY SEE HIM EVEN WHERE HE ISN'T."
WHAT ABOUT SANTA CLAUS? SAINT NICK? DOES HE HAVE ANYTHING TO DO WITH CHRIST?
IS OUR WORSHIP PURE WHEN WE HAVE THIS OLD SAINT NICK IN OUR HEARTS?
IS HE REALLY JOLLY? OR DOES HE LAUGH BECAUSE HE KNOWS...

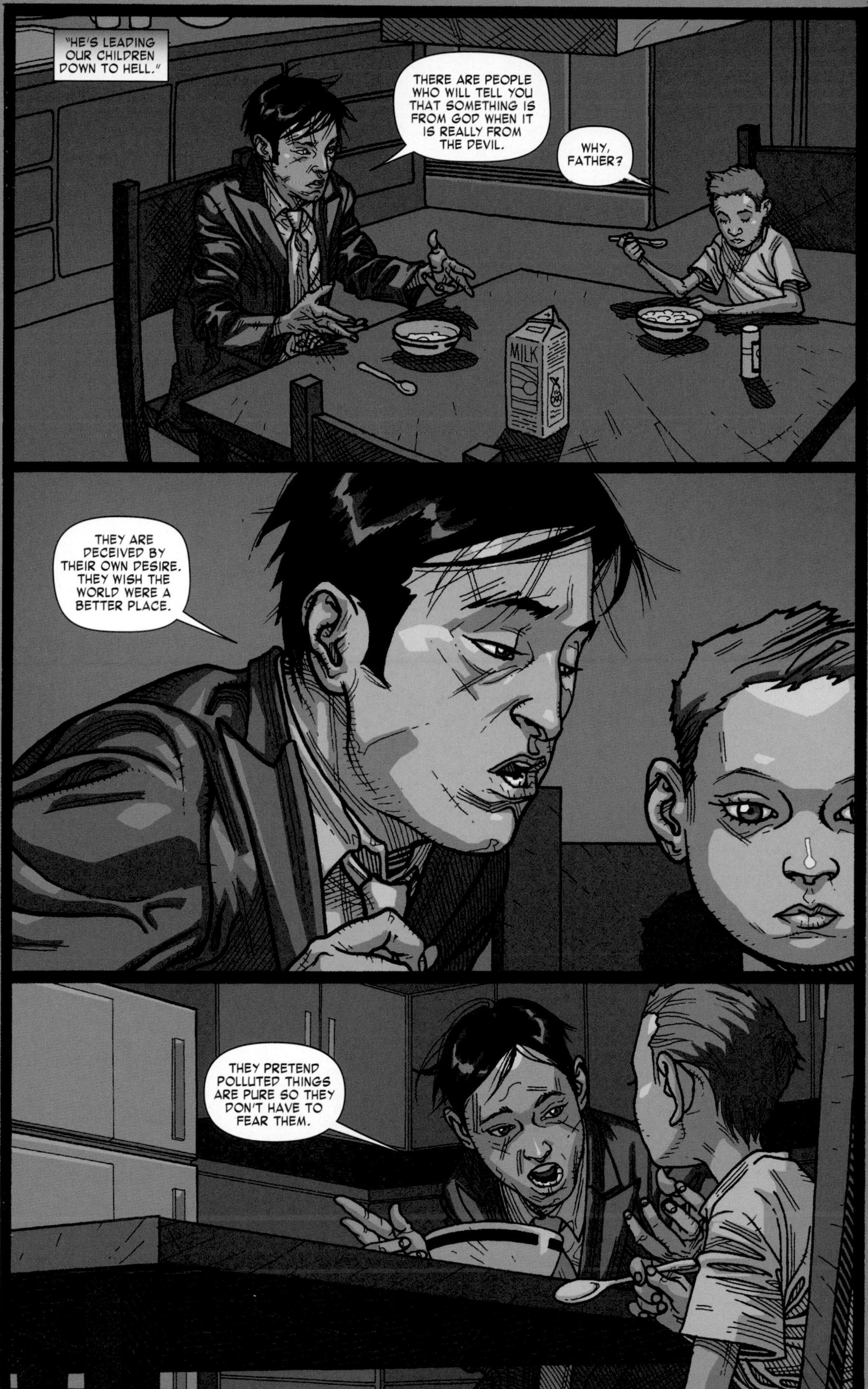
"HE'S LEADING OUR CHILDREN DOWN TO HELL."
THERE ARE PEOPLE WHO WILL TELL YOU THAT SOMETHING IS FROM GOD WHEN IT IS REALLY FROM THE DEVIL.
WHY, FATHER?
MILK
THEY ARE DECEIVED BY THEIR OWN DESIRE. THEY WISH THE WORLD WERE A BETTER PLACE.
THEY PRETEND POLLUTED THINGS ARE PURE SO THEY DON'T HAVE TO FEAR THEM.

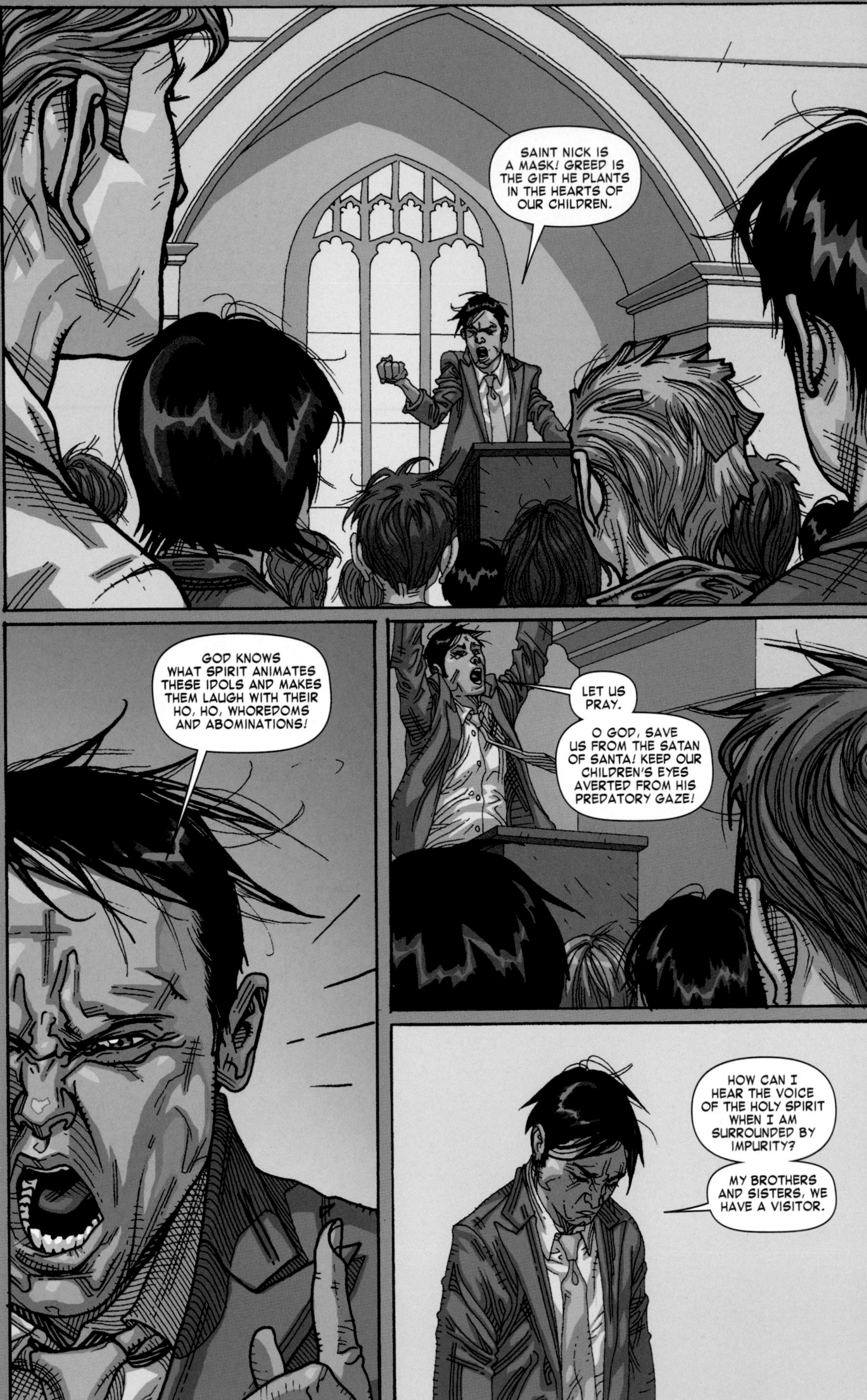
SAINT NICK IS A MASK! GREED IS THE GIFT HE PLANTS IN THE HEARTS OF OUR CHILDREN.
GOD KNOWS WHAT SPIRIT ANIMATES THESE IDOLS AND MAKES THEM LAUGH WITH THEIR HO, HO, WHOREDOMS AND ABOMINATIONS!
LET US PRAY.
O GOD, SAVE US FROM THE SATAN OF SANTA! KEEP OUR CHILDREN'S EYES AVERTED FROM HIS PREDATORY GAZE!
HOW CAN I HEAR THE VOICE OF THE HOLY SPIRIT WHEN I AM SURROUNDED BY IMPURITY?
MY BROTHERS AND SISTERS, WE HAVE A VISITOR.

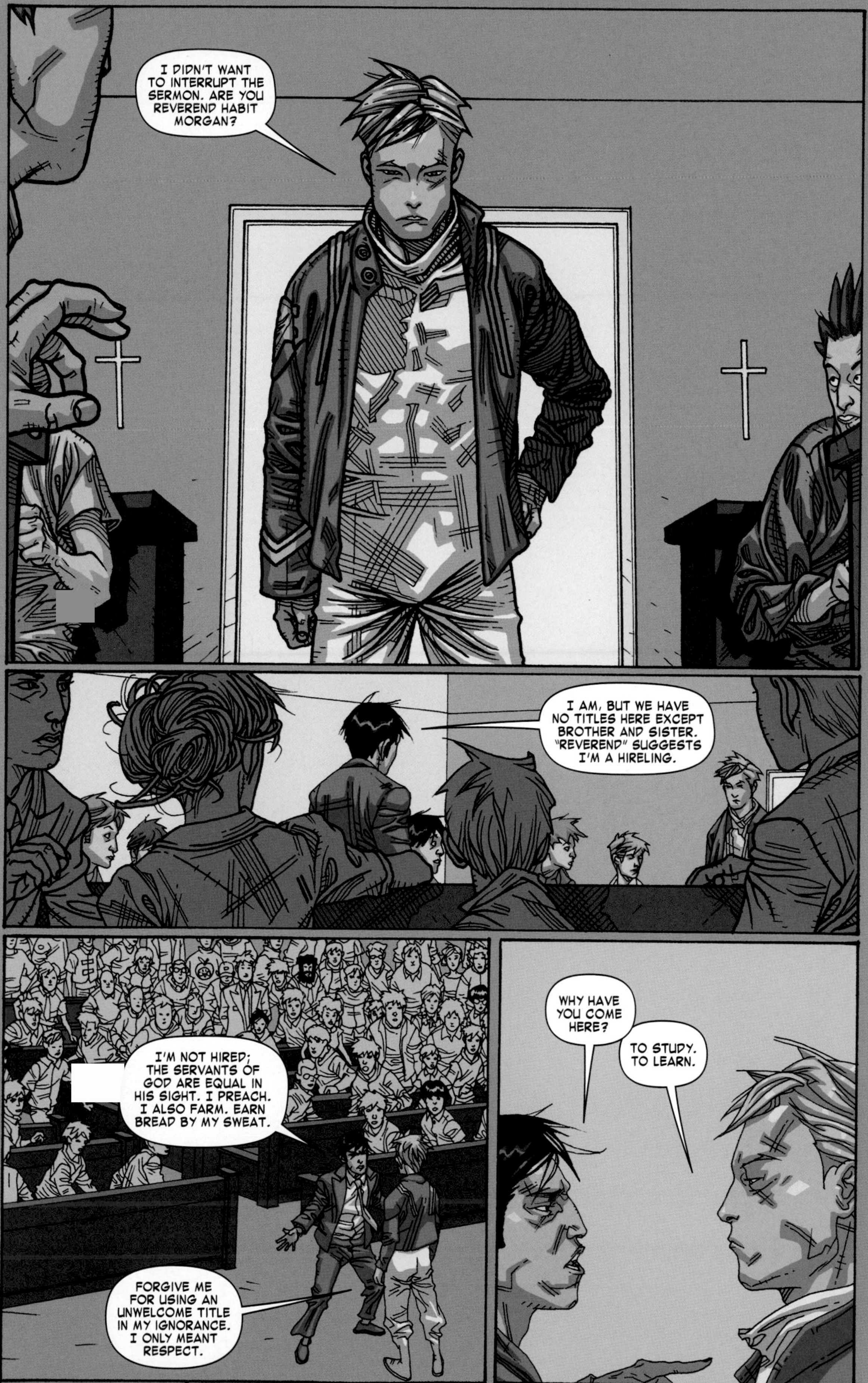
I DIDN'T WANT TO INTERRUPT THE SERMON. ARE YOU REVEREND HABIT MORGAN?
I AM, BUT WE HAVE NO TITLES HERE EXCEPT BROTHER AND SISTER. "REVEREND" SUGGESTS I'M A HIRELING.
I'M NOT HIRED; THE SERVANTS OF GOD ARE EQUAL IN HIS SIGHT. I PREACH. I ALSO FARM. EARN BREAD BY MY SWEAT.
FORGIVE ME FOR USING AN UNWELCOME TITLE IN MY IGNORANCE. I ONLY MEANT RESPECT.
WHY HAVE YOU COME HERE?
TO STUDY. TO LEARN.

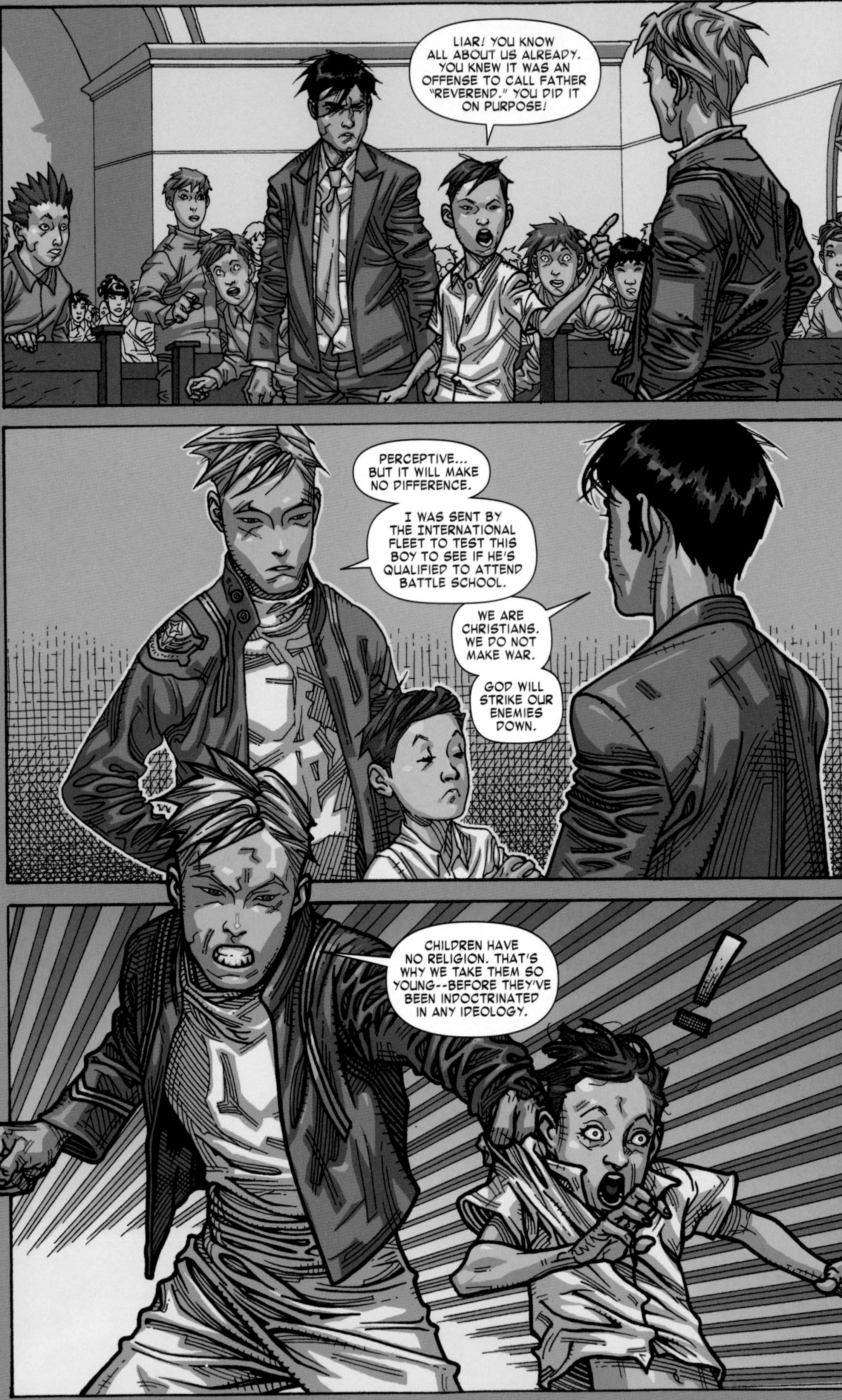
LIAR! YOU KNOW ALL ABOUT US ALREADY. YOU KNEW IT WAS AN OFFENSE TO CALL FATHER "REVEREND." YOU DID IT ON PURPOSE!
PERCEPTIVE... BUT IT WILL MAKE NO DIFFERENCE.
I WAS SENT BY THE INTERNATIONAL FLEET TO TEST THIS BOY TO SEE IF HE'S QUALIFIED TO ATTEND BATTLE SCHOOL.
WE ARE CHRISTIANS. WE DO NOT MAKE WAR.
GOD WILL STRIKE OUR ENEMIES DOWN.
CHILDREN HAVE NO RELIGION. THAT'S WHY WE TAKE THEM SO YOUNG--BEFORE THEY'VE BEEN INDOCTRINATED IN ANY IDEOLOGY.
!

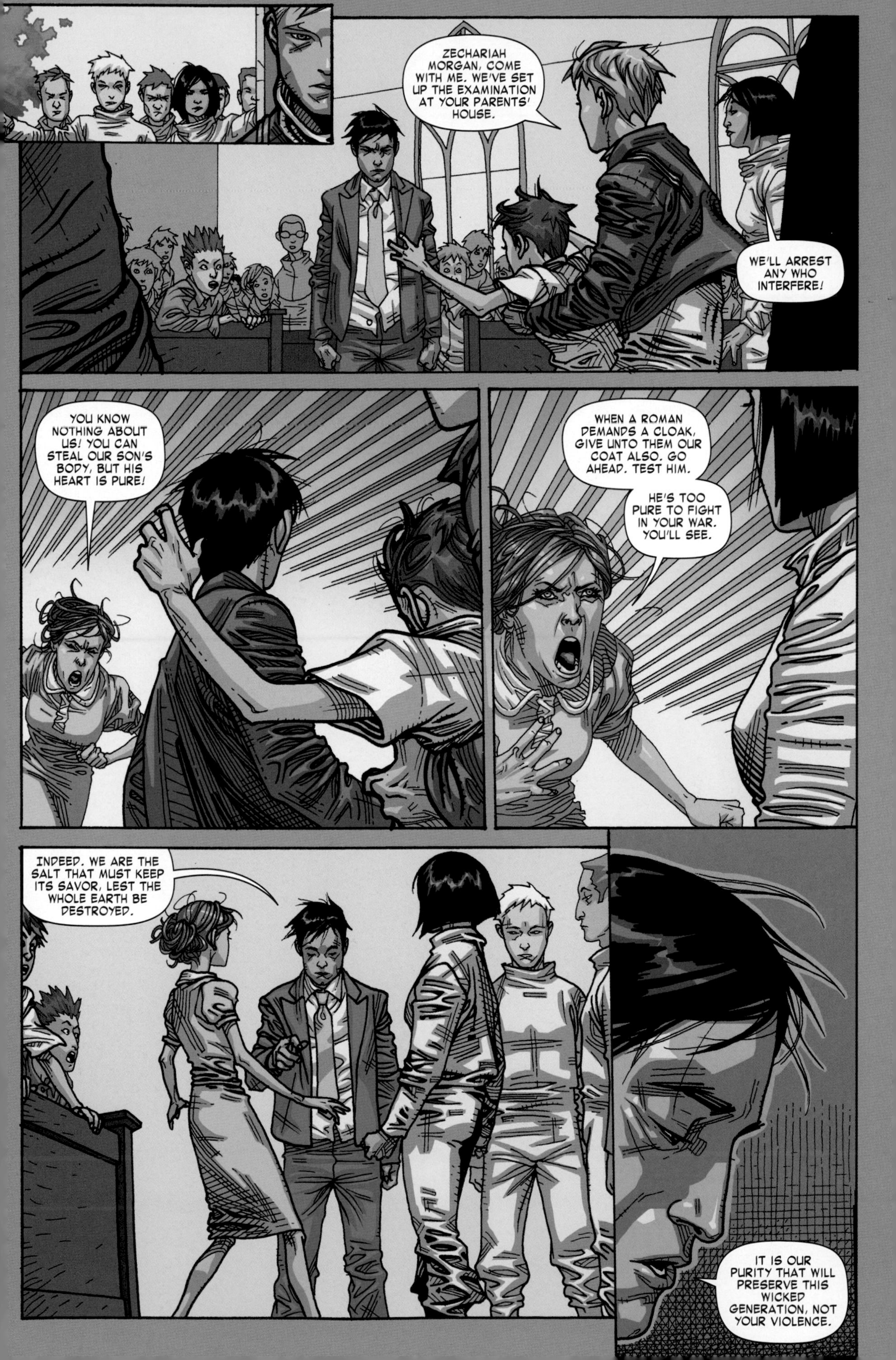
ZECHARIAH MORGAN, COME WITH ME. WE'VE SET UP THE EXAMINATION AT YOUR PARENTS' HOUSE.
WE'LL ARREST ANY WHO INTERFERE!
YOU KNOW NOTHING ABOUT US! YOU CAN STEAL OUR SON'S BODY, BUT HIS HEART IS PURE!
WHEN A ROMAN DEMANDS A CLOAK, GIVE UNTO THEM OUR COAT ALSO. GO AHEAD. TEST HIM.
HE'S TOO PURE TO FIGHT IN YOUR WAR. YOU'LL SEE.
INDEED. WE ARE THE SALT THAT MUST KEEP ITS SAVOR, LEST THE WHOLE EARTH BE DESTROYED.
IT IS OUR PURITY THAT WILL PRESERVE THIS WICKED GENERATION, NOT YOUR VIOLENCE.

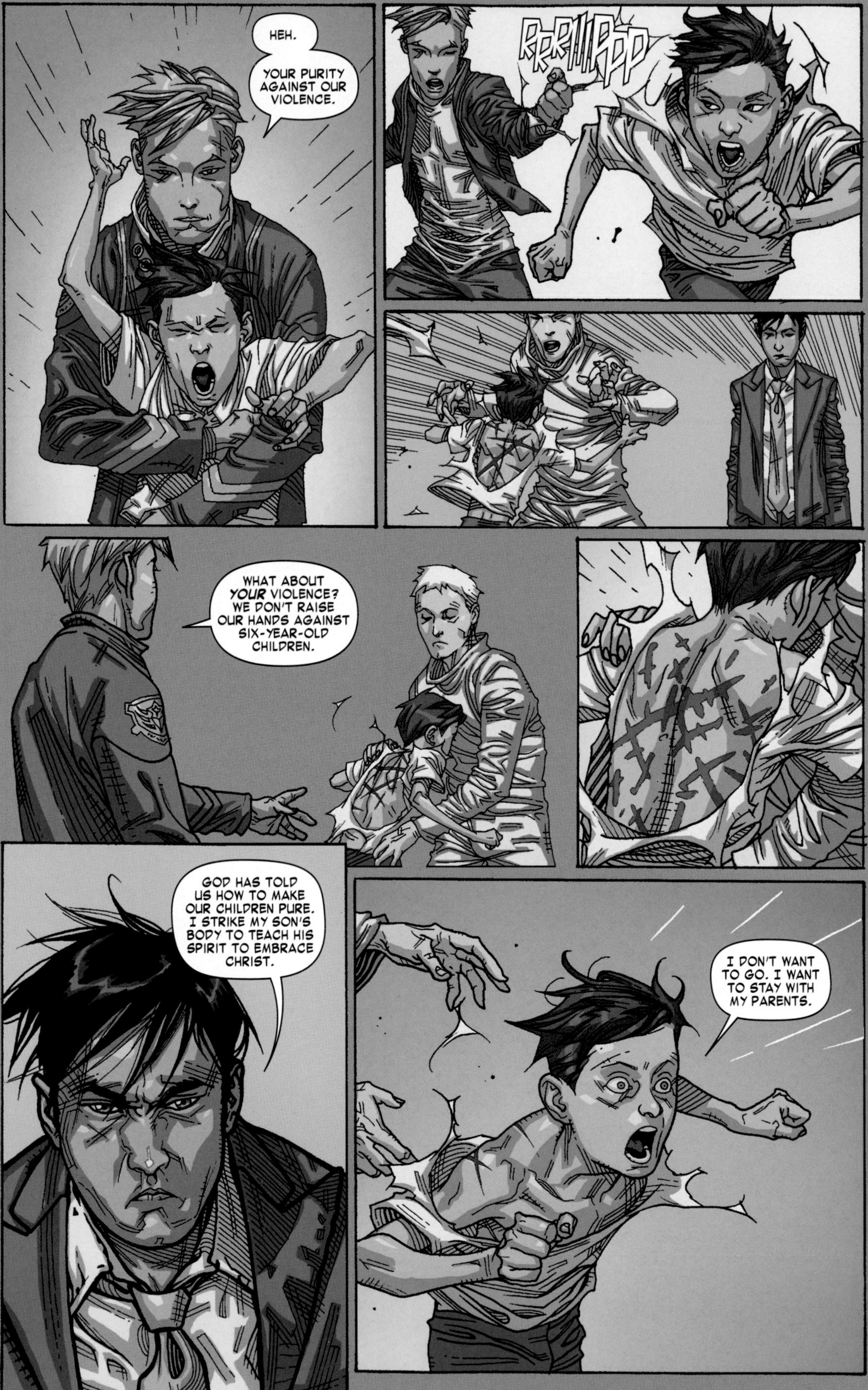
HEH.
YOUR PURITY AGAINST OUR VIOLENCE.
RRRIIIPPP
WHAT ABOUT *YOUR* VIOLENCE? WE DON'T RAISE OUR HANDS AGAINST SIX-YEAR-OLD CHILDREN.
GOD HAS TOLD US HOW TO MAKE OUR CHILDREN PURE. I STRIKE MY SON'S BODY TO TEACH HIS SPIRIT TO EMBRACE CHRIST.
I DON'T WANT TO GO. I WANT TO STAY WITH MY PARENTS.

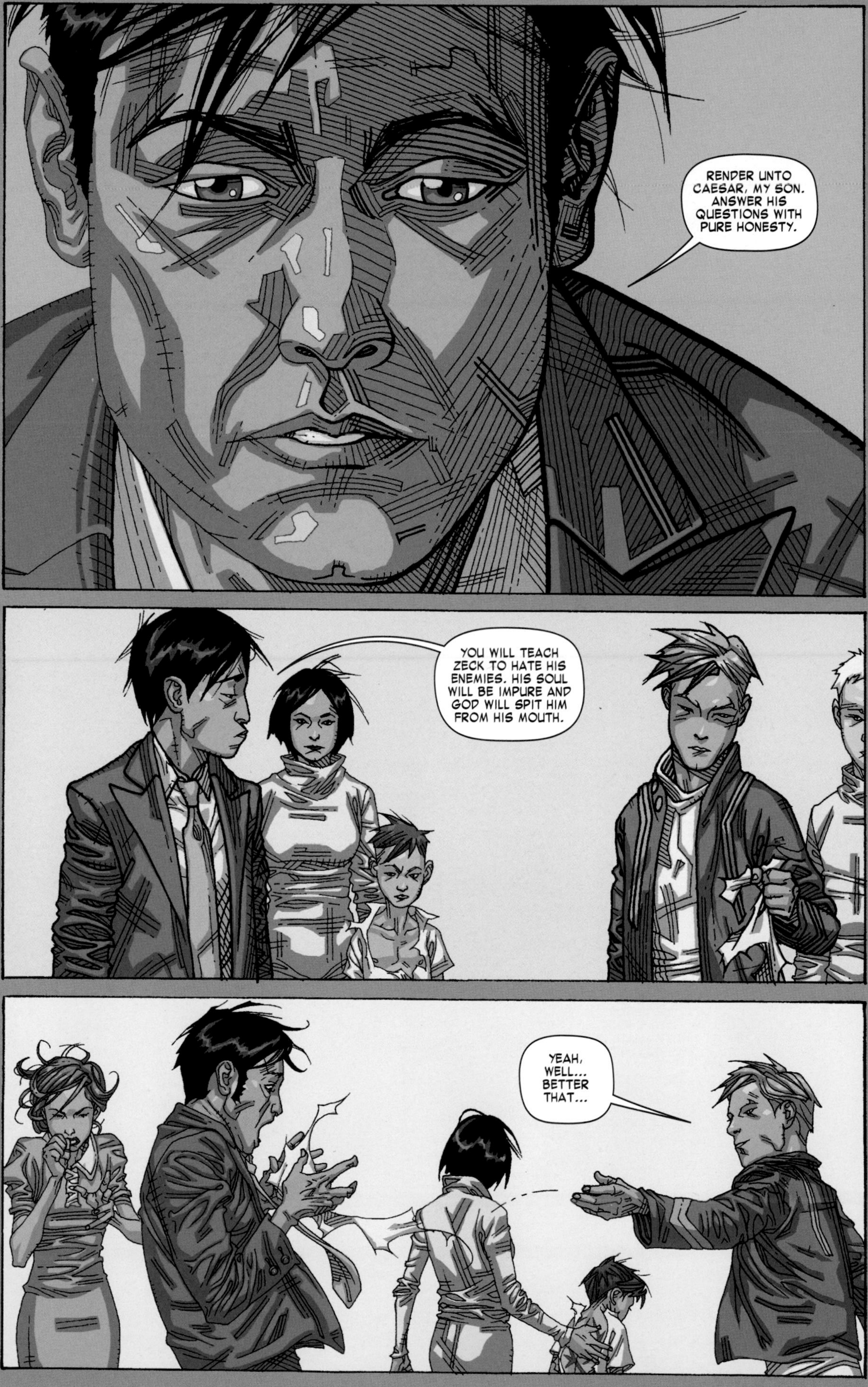
RENDER UNTO CAESAR, MY SON. ANSWER HIS QUESTIONS WITH PURE HONESTY.
YOU WILL TEACH ZECK TO HATE HIS ENEMIES. HIS SOUL WILL BE IMPURE AND GOD WILL SPIT HIM FROM HIS MOUTH.
YEAH, WELL... BETTER THAT...

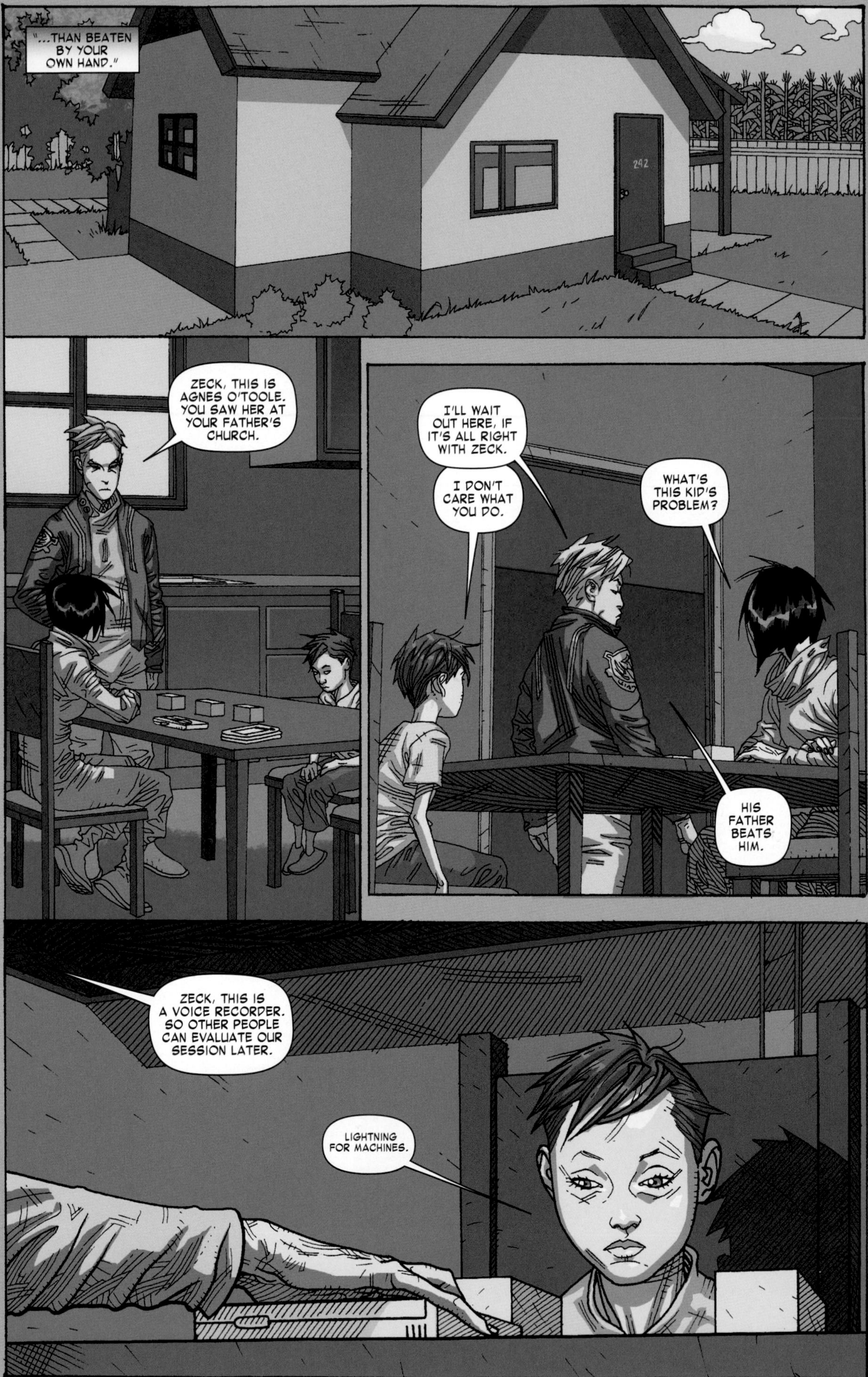
"...THAN BEATEN BY YOUR OWN HAND."
242
ZECK, THIS IS AGNES O'TOOLE. YOU SAW HER AT YOUR FATHER'S CHURCH.
I'LL WAIT OUT HERE, IF IT'S ALL RIGHT WITH ZECK.
I DON'T CARE WHAT YOU DO.
WHAT'S THIS KID'S PROBLEM?
HIS FATHER BEATS HIM.
ZECK, THIS IS A VOICE RECORDER. SO OTHER PEOPLE CAN EVALUATE OUR SESSION LATER.
LIGHTNING FOR MACHINES.

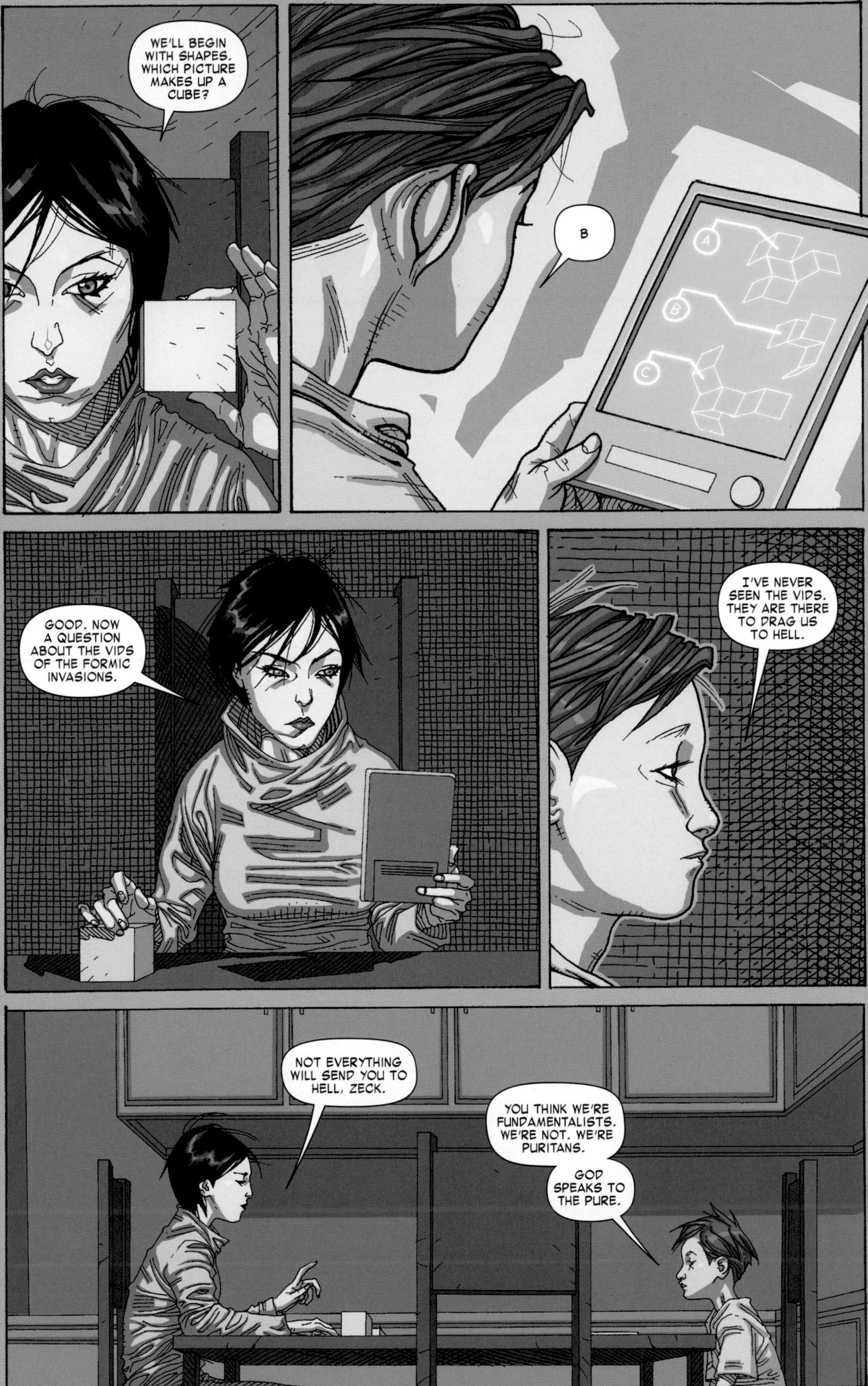
WE'LL BEGIN WITH SHAPES. WHICH PICTURE MAKES UP A CUBE?
A
B
C
B
GOOD. NOW A QUESTION ABOUT THE VIDS OF THE FORMIC INVASIONS.
I'VE NEVER SEEN THE VIDS. THEY ARE THERE TO DRAG US TO HELL.
NOT EVERYTHING WILL SEND YOU TO HELL, ZECK.
YOU THINK WE'RE FUNDAMENTALISTS. WE'RE NOT. WE'RE PURITANS.
GOD SPEAKS TO THE PURE.

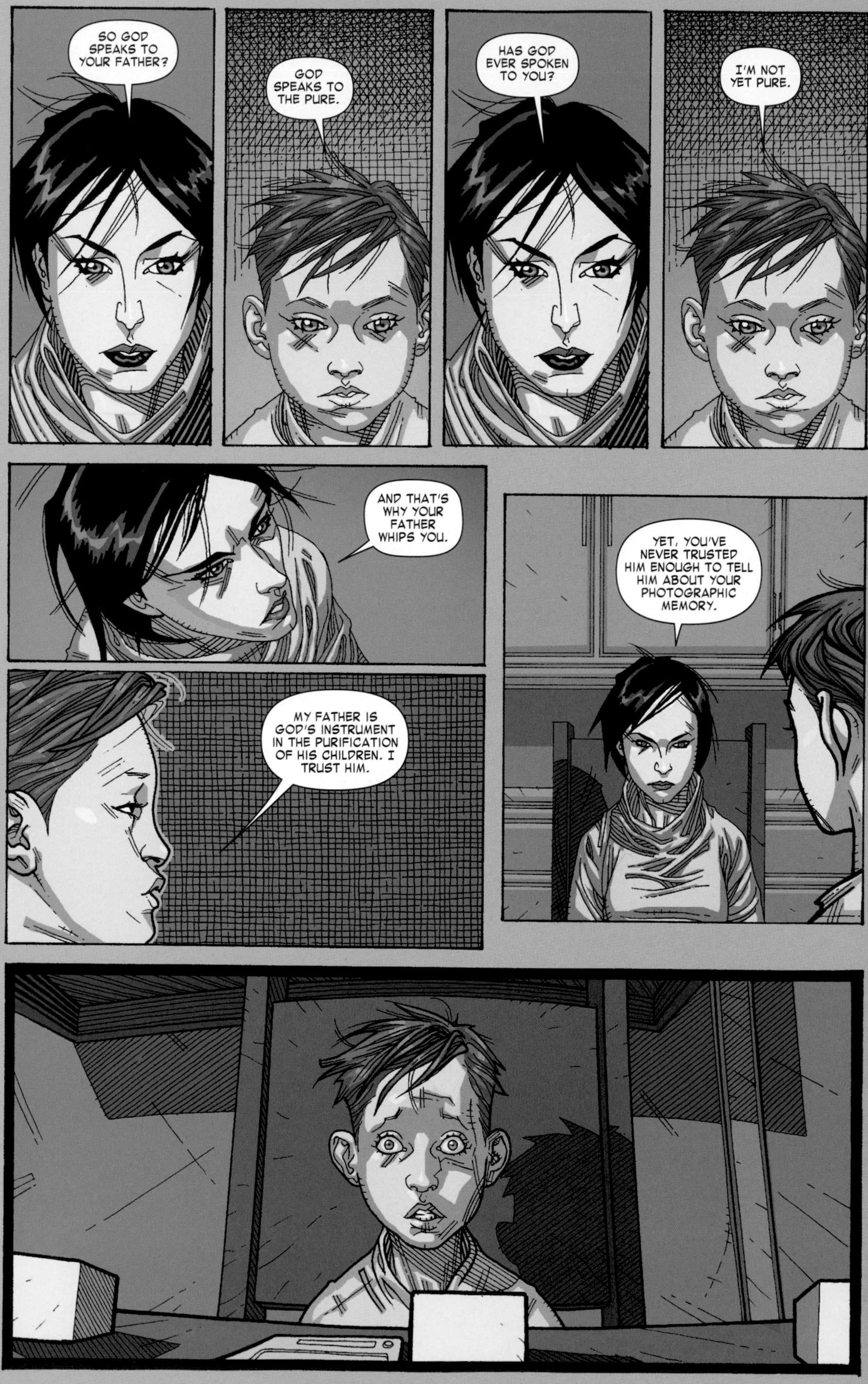
SO GOD SPEAKS TO YOUR FATHER?
GOD SPEAKS TO THE PURE.
HAS GOD EVER SPOKEN TO YOU?
I'M NOT YET PURE.
AND THAT'S WHY YOUR FATHER WHIPS YOU.
YET, YOU'VE NEVER TRUSTED HIM ENOUGH TO TELL HIM ABOUT YOUR PHOTOGRAPHIC MEMORY.
MY FATHER IS GOD'S INSTRUMENT IN THE PURIFICATION OF HIS CHILDREN. I TRUST HIM.

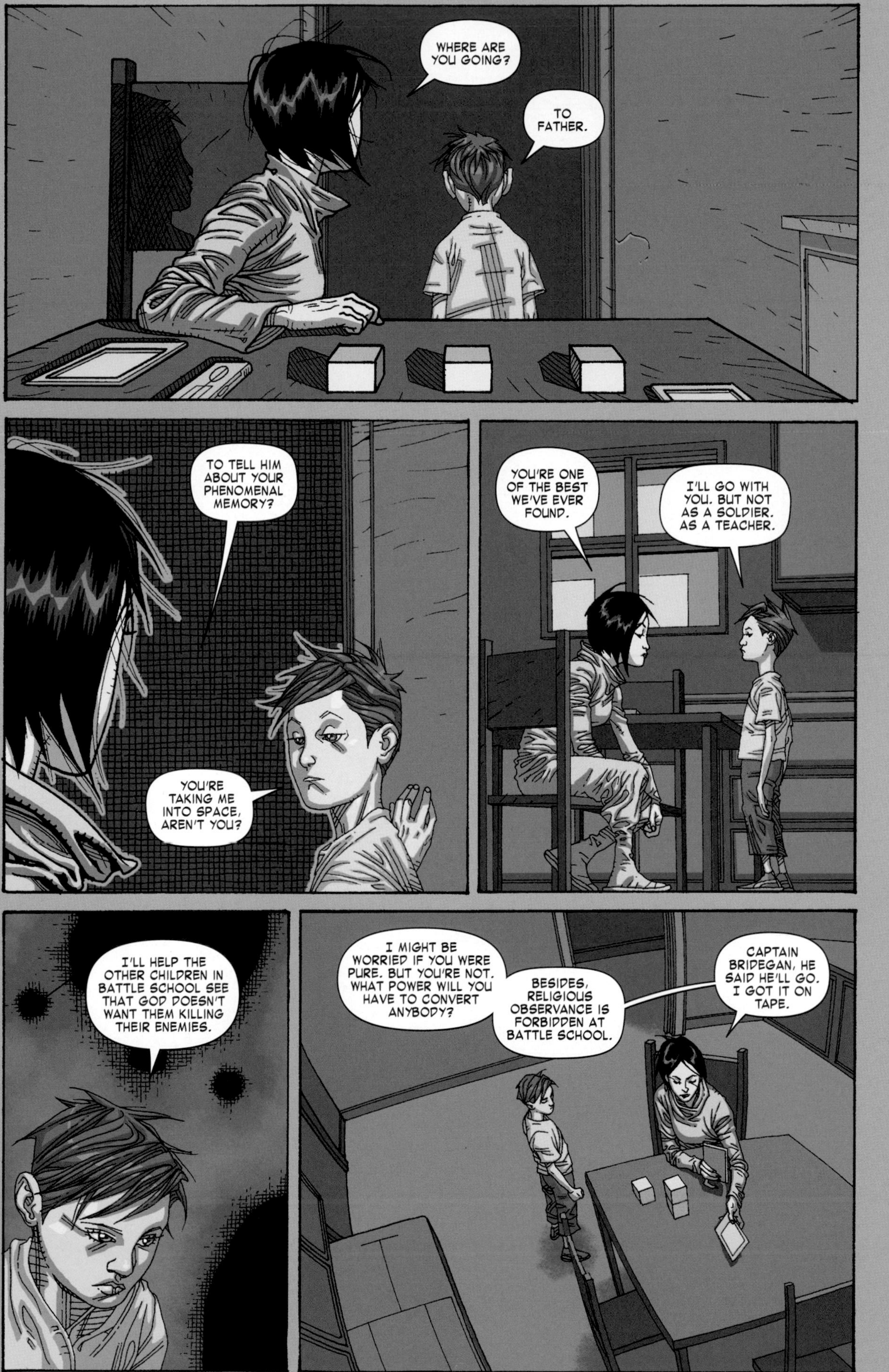
WHERE ARE YOU GOING?
TO FATHER.
TO TELL HIM ABOUT YOUR PHENOMENAL MEMORY?
YOU'RE TAKING ME INTO SPACE, AREN'T YOU?
YOU'RE ONE OF THE BEST WE'VE EVER FOUND.
I'LL GO WITH YOU. BUT NOT AS A SOLDIER. AS A TEACHER.
I'LL HELP THE OTHER CHILDREN IN BATTLE SCHOOL SEE THAT GOD DOESN'T WANT THEM KILLING THEIR ENEMIES.
I MIGHT BE WORRIED IF YOU WERE PURE. BUT YOU'RE NOT. WHAT POWER WILL YOU HAVE TO CONVERT ANYBODY?
BESIDES, RELIGIOUS OBSERVANCE IS FORBIDDEN AT BATTLE SCHOOL.
CAPTAIN BRIDEGAN, HE SAID HE'LL GO. I GOT IT ON TAPE.

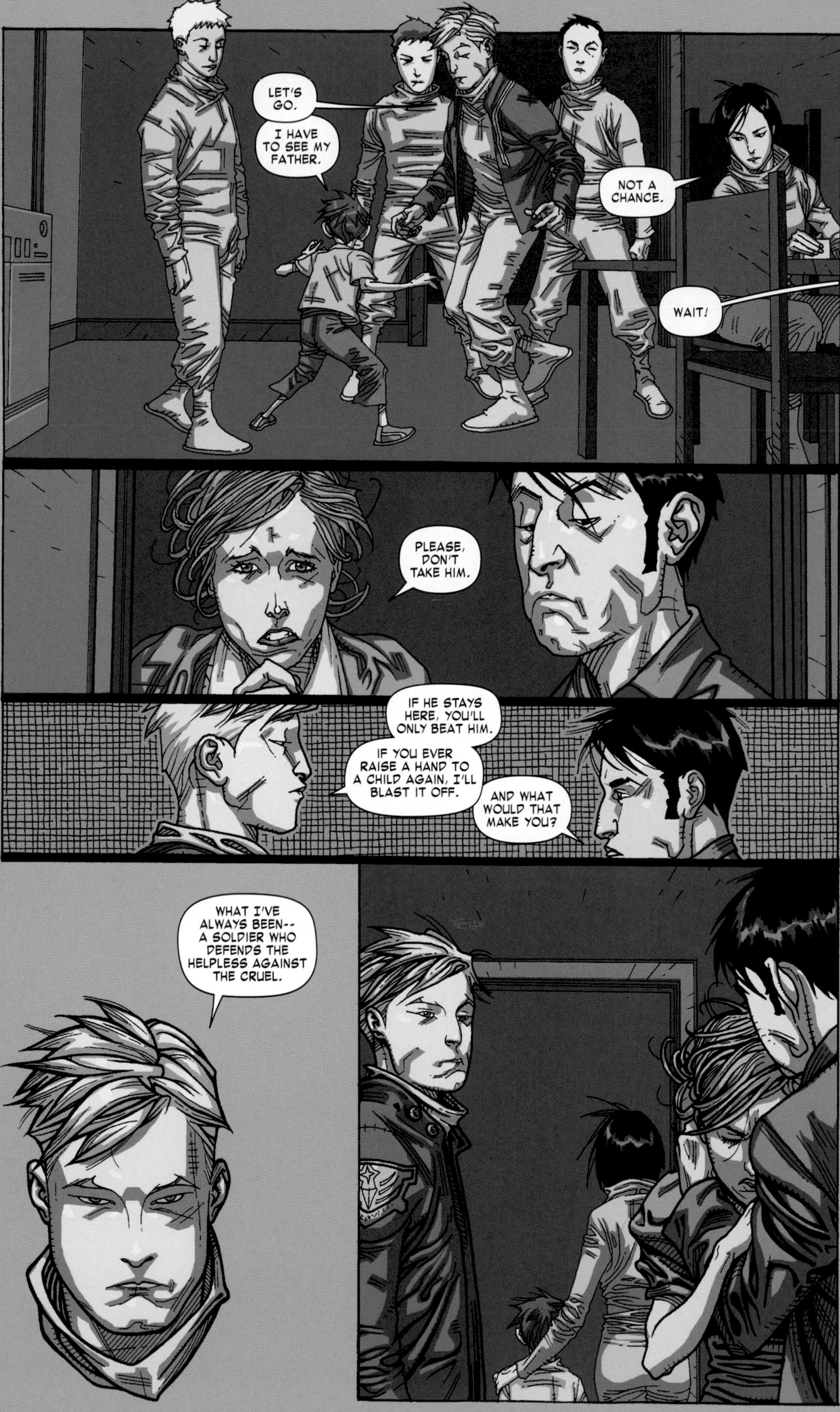
LET'S GO.
I HAVE TO SEE MY FATHER.
NOT A CHANCE.
WAIT!
PLEASE, DON'T TAKE HIM.
IF HE STAYS HERE, YOU'LL ONLY BEAT HIM.
IF YOU EVER RAISE A HAND TO A CHILD AGAIN, I'LL BLAST IT OFF.
AND WHAT WOULD THAT MAKE YOU?
WHAT I'VE ALWAYS BEEN-- A SOLDIER WHO DEFENDS THE HELPLESS AGAINST THE CRUEL.

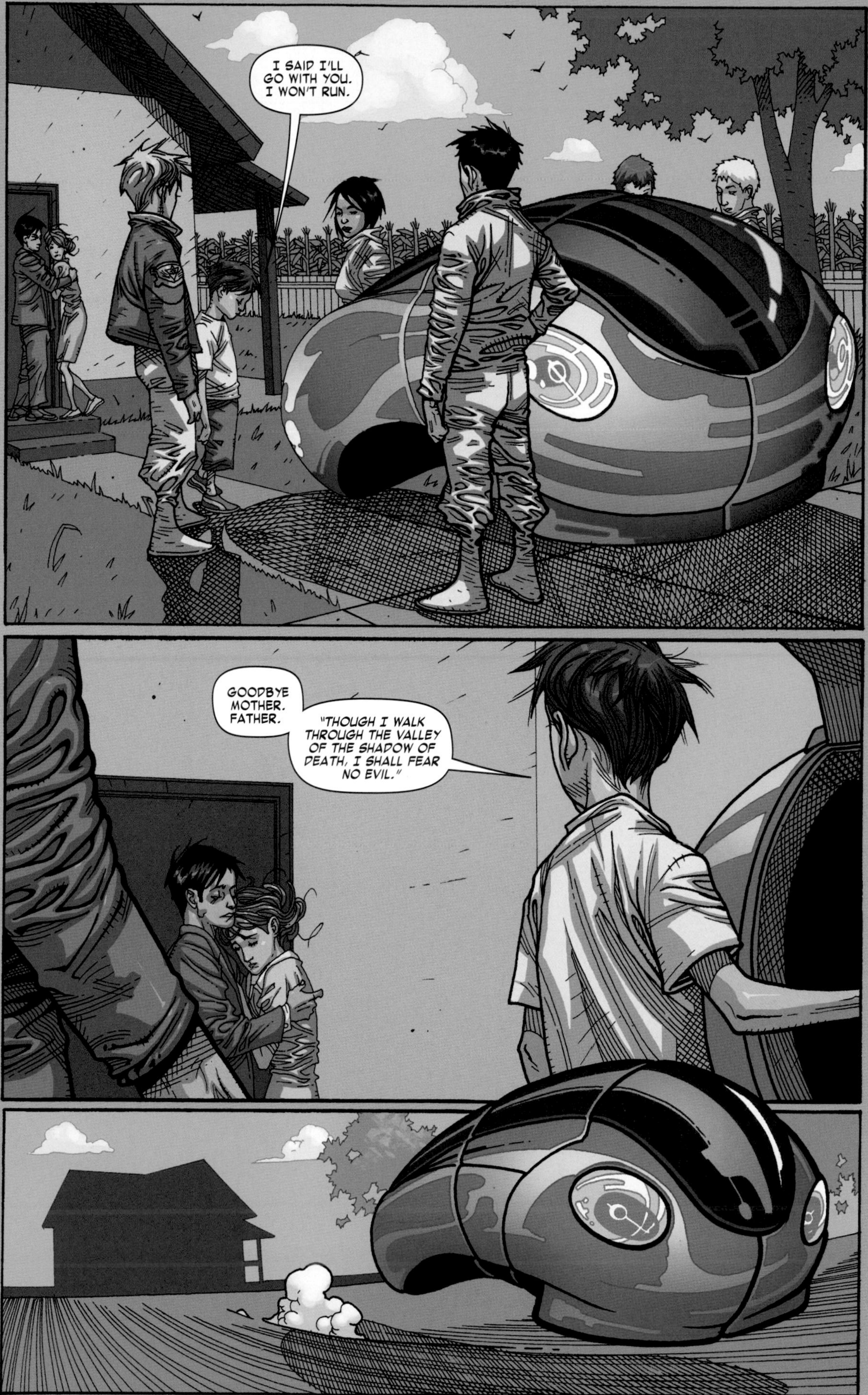
I SAID I'LL GO WITH YOU. I WON'T RUN.
GOODBYE MOTHER. FATHER.
"THOUGH I WALK THROUGH THE VALLEY OF THE SHADOW OF DEATH, I SHALL FEAR NO EVIL."

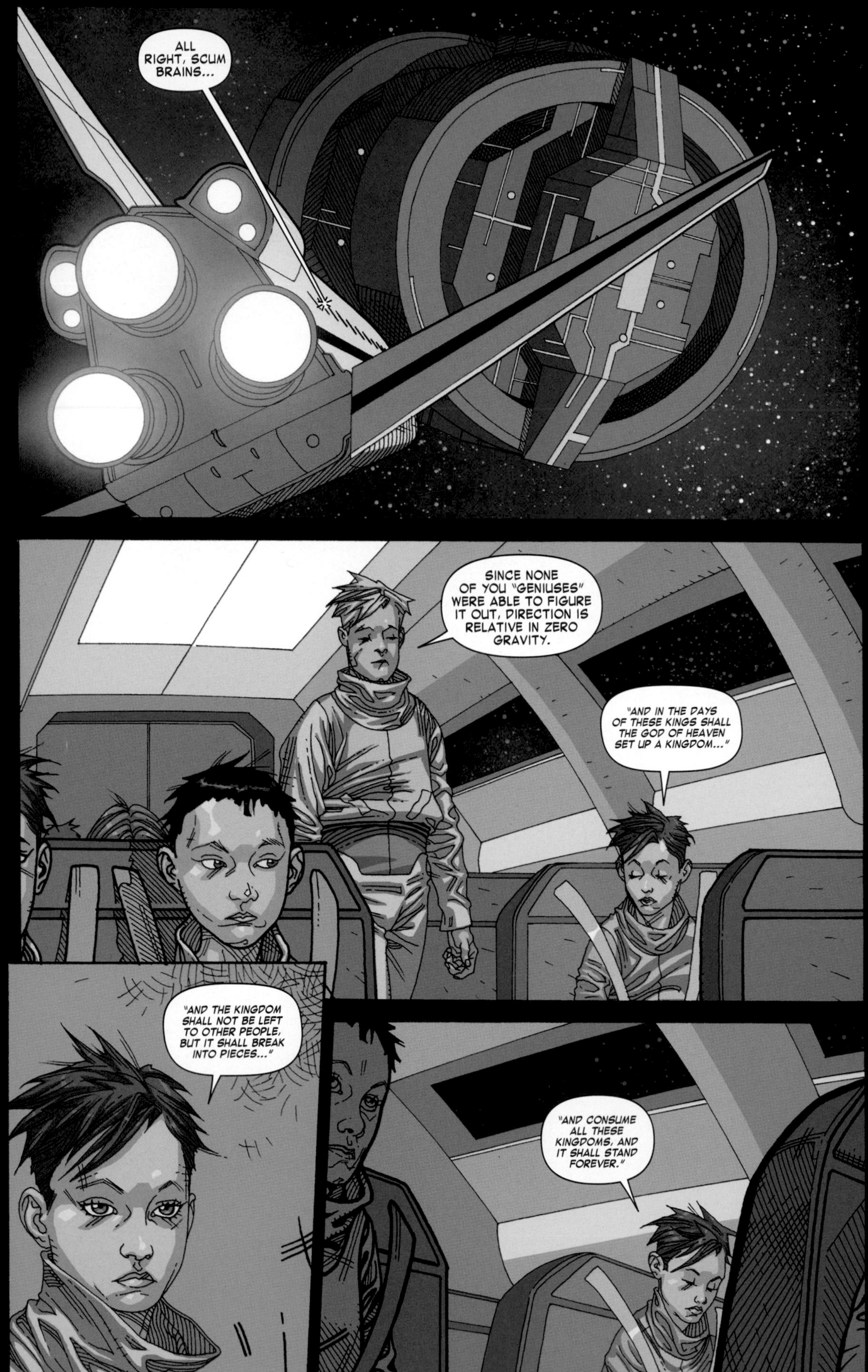
ALL RIGHT, SCUM BRAINS...
SINCE NONE OF YOU "GENIUSES" WERE ABLE TO FIGURE IT OUT, DIRECTION IS RELATIVE IN ZERO GRAVITY.
"AND IN THE DAYS OF THESE KINGS SHALL THE GOD OF HEAVEN SET UP A KINGDOM..."
"AND THE KINGDOM SHALL NOT BE LEFT TO OTHER PEOPLE, BUT IT SHALL BREAK INTO PIECES..."
"AND CONSUME ALL THESE KINGDOMS, AND IT SHALL STAND FOREVER."

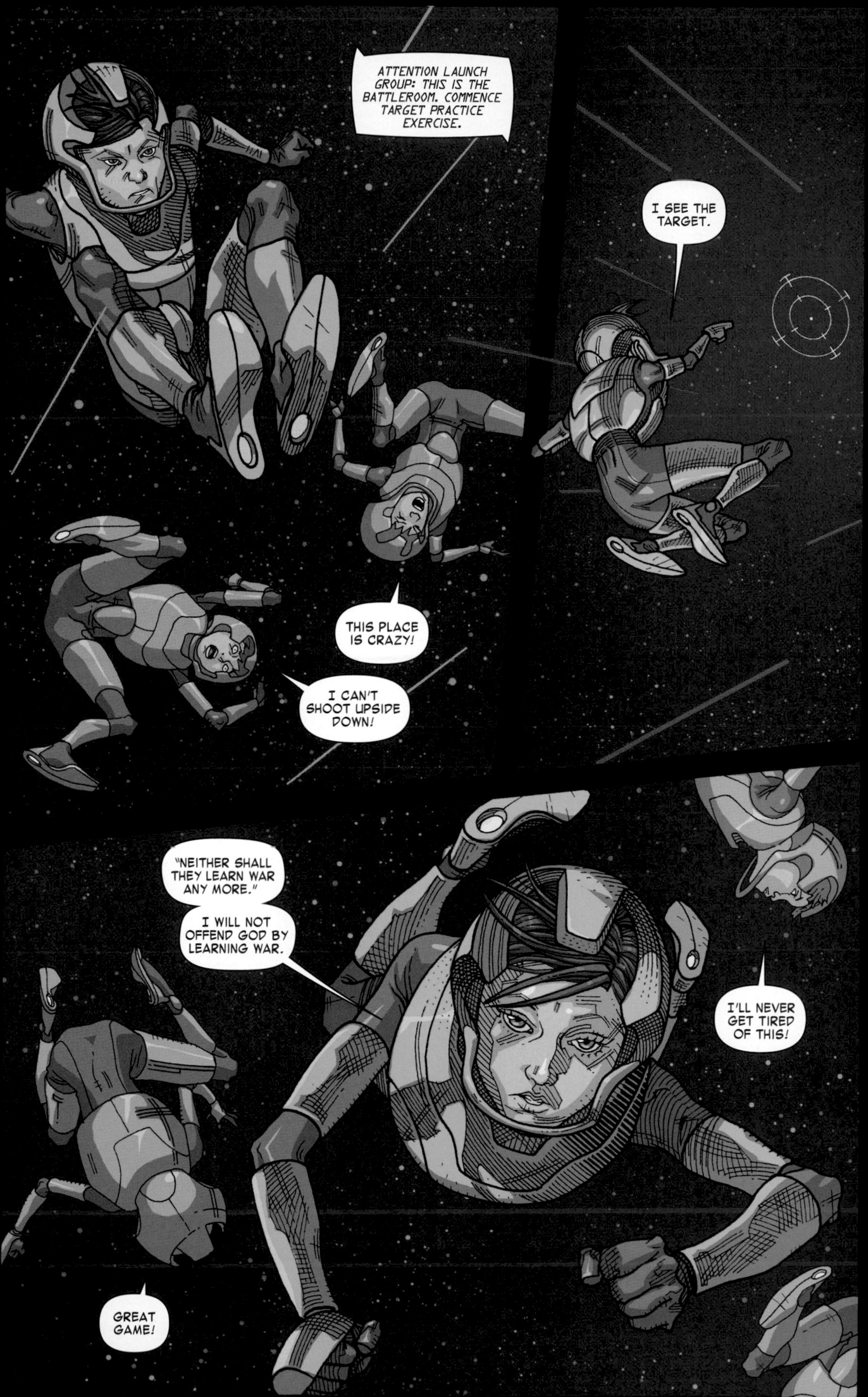
ATTENTION LAUNCH GROUP: THIS IS THE BATTLEROOM. COMMENCE TARGET PRACTICE EXERCISE.
I SEE THE TARGET.
THIS PLACE IS CRAZY!
I CAN'T SHOOT UPSIDE DOWN!
"NEITHER SHALL THEY LEARN WAR ANY MORE."
I WILL NOT OFFEND GOD BY LEARNING WAR.
I'LL NEVER GET TIRED OF THIS!
GREAT GAME!

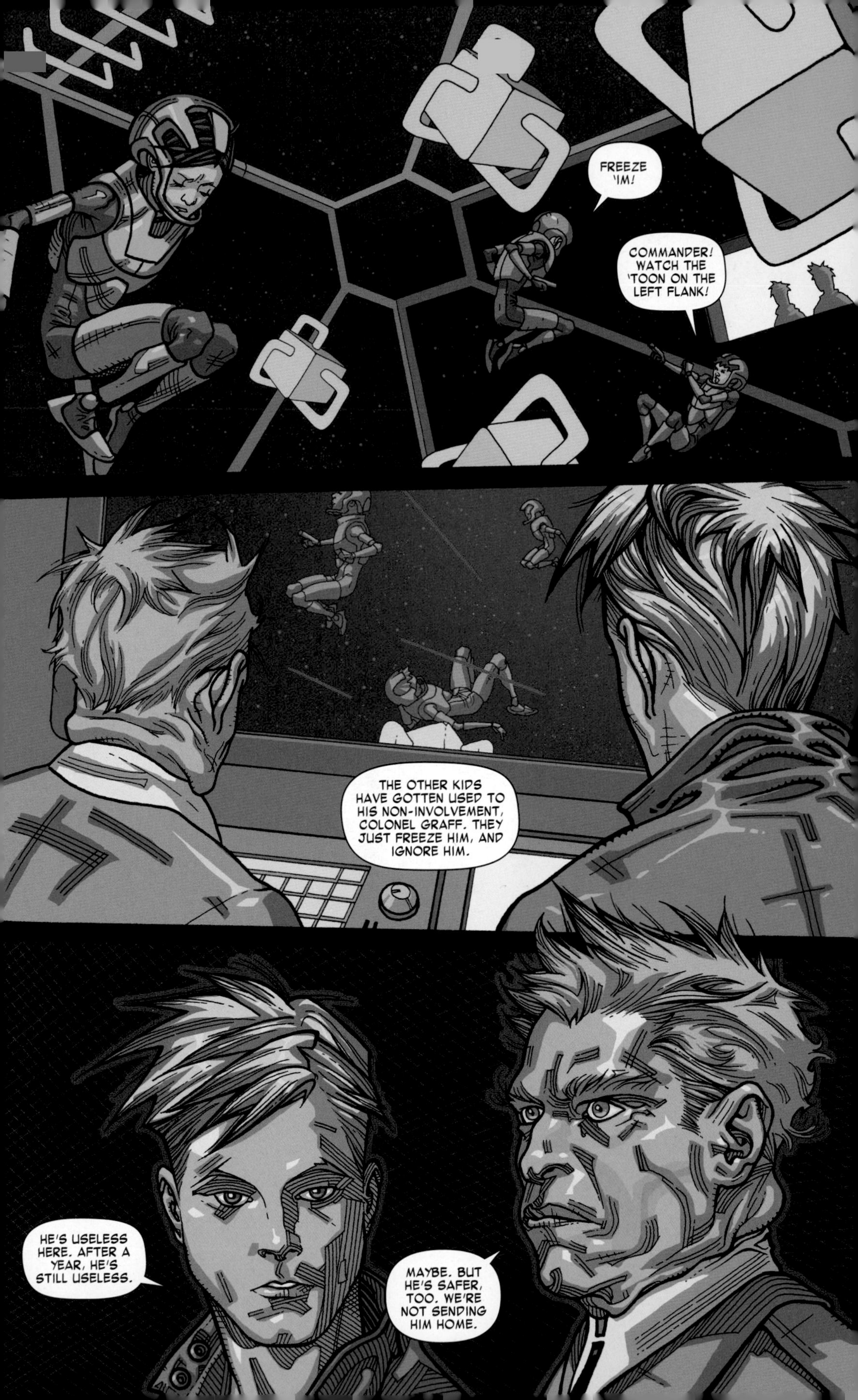
FREEZE 'IM!
COMMANDER! WATCH THE 'TOON ON THE LEFT FLANK!
THE OTHER KIDS HAVE GOTTEN USED TO HIS NON-INVOLVEMENT, COLONEL GRAFF. THEY JUST FREEZE HIM, AND IGNORE HIM.
HE'S USELESS HERE. AFTER A YEAR, HE'S STILL USELESS.
MAYBE. BUT HE'S SAFER, TOO. WE'RE NOT SENDING HIM HOME.

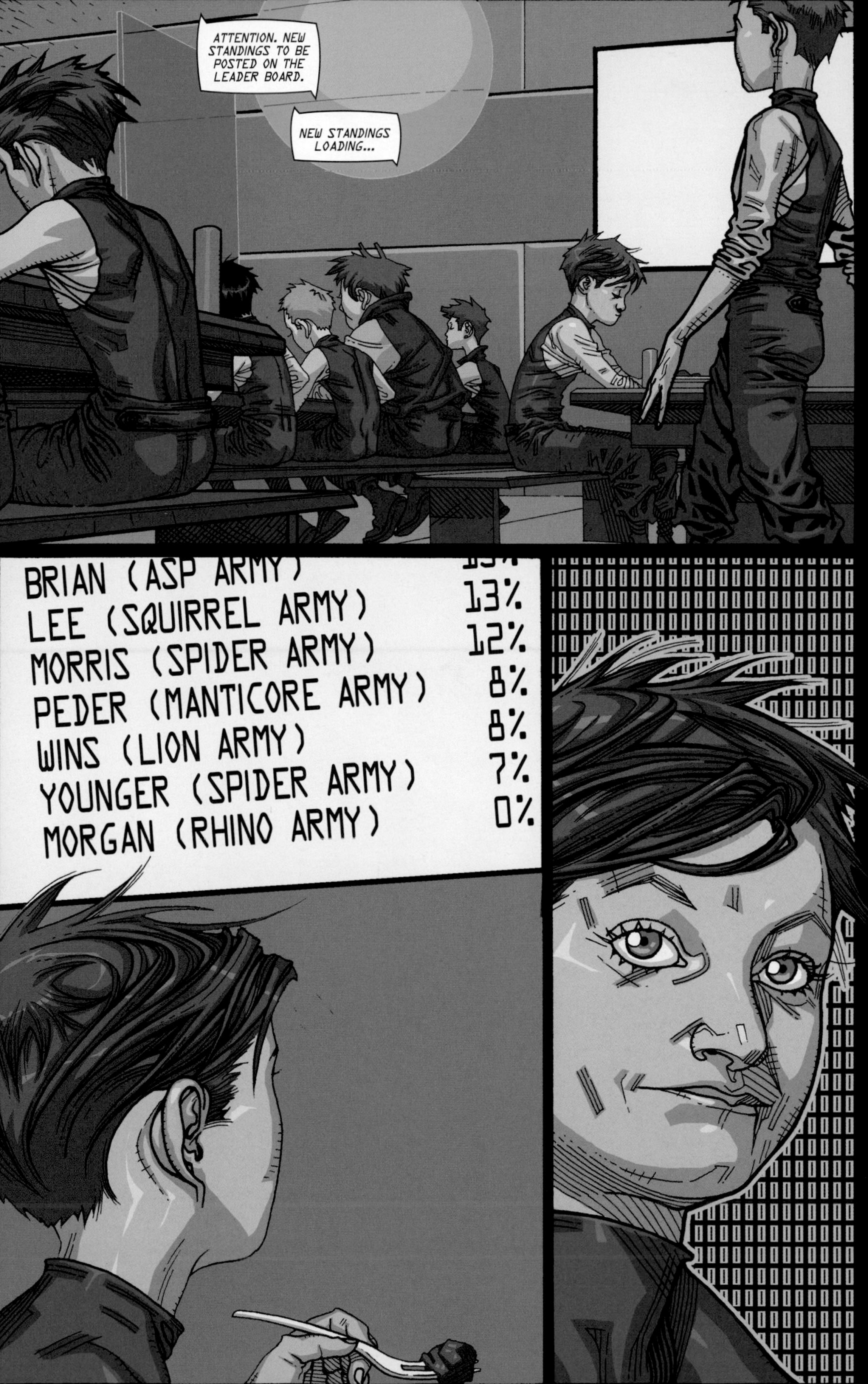
ATTENTION. NEW STANDINGS TO BE POSTED ON THE LEADER BOARD.
NEW STANDINGS LOADING...
BRIAN (ASP ARMY)
LEE (SQUIRREL ARMY) 13%
MORRIS (SPIDER ARMY) 12%
PEDER (MANTICORE ARMY) 8%
WINS (LION ARMY) 8%
YOUNGER (SPIDER ARMY) 7%
MORGAN (RHINO ARMY) 0%

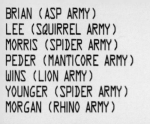

BRIAN (ASP ARMY) 15%
LEE (SQUIRREL ARMY) 13%
MORRIS (SPIDER ARMY) 12%
PEDER (MANTICORE ARMY) 8%
WINS (LION ARMY) 8%
YOUNGER (SPIDER ARMY) 7%
MORGAN (RHINO ARMY) 0%

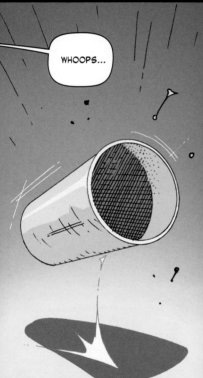

WHOOPS...

I'M IN LAST PLACE BECAUSE I CHOOSE TO BE. TO SHOW THEM THAT I SERVE YOU, GOD, NOT THEM.

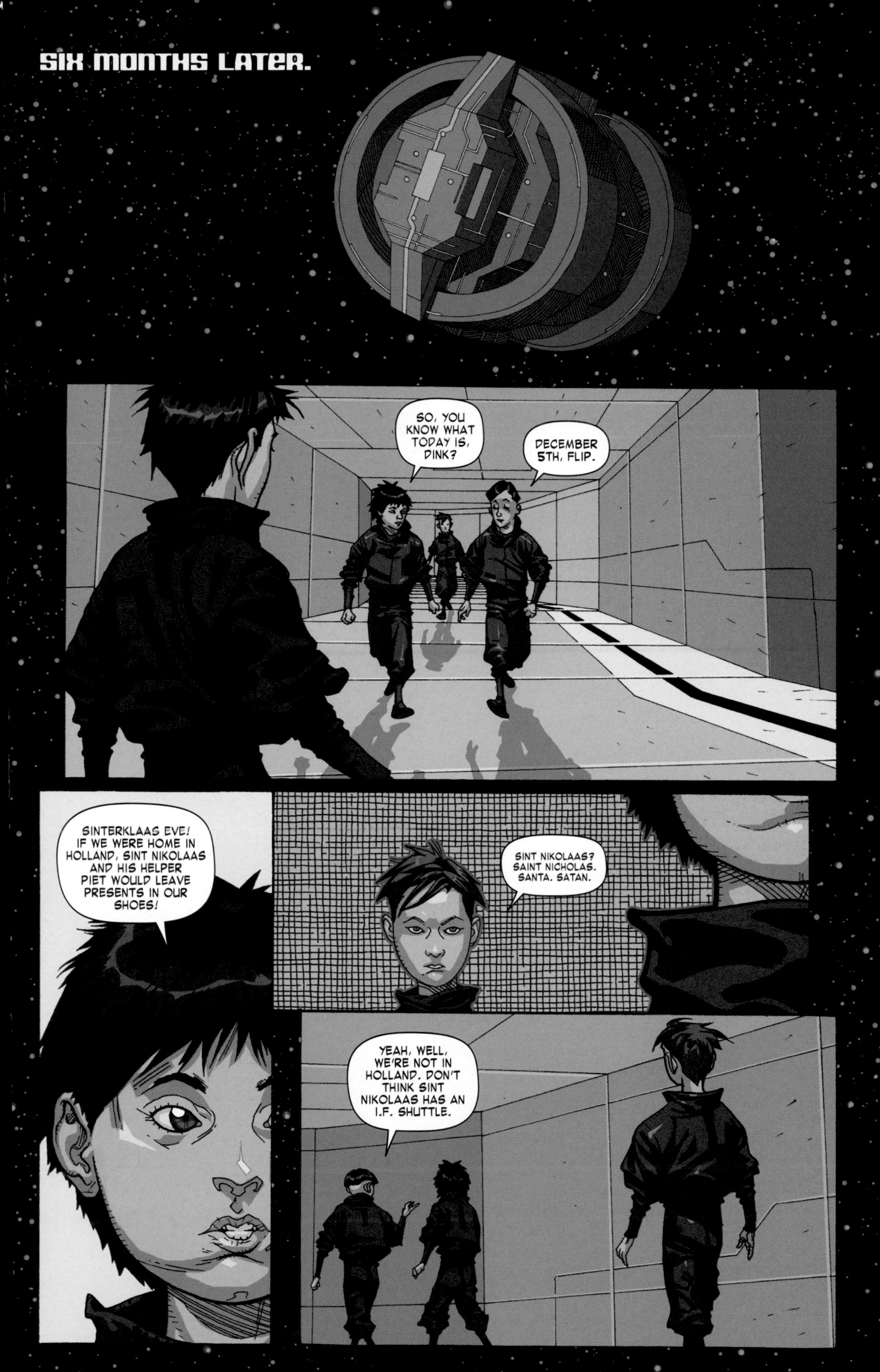
SIX MONTHS LATER.
SO, YOU KNOW WHAT TODAY IS, DINK?
DECEMBER 5TH, FLIP.
SINTERKLAAS EVE! IF WE WERE HOME IN HOLLAND, SINT NIKOLAAS AND HIS HELPER PIET WOULD LEAVE PRESENTS IN OUR SHOES!
SINT NIKOLAAS? SAINT NICHOLAS. SANTA. SATAN.
YEAH, WELL, WE'RE NOT IN HOLLAND. DON'T THINK SINT NIKOLAAS HAS AN I.F. SHUTTLE.

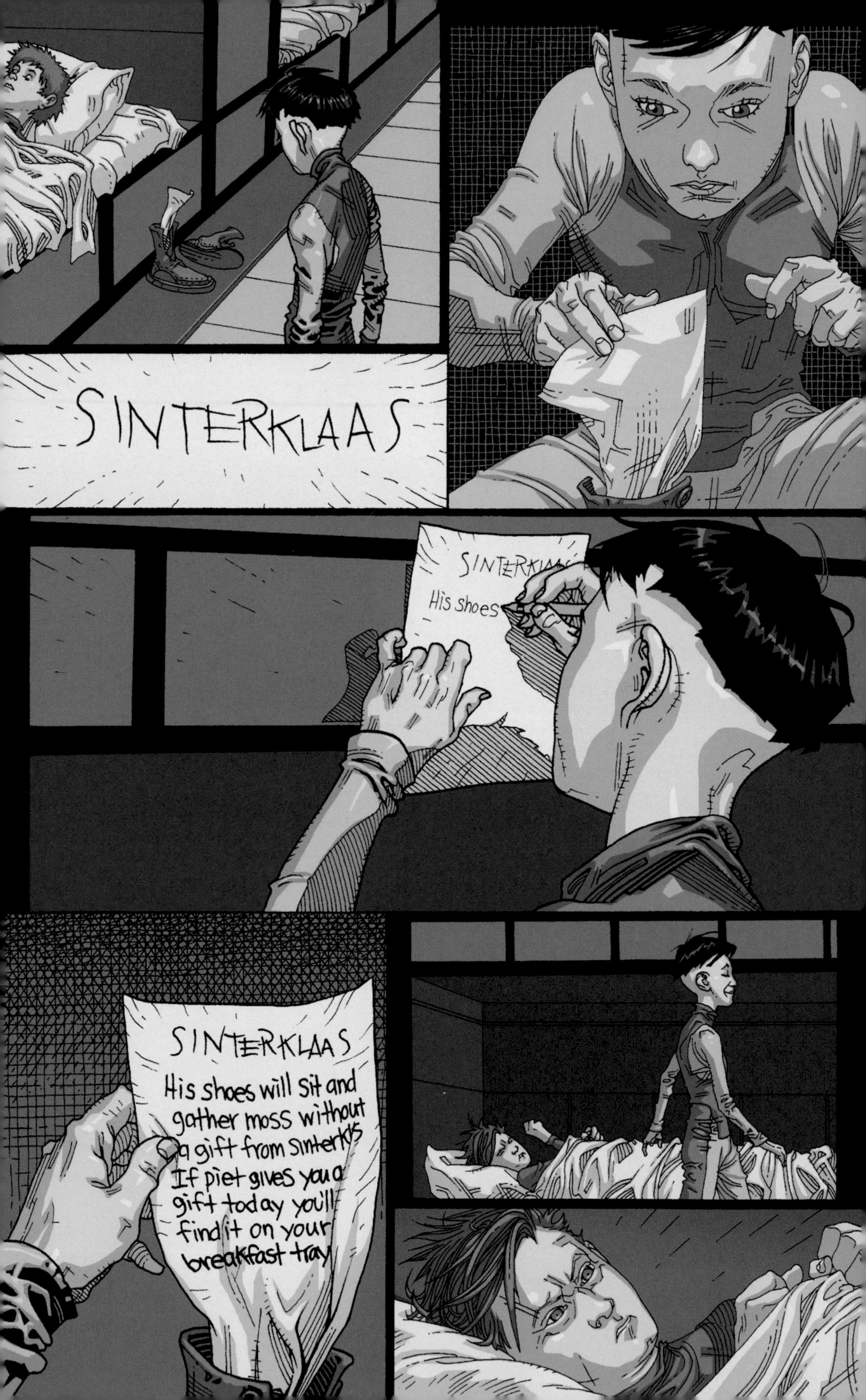
SINTERKLAAS
SINTERKLAAS
His shoes
SINTERKLAAS
His shoes will sit and gather moss without a gift from Sinterklaas
If piet gives you a gift today you'll find it on your breakfast tray

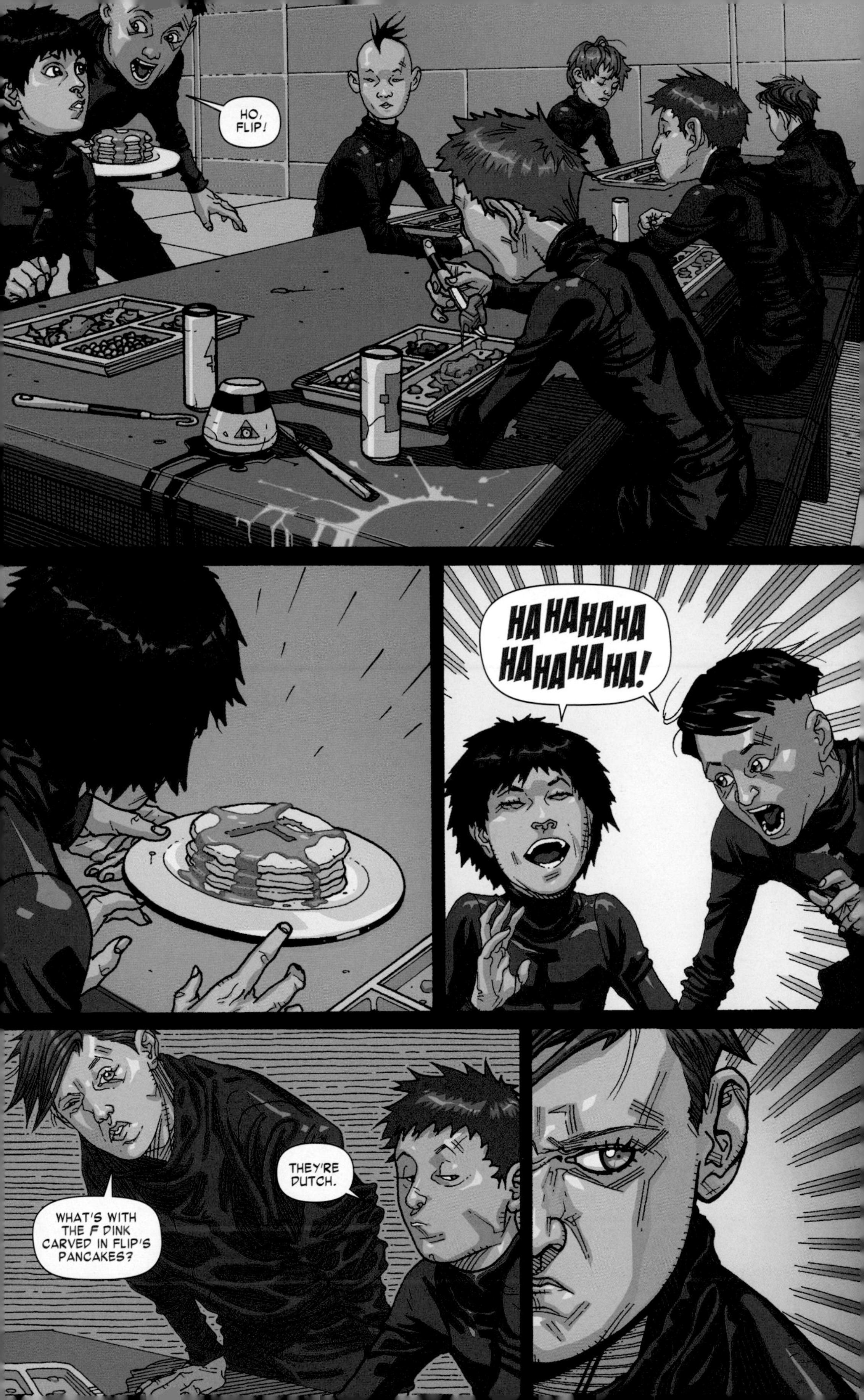
HO, FLIP!
HAHAHAHA HAHAHAHA!
WHAT'S WITH THE F DINK CARVED IN FLIP'S PANCAKES?
THEY'RE DUTCH.

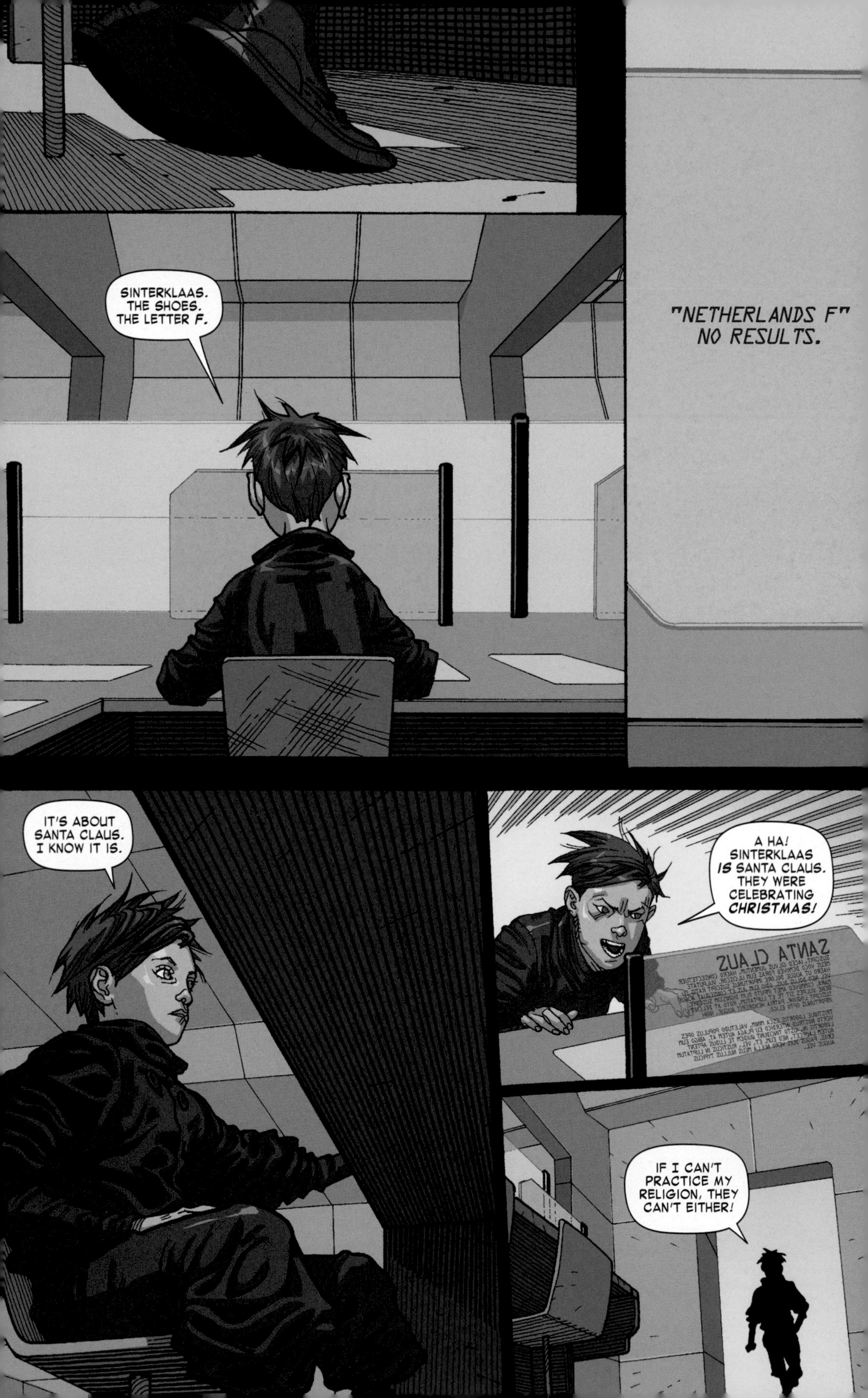
SINTERKLAAS. THE SHOES. THE LETTER F.
"NETHERLANDS F" NO RESULTS.
IT'S ABOUT SANTA CLAUS. I KNOW IT IS.
A HA! SINTERKLAAS IS SANTA CLAUS. THEY WERE CELEBRATING CHRISTMAS!
IF I CAN'T PRACTICE MY RELIGION, THEY CAN'T EITHER!

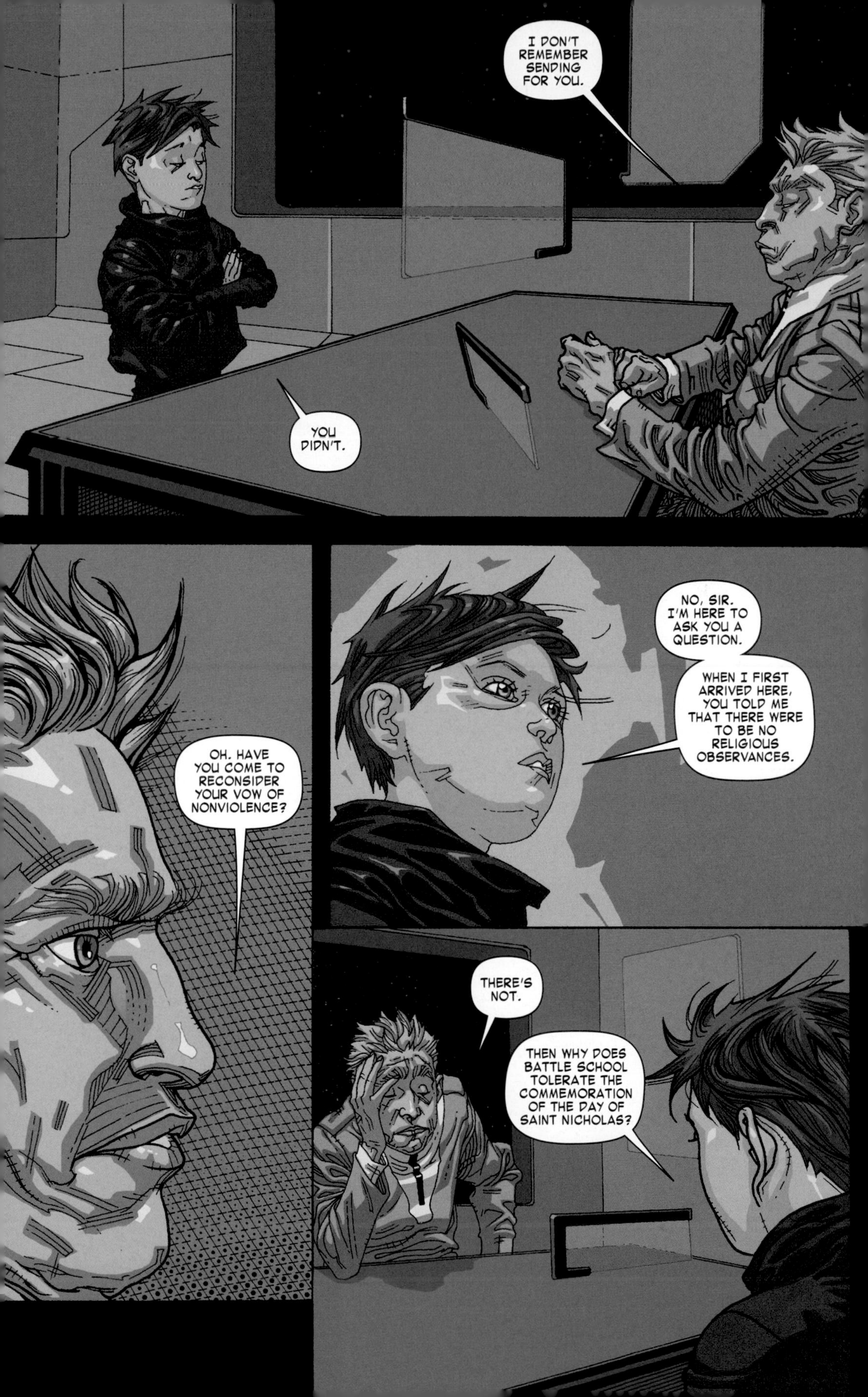
I DON'T REMEMBER SENDING FOR YOU.
YOU DIDN'T.
NO, SIR. I'M HERE TO ASK YOU A QUESTION.
WHEN I FIRST ARRIVED HERE, YOU TOLD ME THAT THERE WERE TO BE NO RELIGIOUS OBSERVANCES.
OH. HAVE YOU COME TO RECONSIDER YOUR VOW OF NONVIOLENCE?
THERE'S NOT.
THEN WHY DOES BATTLE SCHOOL TOLERATE THE COMMEMORATION OF THE DAY OF SAINT NICHOLAS?

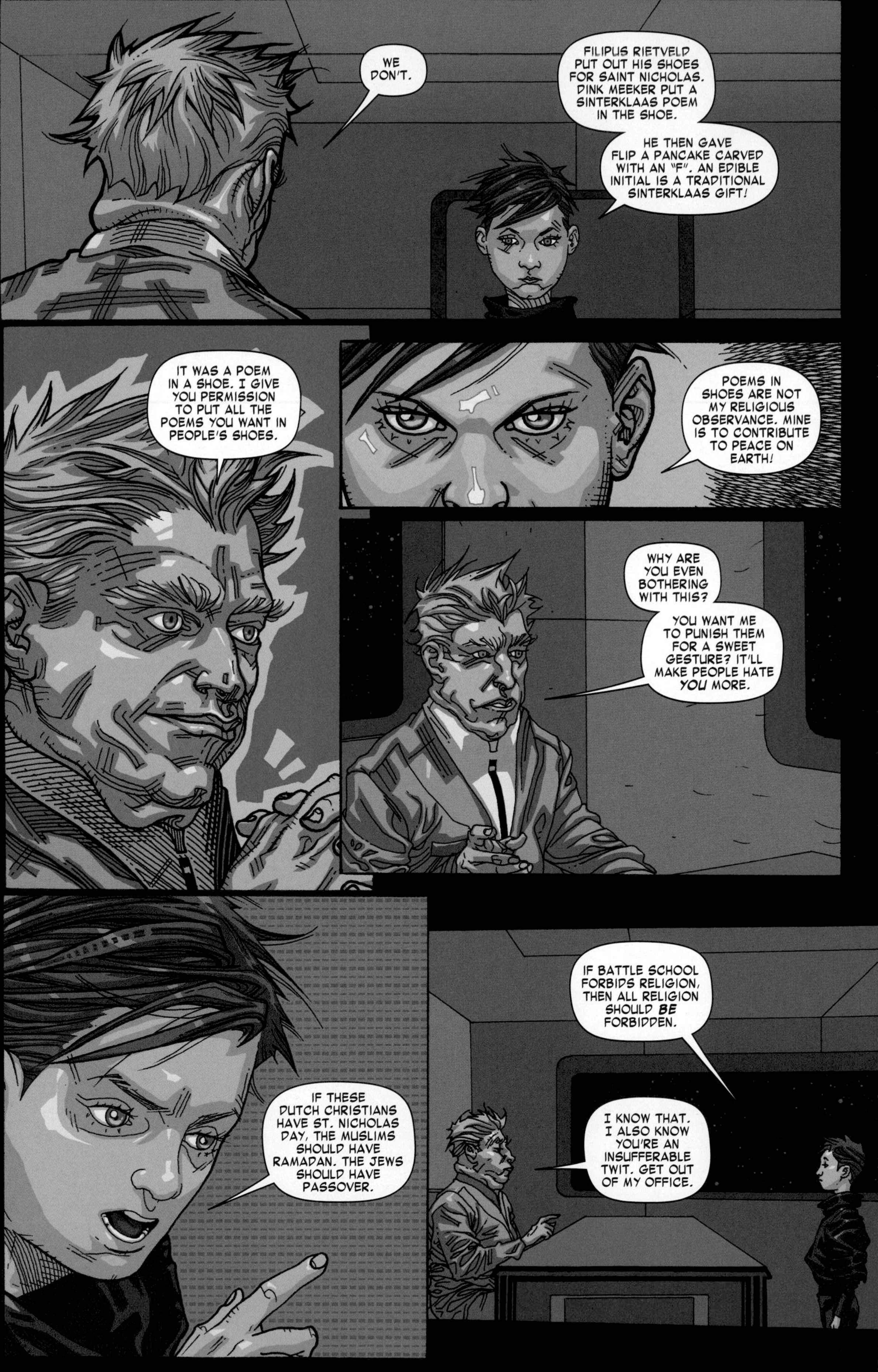
WE DON'T.
FILIPUS RIETVELD PUT OUT HIS SHOES FOR SAINT NICHOLAS. DINK MEEKER PUT A SINTERKLAAS POEM IN THE SHOE.
HE THEN GAVE FLIP A PANCAKE CARVED WITH AN "F". AN EDIBLE INITIAL IS A TRADITIONAL SINTERKLAAS GIFT!
IT WAS A POEM IN A SHOE. I GIVE YOU PERMISSION TO PUT ALL THE POEMS YOU WANT IN PEOPLE'S SHOES.
POEMS IN SHOES ARE NOT MY RELIGIOUS OBSERVANCE. MINE IS TO CONTRIBUTE TO PEACE ON EARTH!
WHY ARE YOU EVEN BOTHERING WITH THIS?
YOU WANT ME TO PUNISH THEM FOR A SWEET GESTURE? IT'LL MAKE PEOPLE HATE *YOU* MORE.
IF THESE DUTCH CHRISTIANS HAVE ST. NICHOLAS DAY, THE MUSLIMS SHOULD HAVE RAMADAN. THE JEWS SHOULD HAVE PASSOVER.
IF BATTLE SCHOOL FORBIDS RELIGION, THEN ALL RELIGION SHOULD *BE* FORBIDDEN.
I KNOW THAT. I ALSO KNOW YOU'RE AN INSUFFERABLE TWIT. GET OUT OF MY OFFICE.

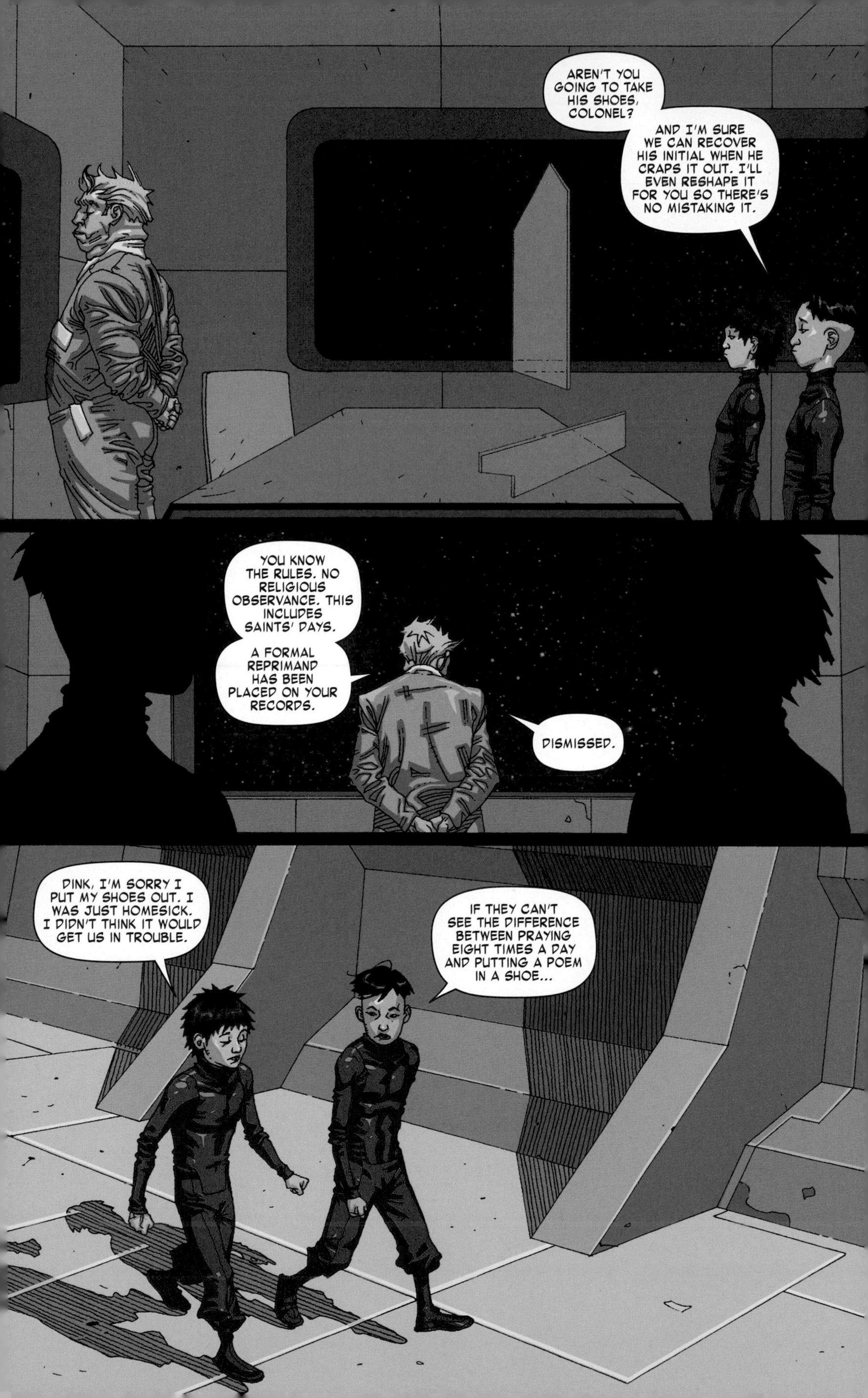
AREN'T YOU GOING TO TAKE HIS SHOES, COLONEL?
AND I'M SURE WE CAN RECOVER HIS INITIAL WHEN HE CRAPS IT OUT. I'LL EVEN RESHAPE IT FOR YOU SO THERE'S NO MISTAKING IT.
YOU KNOW THE RULES. NO RELIGIOUS OBSERVANCE. THIS INCLUDES SAINTS' DAYS.
A FORMAL REPRIMAND HAS BEEN PLACED ON YOUR RECORDS.
DISMISSED.
DINK, I'M SORRY I PUT MY SHOES OUT. I WAS JUST HOMESICK. I DIDN'T THINK IT WOULD GET US IN TROUBLE.
IF THEY CAN'T SEE THE DIFFERENCE BETWEEN PRAYING EIGHT TIMES A DAY AND PUTTING A POEM IN A SHOE...

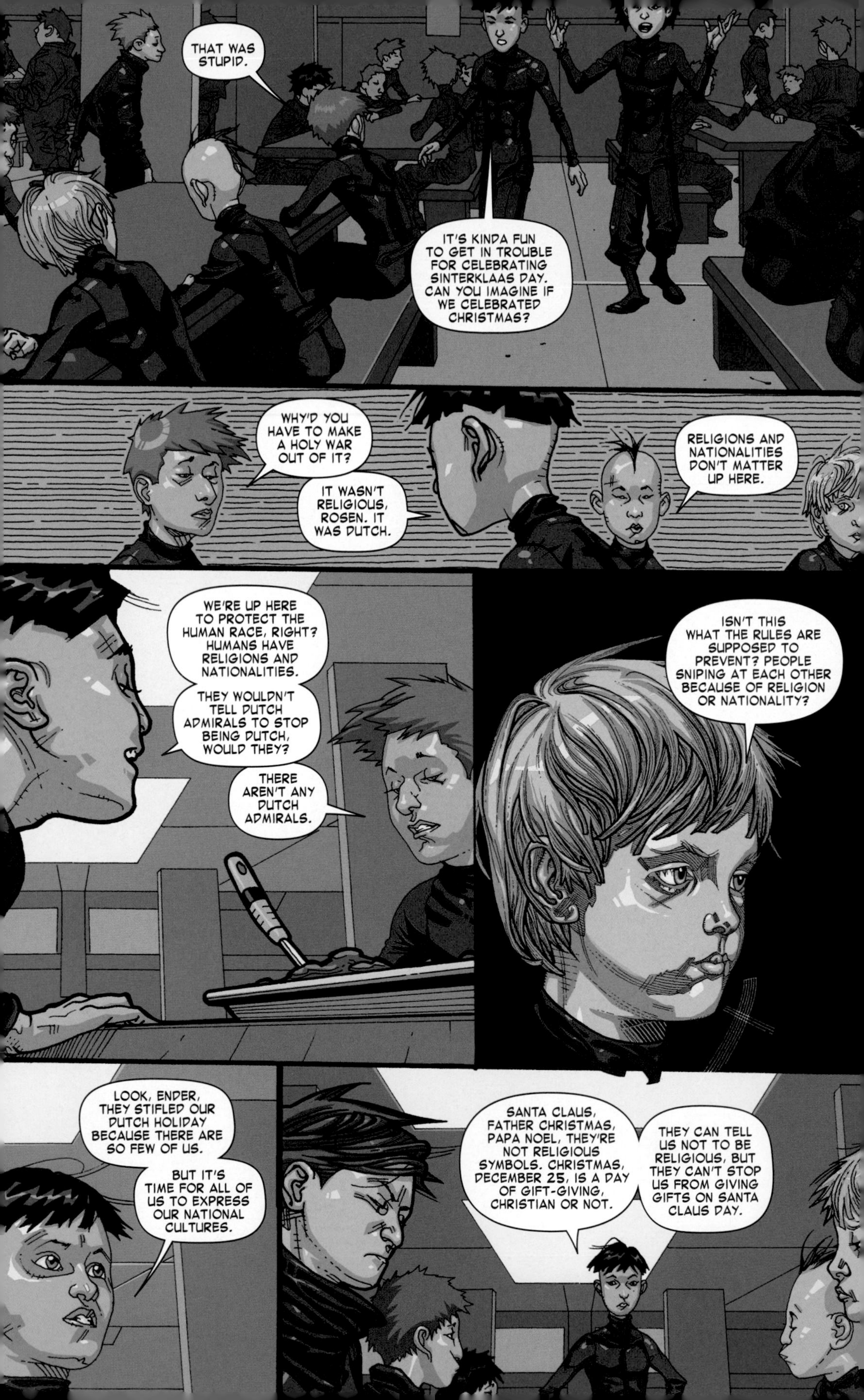
THAT WAS STUPID.
IT'S KINDA FUN TO GET IN TROUBLE FOR CELEBRATING SINTERKLAAS DAY. CAN YOU IMAGINE IF WE CELEBRATED CHRISTMAS?
WHY'D YOU HAVE TO MAKE A HOLY WAR OUT OF IT?
IT WASN'T RELIGIOUS, ROSEN. IT WAS DUTCH.
RELIGIONS AND NATIONALITIES DON'T MATTER UP HERE.
WE'RE UP HERE TO PROTECT THE HUMAN RACE, RIGHT? HUMANS HAVE RELIGIONS AND NATIONALITIES.
THEY WOULDN'T TELL DUTCH ADMIRALS TO STOP BEING DUTCH, WOULD THEY?
THERE AREN'T ANY DUTCH ADMIRALS.
ISN'T THIS WHAT THE RULES ARE SUPPOSED TO PREVENT? PEOPLE SNIPING AT EACH OTHER BECAUSE OF RELIGION OR NATIONALITY?
LOOK, ENDER, THEY STIFLED OUR DUTCH HOLIDAY BECAUSE THERE ARE SO FEW OF US.
BUT IT'S TIME FOR ALL OF US TO EXPRESS OUR NATIONAL CULTURES.
SANTA CLAUS, FATHER CHRISTMAS, PAPA NOEL, THEY'RE NOT RELIGIOUS SYMBOLS. CHRISTMAS, DECEMBER 25, IS A DAY OF GIFT-GIVING, CHRISTIAN OR NOT.
THEY CAN TELL US NOT TO BE RELIGIOUS, BUT THEY CAN'T STOP US FROM GIVING GIFTS ON SANTA CLAUS DAY.

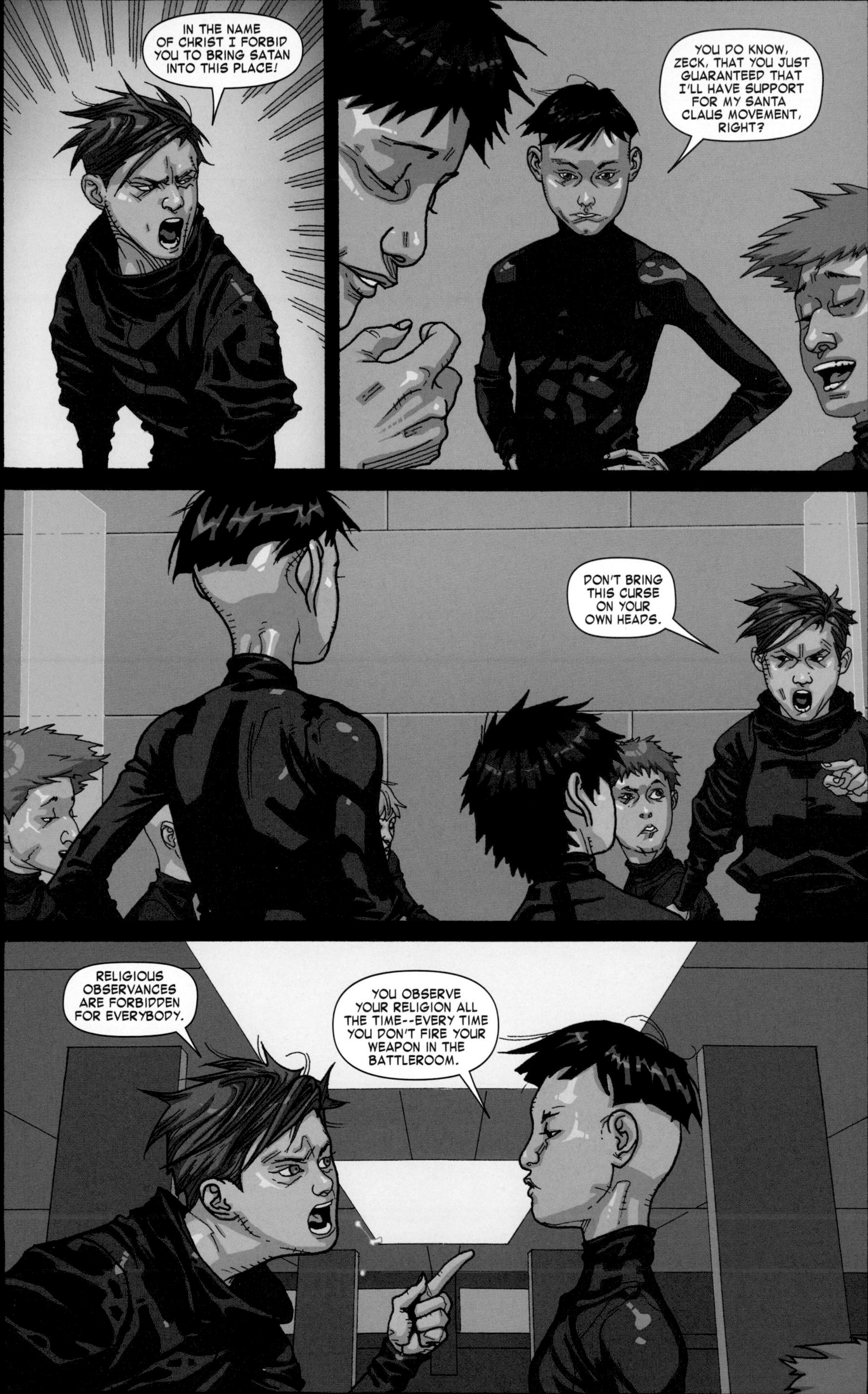
IN THE NAME OF CHRIST I FORBID YOU TO BRING SATAN INTO THIS PLACE!
YOU DO KNOW, ZECK, THAT YOU JUST GUARANTEED THAT I'LL HAVE SUPPORT FOR MY SANTA CLAUS MOVEMENT, RIGHT?
DON'T BRING THIS CURSE ON YOUR OWN HEADS.
RELIGIOUS OBSERVANCES ARE FORBIDDEN FOR EVERYBODY.
YOU OBSERVE YOUR RELIGION ALL THE TIME--EVERY TIME YOU DON'T FIRE YOUR WEAPON IN THE BATTLEROOM.

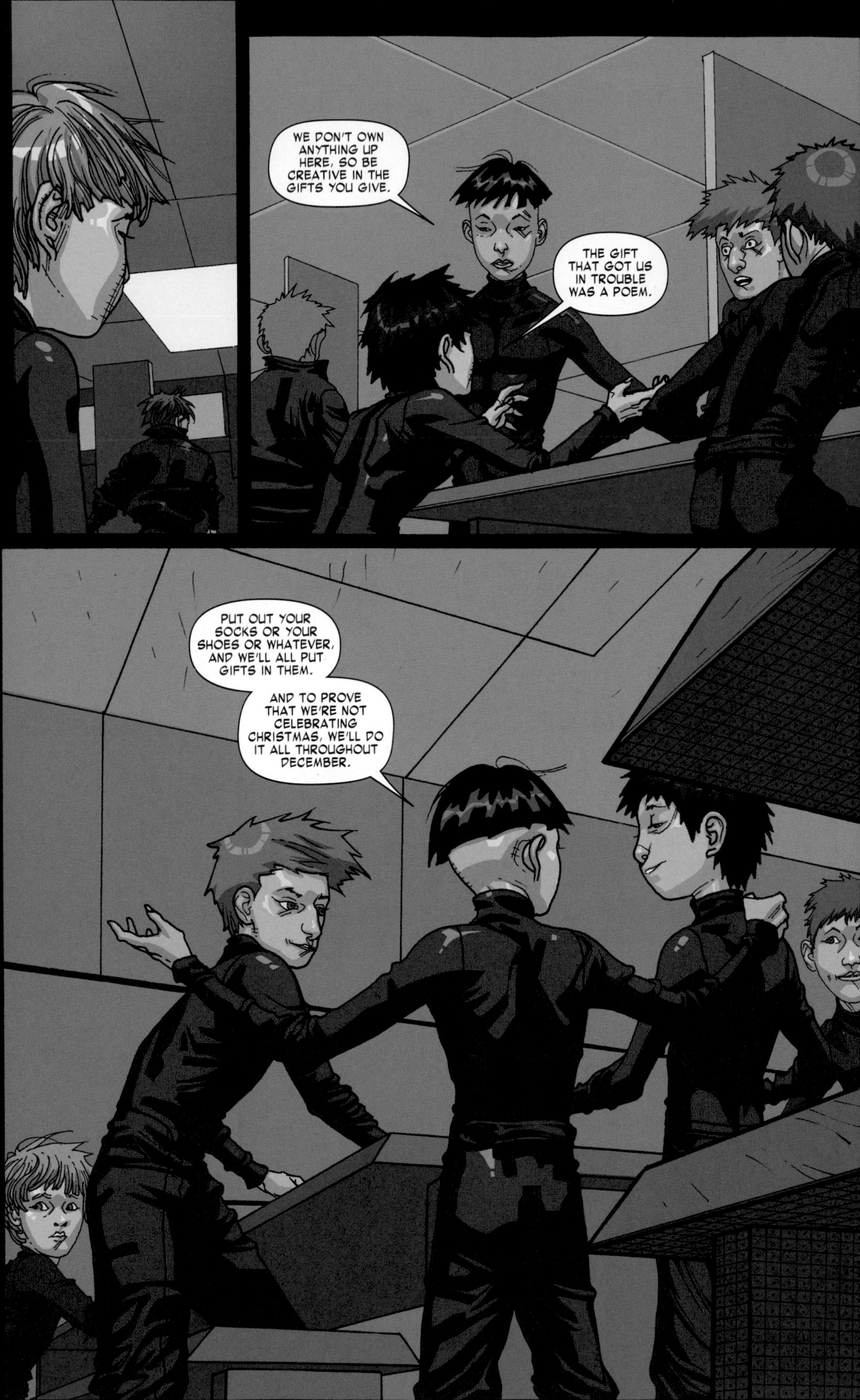
WE DON'T OWN ANYTHING UP HERE, SO BE CREATIVE IN THE GIFTS YOU GIVE.
THE GIFT THAT GOT US IN TROUBLE WAS A POEM.
PUT OUT YOUR SOCKS OR YOUR SHOES OR WHATEVER, AND WE'LL ALL PUT GIFTS IN THEM.
AND TO PROVE THAT WE'RE NOT CELEBRATING CHRISTMAS, WE'LL DO IT ALL THROUGHOUT DECEMBER.

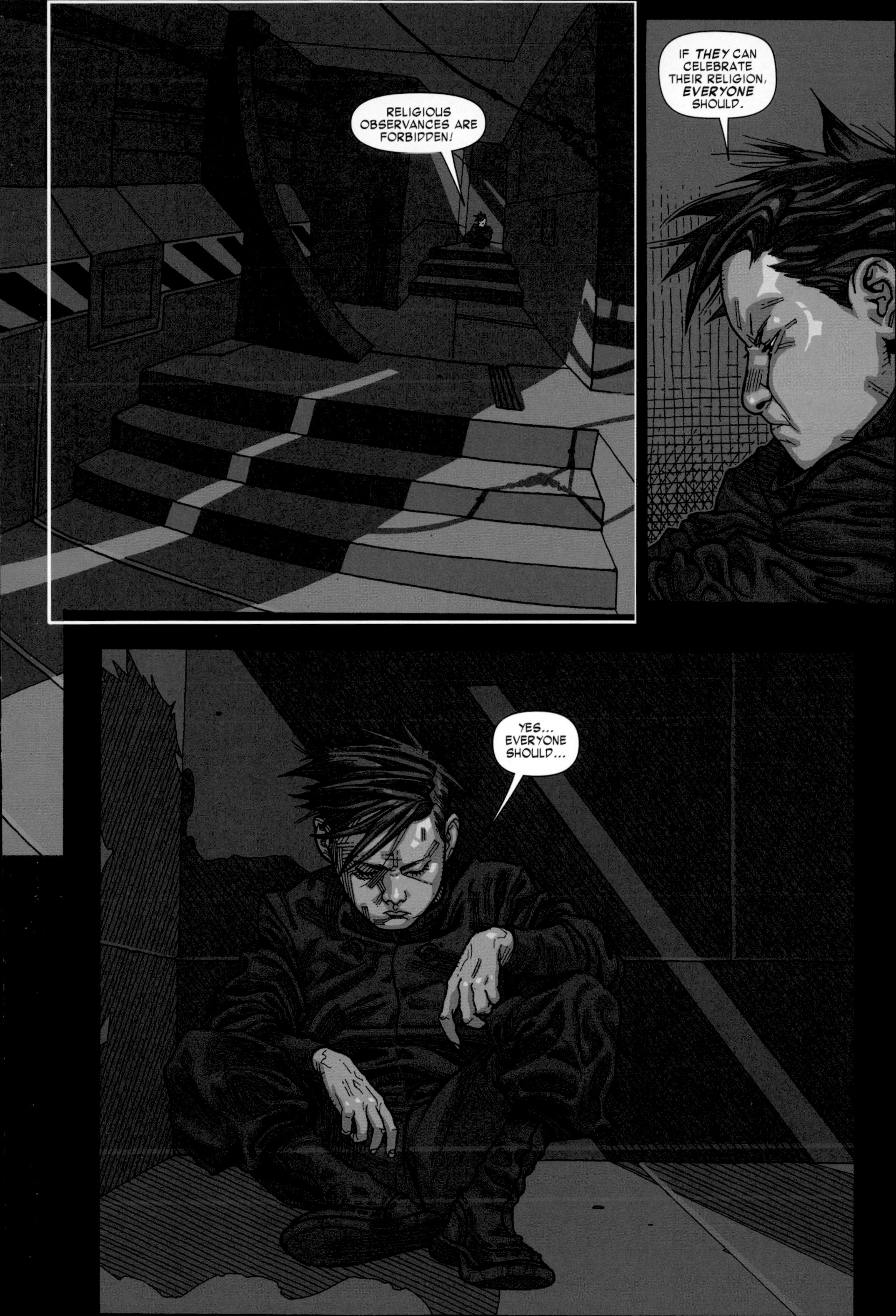
RELIGIOUS OBSERVANCES ARE FORBIDDEN!
IF THEY CAN CELEBRATE THEIR RELIGION, EVERYONE SHOULD.
YES... EVERYONE SHOULD...

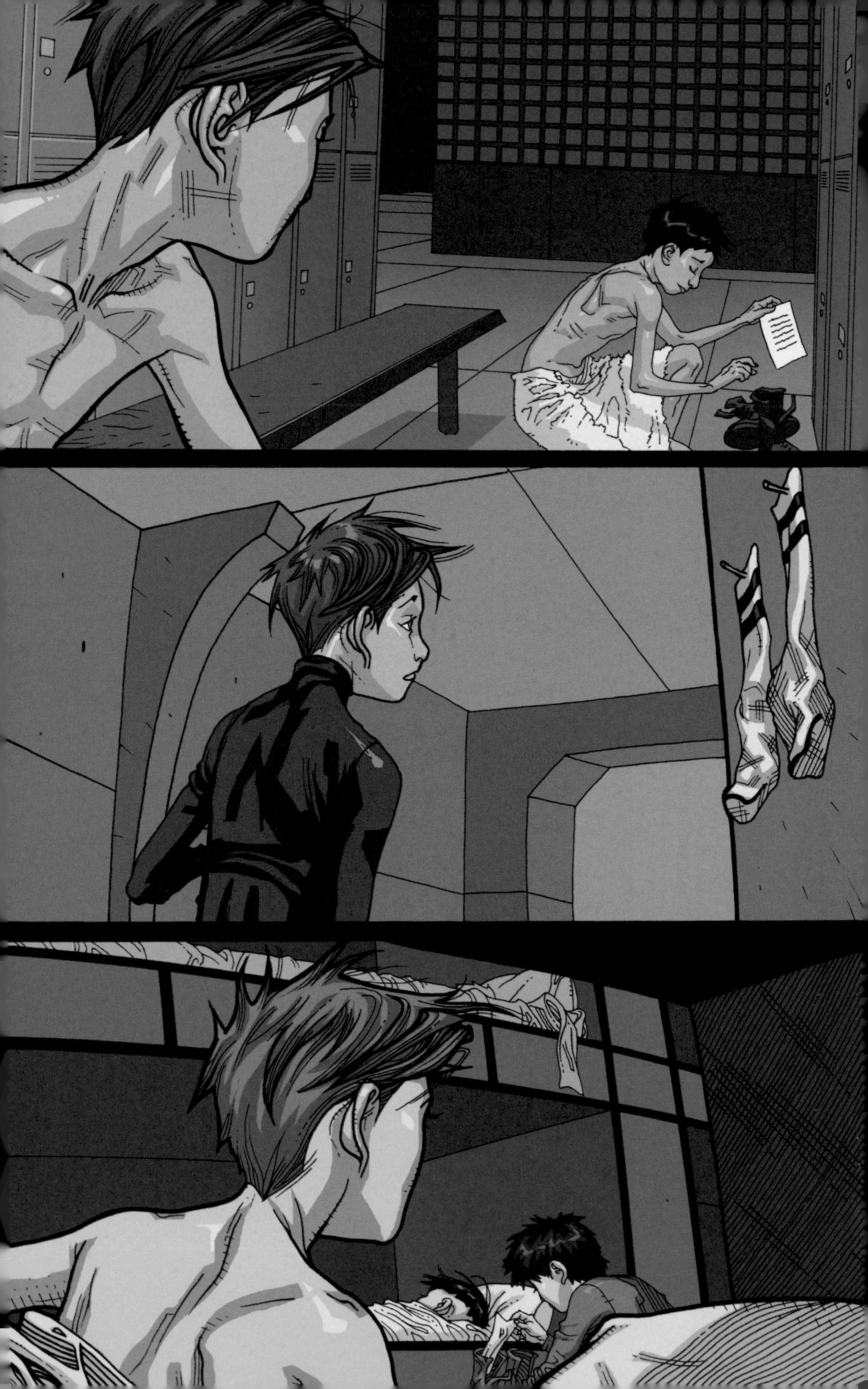

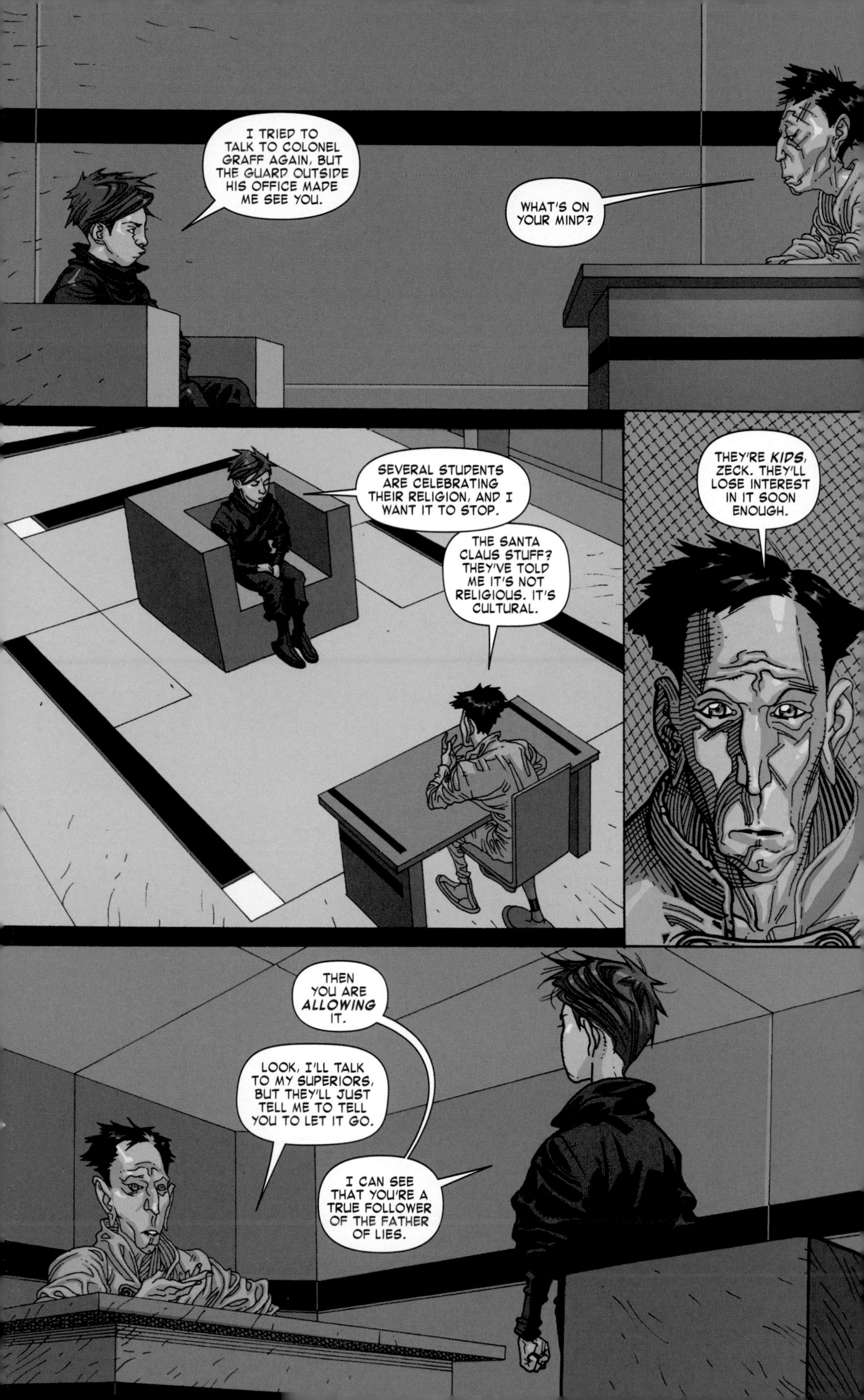
I TRIED TO TALK TO COLONEL GRAFF AGAIN, BUT THE GUARD OUTSIDE HIS OFFICE MADE ME SEE YOU.
WHAT'S ON YOUR MIND?
SEVERAL STUDENTS ARE CELEBRATING THEIR RELIGION, AND I WANT IT TO STOP.
THE SANTA CLAUS STUFF? THEY'VE TOLD ME IT'S NOT RELIGIOUS. IT'S CULTURAL.
THEY'RE KIDS, ZECK. THEY'LL LOSE INTEREST IN IT SOON ENOUGH.
THEN YOU ARE ALLOWING IT.
LOOK, I'LL TALK TO MY SUPERIORS, BUT THEY'LL JUST TELL ME TO TELL YOU TO LET IT GO.
I CAN SEE THAT YOU'RE A TRUE FOLLOWER OF THE FATHER OF LIES.

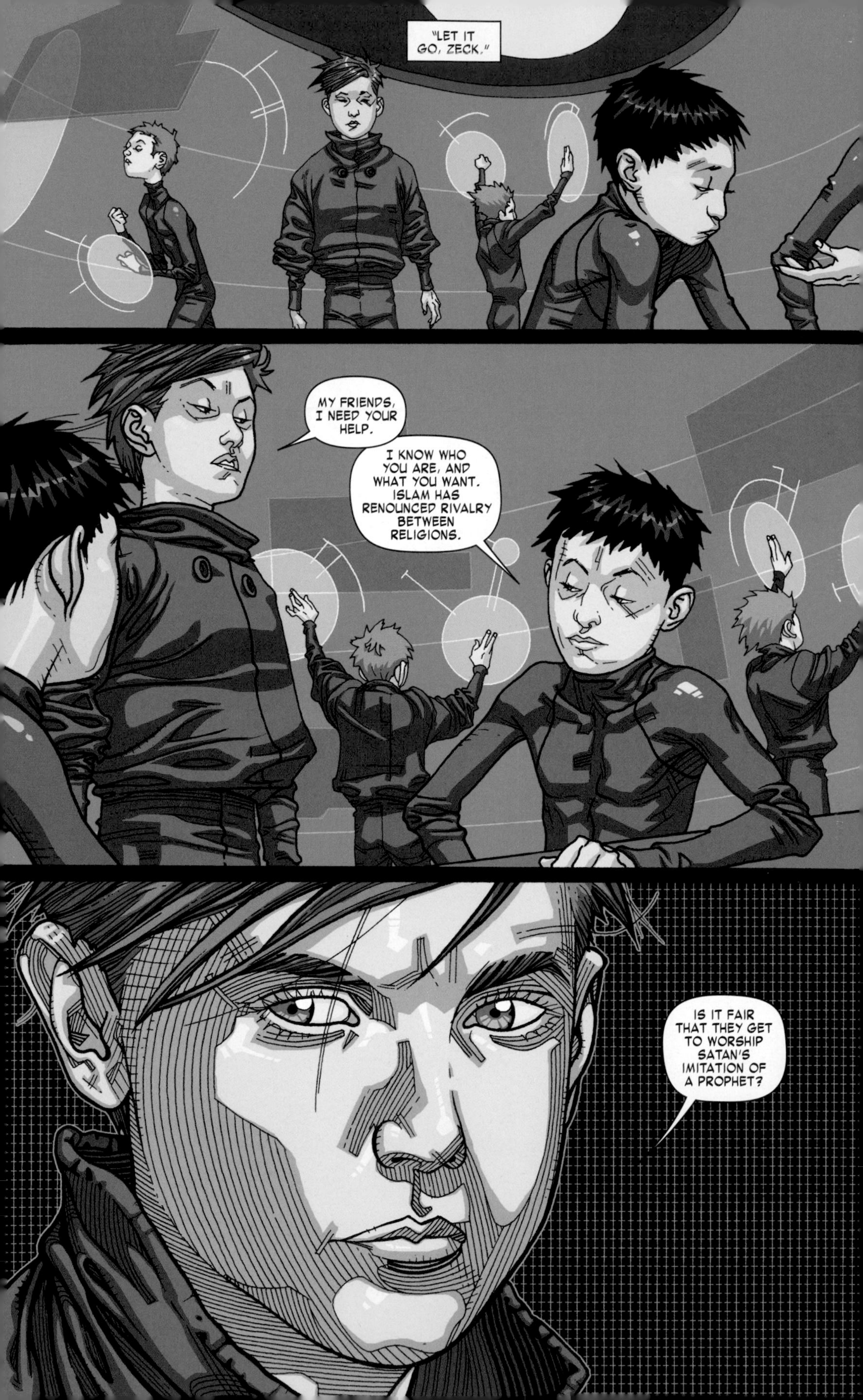
"LET IT GO, ZECK."
MY FRIENDS, I NEED YOUR HELP.
I KNOW WHO YOU ARE, AND WHAT YOU WANT. ISLAM HAS RENOUNCED RIVALRY BETWEEN RELIGIONS.
IS IT FAIR THAT THEY GET TO WORSHIP SATAN'S IMITATION OF A PROPHET?

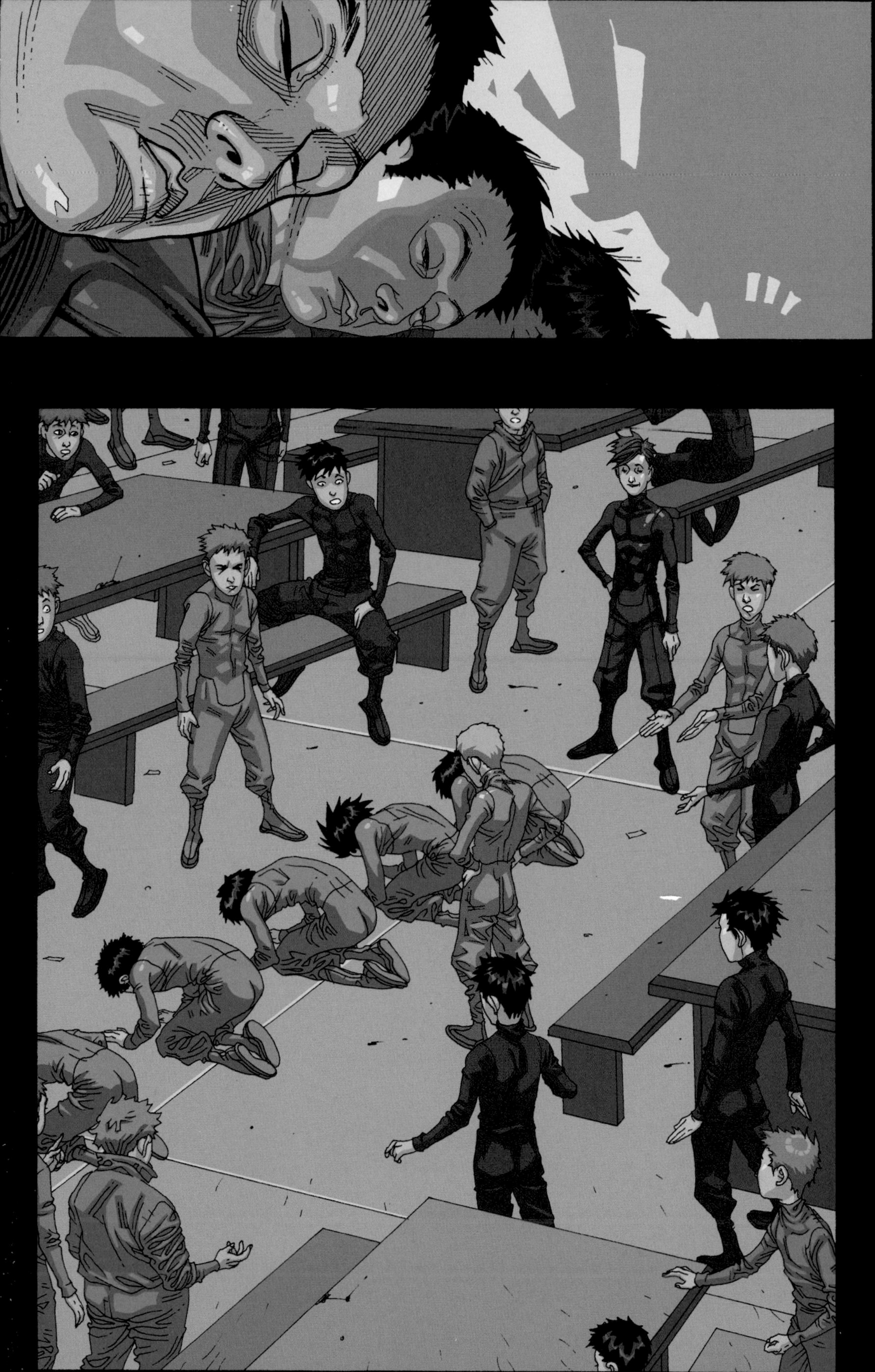

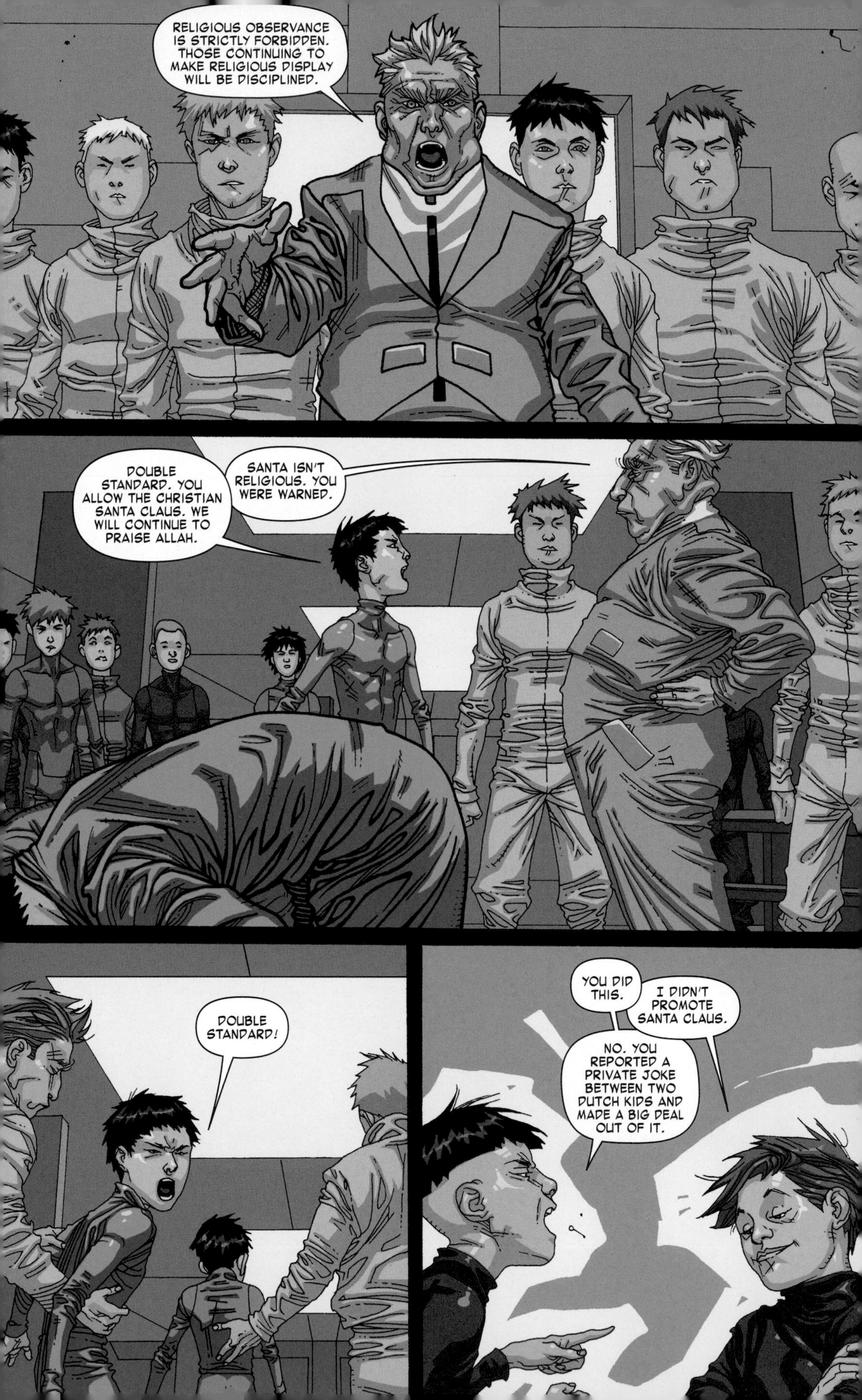
RELIGIOUS OBSERVANCE IS STRICTLY FORBIDDEN. THOSE CONTINUING TO MAKE RELIGIOUS DISPLAY WILL BE DISCIPLINED.
DOUBLE STANDARD. YOU ALLOW THE CHRISTIAN SANTA CLAUS. WE WILL CONTINUE TO PRAISE ALLAH.
SANTA ISN'T RELIGIOUS. YOU WERE WARNED.
DOUBLE STANDARD!
YOU DID THIS.
I DIDN'T PROMOTE SANTA CLAUS.
NO. YOU REPORTED A PRIVATE JOKE BETWEEN TWO DUTCH KIDS AND MADE A BIG DEAL OUT OF IT.

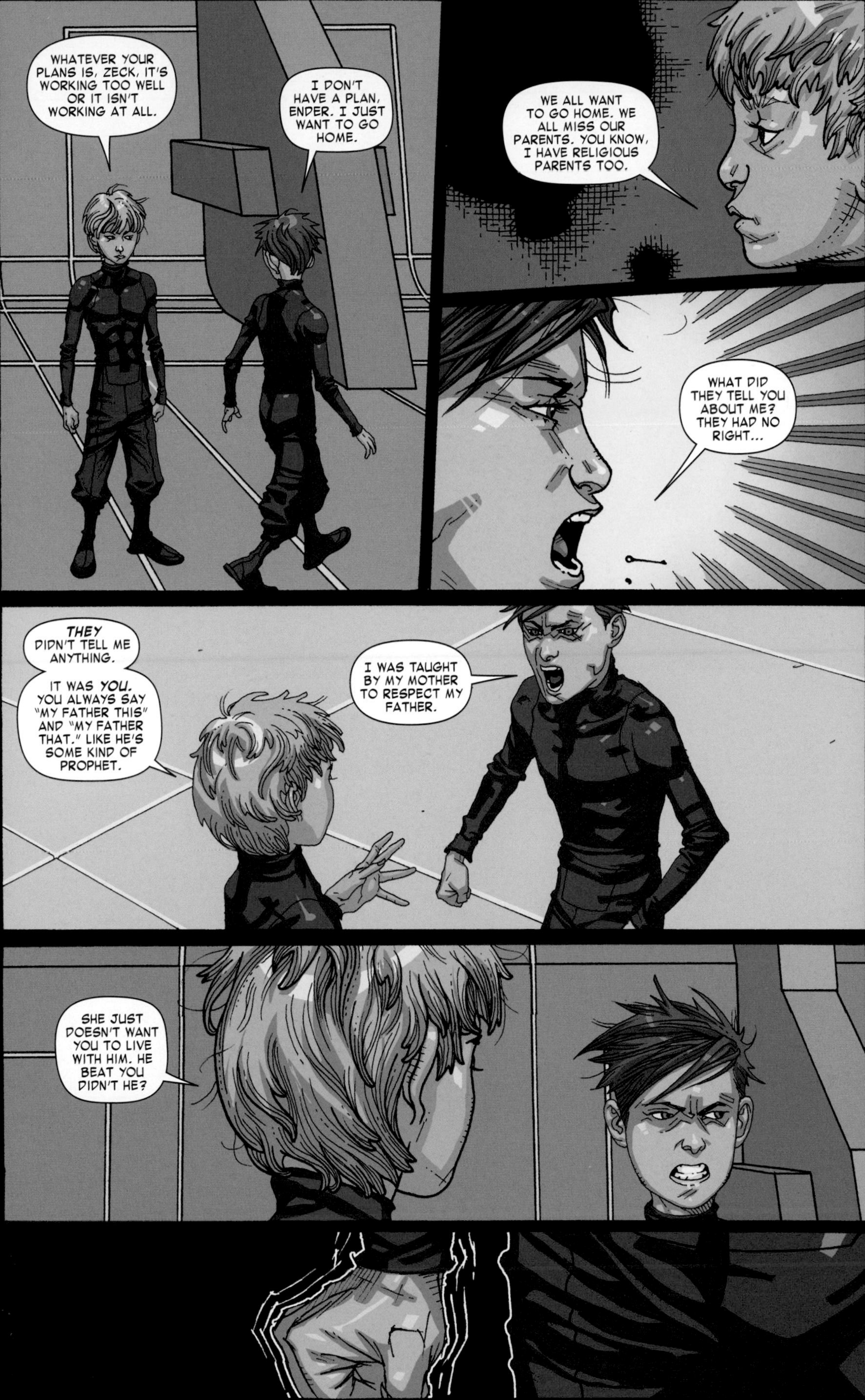
WHATEVER YOUR PLANS IS, ZECK, IT'S WORKING TOO WELL OR IT ISN'T WORKING AT ALL.
I DON'T HAVE A PLAN, ENDER. I JUST WANT TO GO HOME.
WE ALL WANT TO GO HOME. WE ALL MISS OUR PARENTS. YOU KNOW, I HAVE RELIGIOUS PARENTS TOO.
WHAT DID THEY TELL YOU ABOUT ME? THEY HAD NO RIGHT...
THEY DIDN'T TELL ME ANYTHING.
IT WAS *YOU.* YOU ALWAYS SAY "MY FATHER THIS" AND "MY FATHER THAT." LIKE HE'S SOME KIND OF PROPHET.
I WAS TAUGHT BY MY MOTHER TO RESPECT MY FATHER.
SHE JUST DOESN'T WANT YOU TO LIVE WITH HIM. HE BEAT YOU DIDN'T HE?

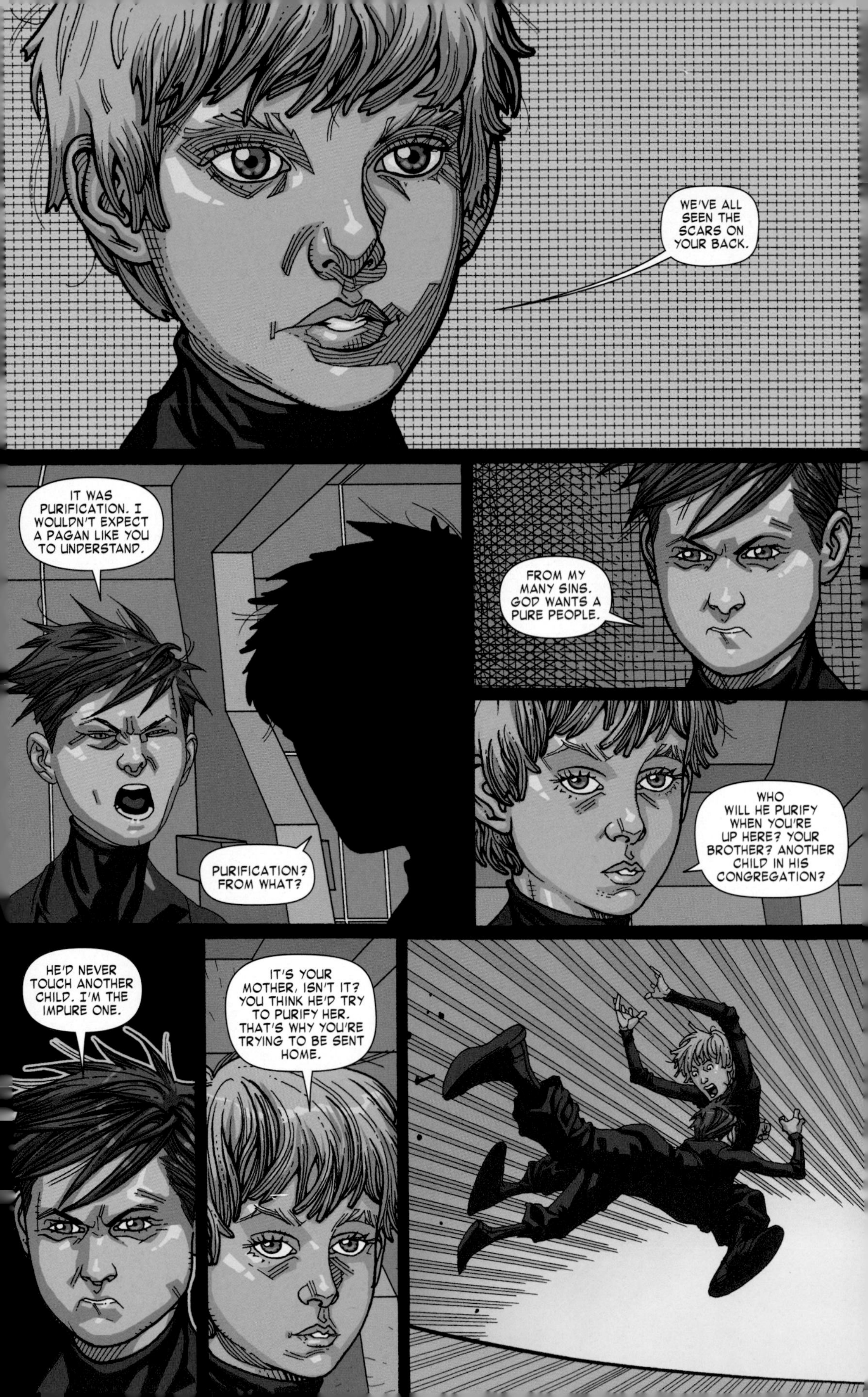
WE'VE ALL SEEN THE SCARS ON YOUR BACK.
IT WAS PURIFICATION. I WOULDN'T EXPECT A PAGAN LIKE YOU TO UNDERSTAND.
PURIFICATION? FROM WHAT?
FROM MY MANY SINS. GOD WANTS A PURE PEOPLE.
WHO WILL HE PURIFY WHEN YOU'RE UP HERE? YOUR BROTHER? ANOTHER CHILD IN HIS CONGREGATION?
HE'D NEVER TOUCH ANOTHER CHILD. I'M THE IMPURE ONE.
IT'S YOUR MOTHER, ISN'T IT? YOU THINK HE'D TRY TO PURIFY HER. THAT'S WHY YOU'RE TRYING TO BE SENT HOME.

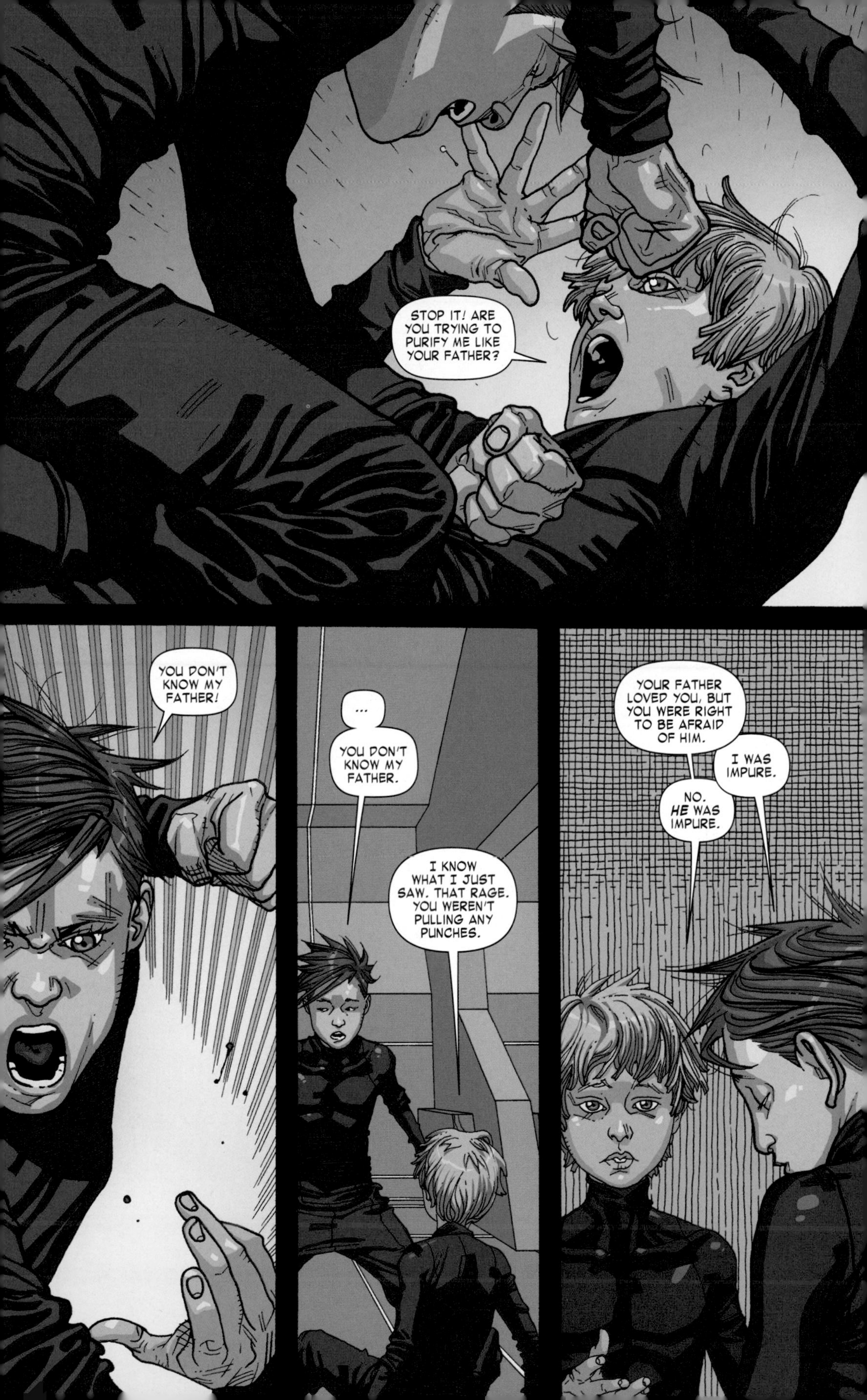
STOP IT! ARE YOU TRYING TO PURIFY ME LIKE YOUR FATHER?
YOU DON'T KNOW MY FATHER!
...
YOU DON'T KNOW MY FATHER.
I KNOW WHAT I JUST SAW. THAT RAGE. YOU WEREN'T PULLING ANY PUNCHES.
YOUR FATHER LOVED YOU, BUT YOU WERE RIGHT TO BE AFRAID OF HIM.
I WAS IMPURE.
NO. HE WAS IMPURE.

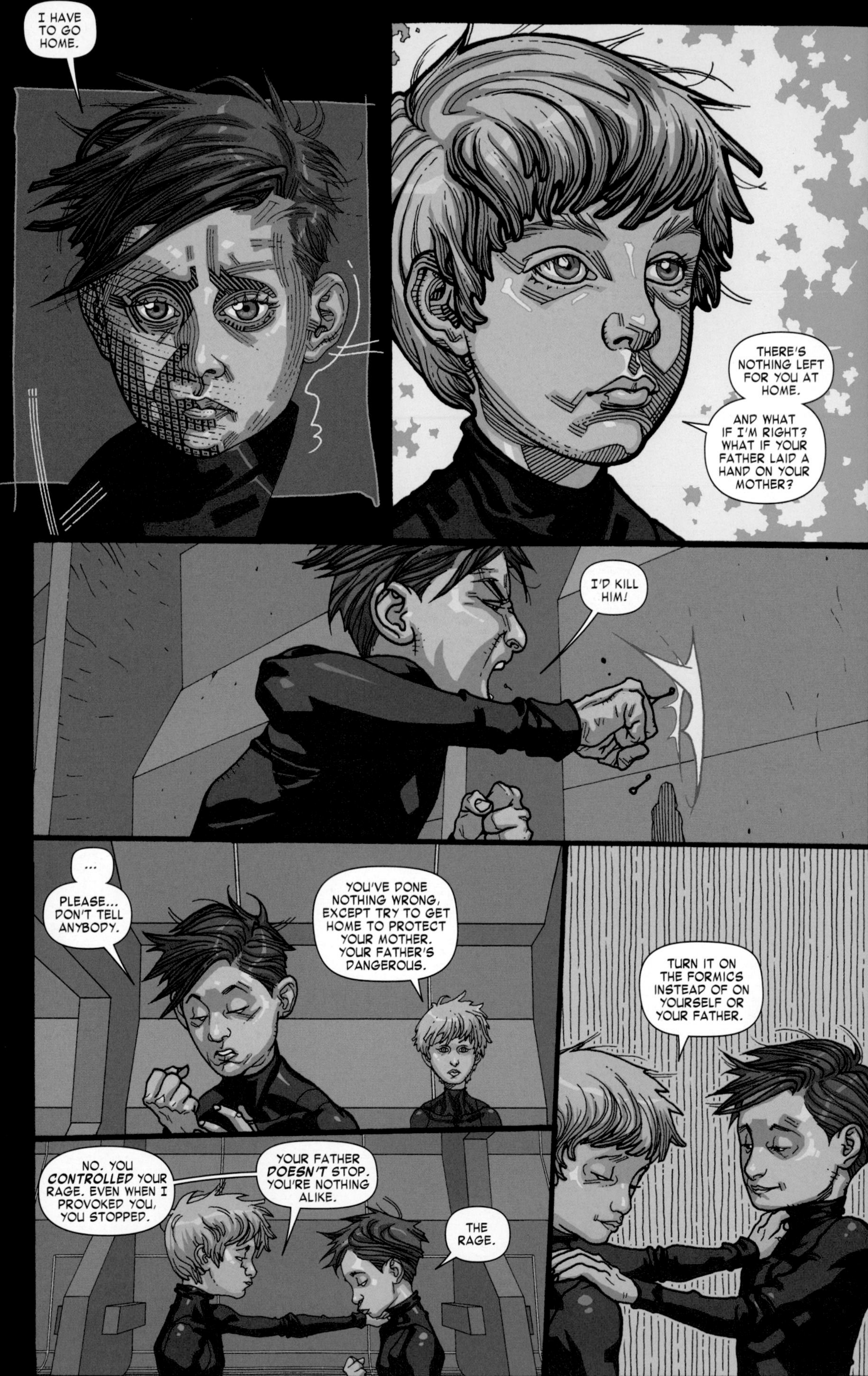
I HAVE TO GO HOME.
THERE'S NOTHING LEFT FOR YOU AT HOME.
AND WHAT IF I'M RIGHT? WHAT IF YOUR FATHER LAID A HAND ON YOUR MOTHER?
I'D KILL HIM!
...
PLEASE... DON'T TELL ANYBODY.
YOU'VE DONE NOTHING WRONG, EXCEPT TRY TO GET HOME TO PROTECT YOUR MOTHER. YOUR FATHER'S DANGEROUS.
NO. YOU CONTROLLED YOUR RAGE. EVEN WHEN I PROVOKED YOU, YOU STOPPED.
YOUR FATHER DOESN'T STOP. YOU'RE NOTHING ALIKE.
THE RAGE.
TURN IT ON THE FORMICS INSTEAD OF ON YOURSELF OR YOUR FATHER.

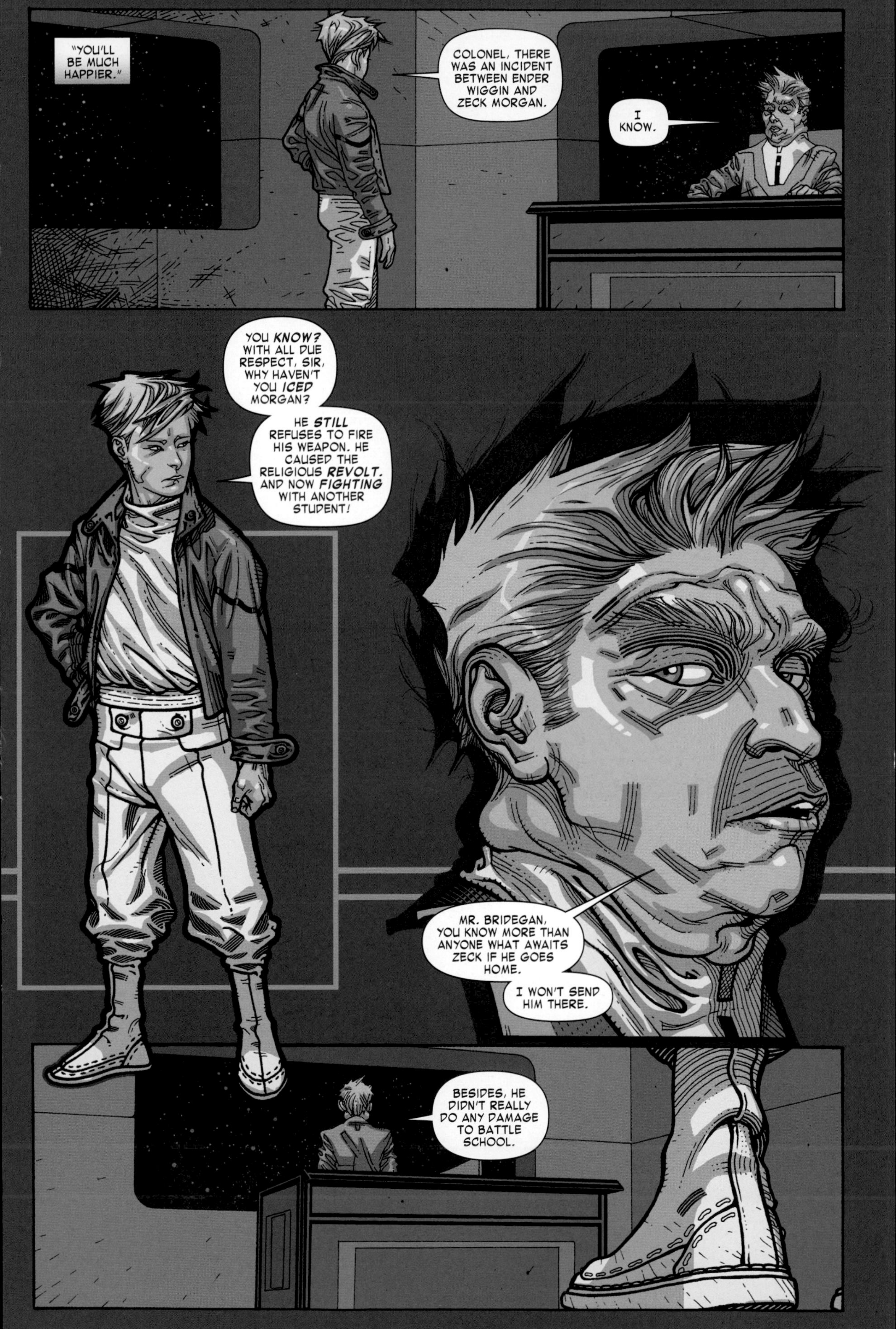
"YOU'LL BE MUCH HAPPIER."
COLONEL, THERE WAS AN INCIDENT BETWEEN ENDER WIGGIN AND ZECK MORGAN.
I KNOW.
YOU KNOW? WITH ALL DUE RESPECT, SIR, WHY HAVEN'T YOU ICED MORGAN?
HE STILL REFUSES TO FIRE HIS WEAPON. HE CAUSED THE RELIGIOUS REVOLT. AND NOW FIGHTING WITH ANOTHER STUDENT!
MR. BRIDEGAN, YOU KNOW MORE THAN ANYONE WHAT AWAITS ZECK IF HE GOES HOME.
I WON'T SEND HIM THERE.
BESIDES, HE DIDN'T REALLY DO ANY DAMAGE TO BATTLE SCHOOL.

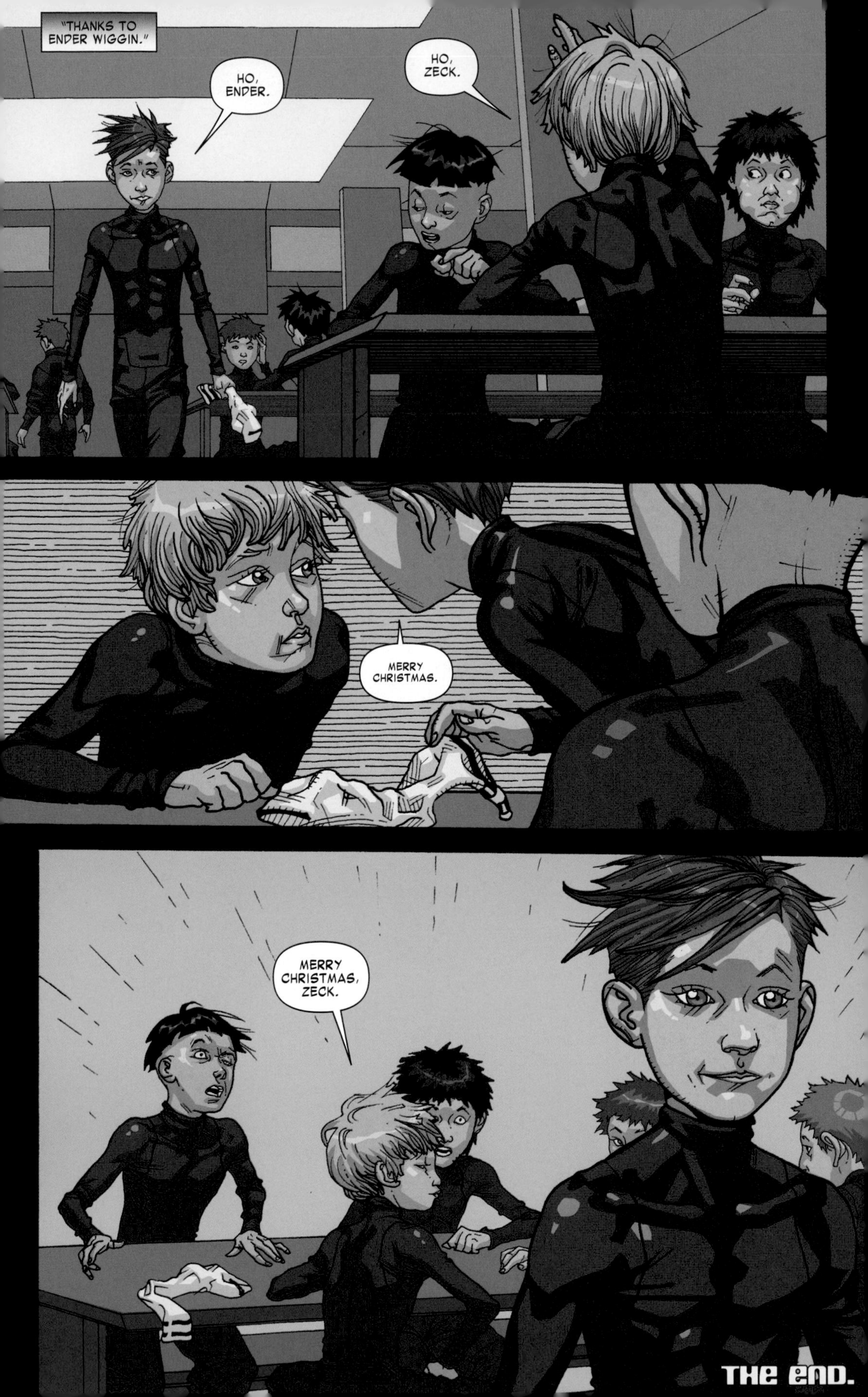
"THANKS TO ENDER WIGGIN."
HO, ENDER.
HO, ZECK.
MERRY CHRISTMAS.
MERRY CHRISTMAS, ZECK.
THE END.

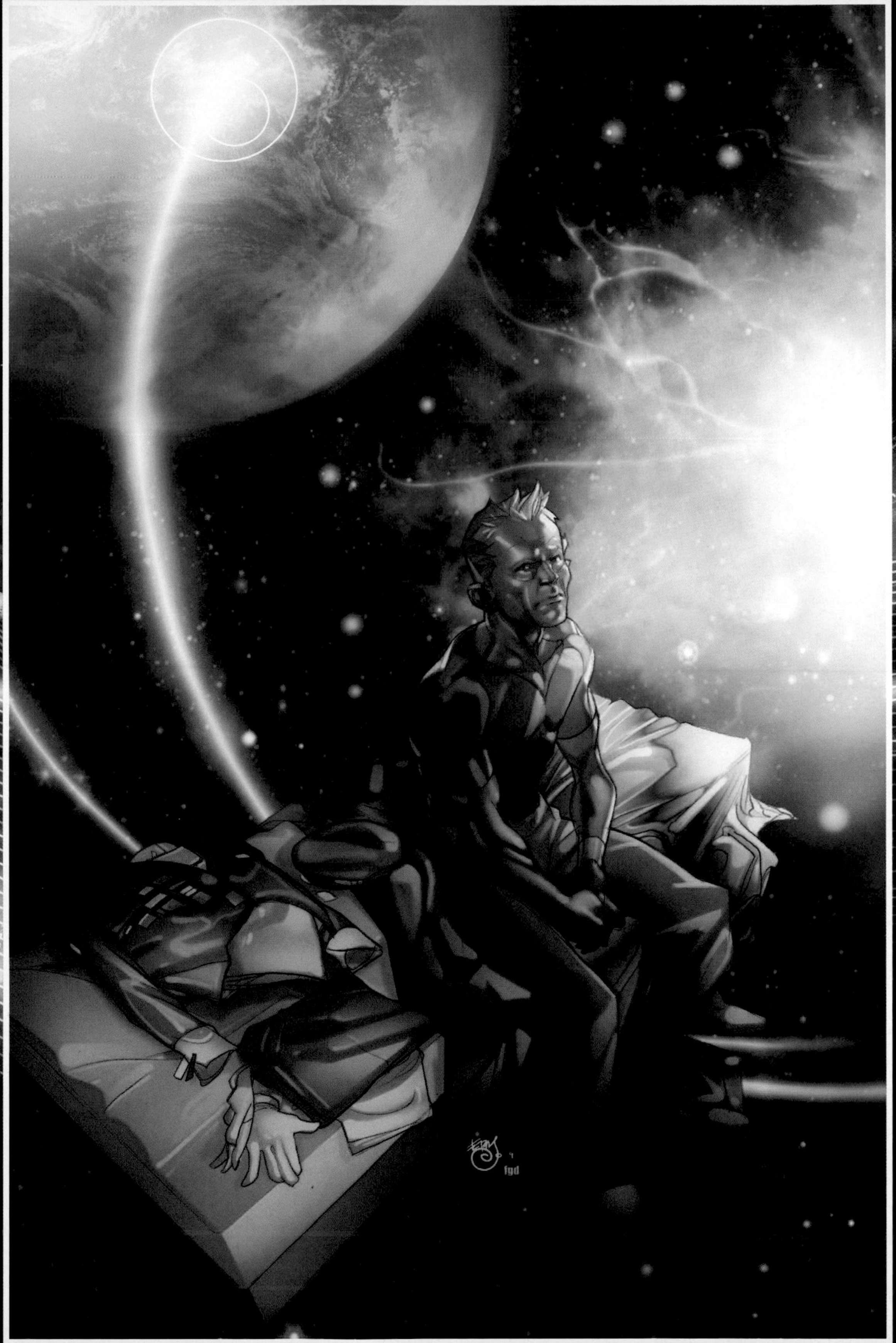

MAZER IN PRISON

"Rackham wants to know if we're looking for his replacement."

"To command the fleet? They won't reach the Formic planet for another thirty years."

"Yes, but his ship is moving at relativistic speeds. Thirty years for us is only a few years for him. He's antsy."

"He's asking the impossible. How can we know who will make a great commander thirty years from now?"

"He's approaching the halfway point. I have to give him something."

"Tell him we got someone working on it."

"Lie?"

"No. I'll send you someone. A junior officer."

"What will that accomplish?"

"Nothing. But that's the point. I'm not about to taint my record by investing resources in some fruitless exercise. We already have our man. Mazer Rackham."

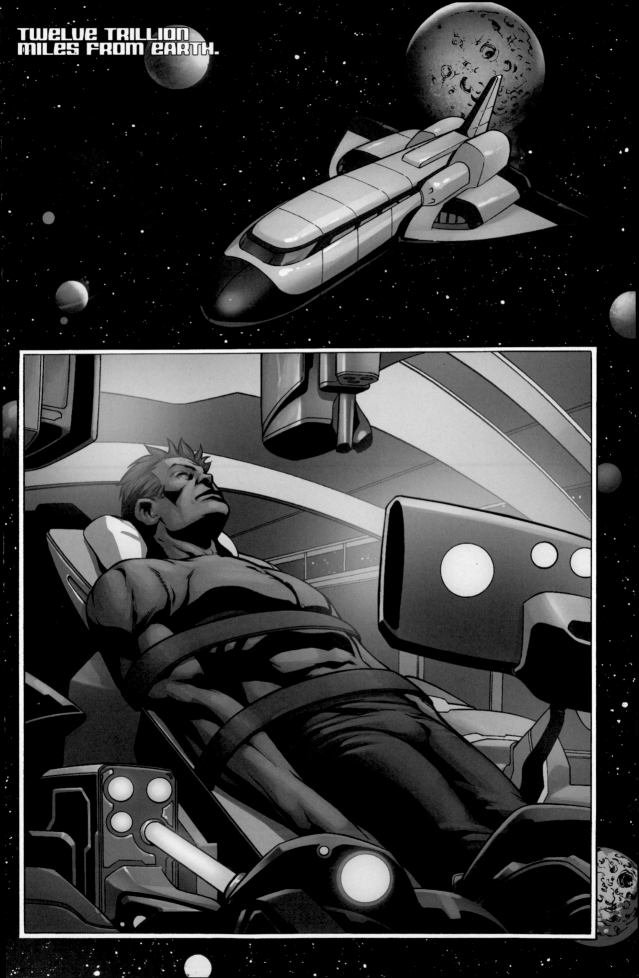

TWELVE TRILLION
MILES FROM EARTH.

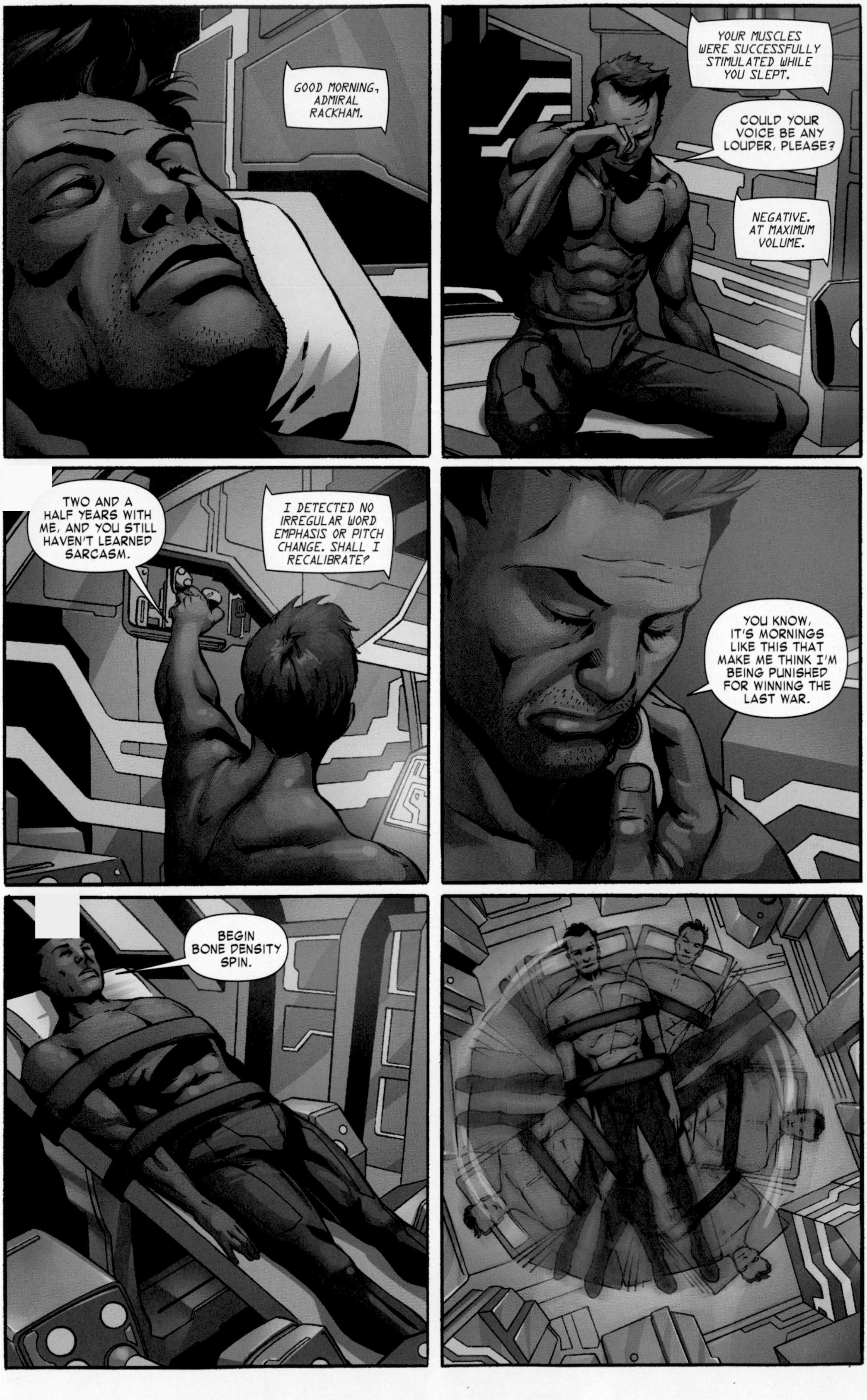
GOOD MORNING, ADMIRAL RACKHAM.
YOUR MUSCLES WERE SUCCESSFULLY STIMULATED WHILE YOU SLEPT.
COULD YOUR VOICE BE ANY LOUDER, PLEASE?
NEGATIVE. AT MAXIMUM VOLUME.
TWO AND A HALF YEARS WITH ME, AND YOU STILL HAVEN'T LEARNED SARCASM.
I DETECTED NO IRREGULAR WORD EMPHASIS OR PITCH CHANGE. SHALL I RECALIBRATE?
YOU KNOW, IT'S MORNINGS LIKE THIS THAT MAKE ME THINK I'M BEING PUNISHED FOR WINNING THE LAST WAR.
BEGIN BONE DENSITY SPIN.

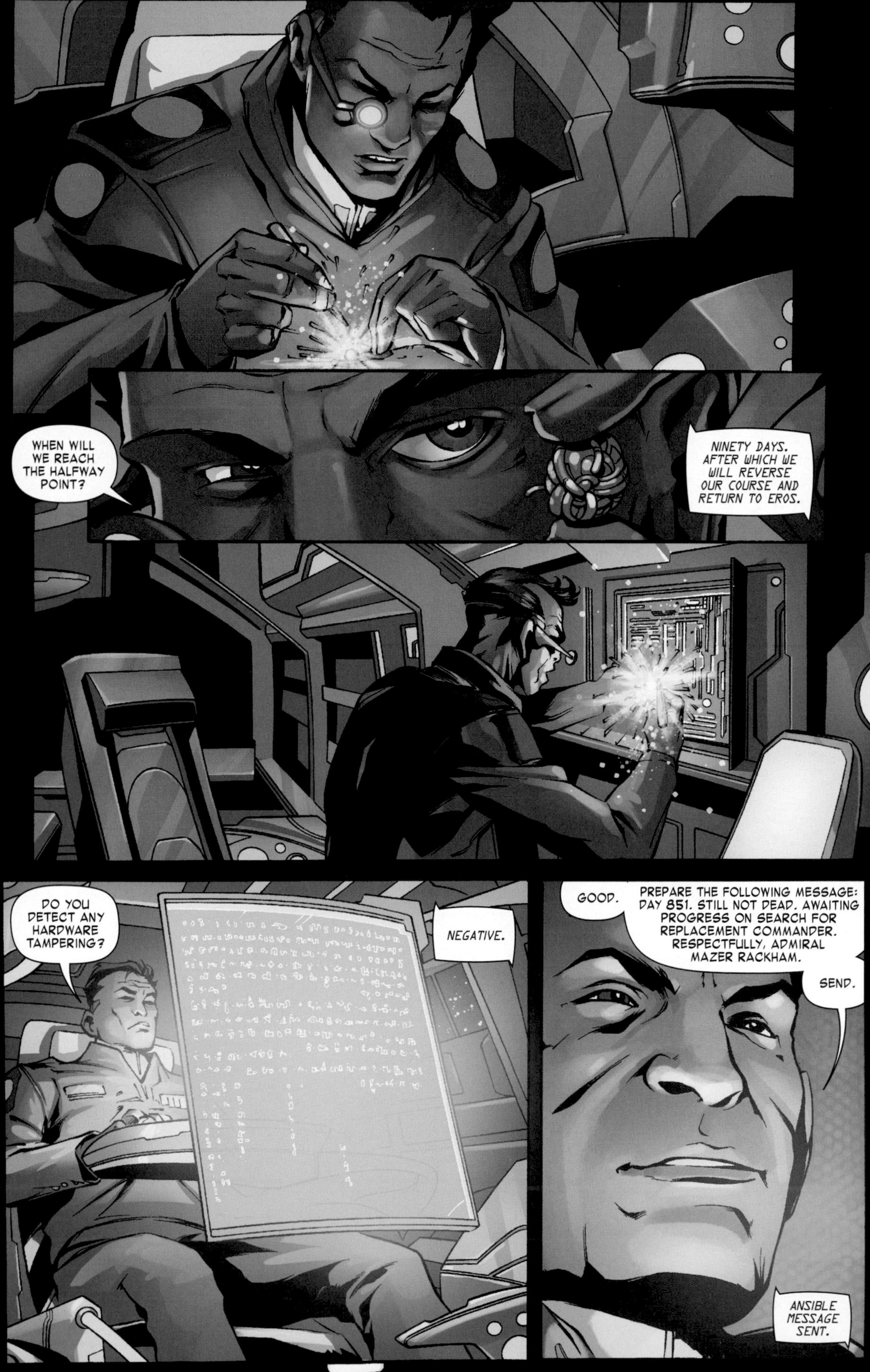
WHEN WILL WE REACH THE HALFWAY POINT?
NINETY DAYS. AFTER WHICH WE WILL REVERSE OUR COURSE AND RETURN TO EROS.
DO YOU DETECT ANY HARDWARE TAMPERING?
NEGATIVE.
GOOD.
PREPARE THE FOLLOWING MESSAGE: DAY 851. STILL NOT DEAD. AWAITING PROGRESS ON SEARCH FOR REPLACEMENT COMMANDER. RESPECTFULLY, ADMIRAL MAZER RACKHAM.
SEND.
ANSIBLE MESSAGE SENT.

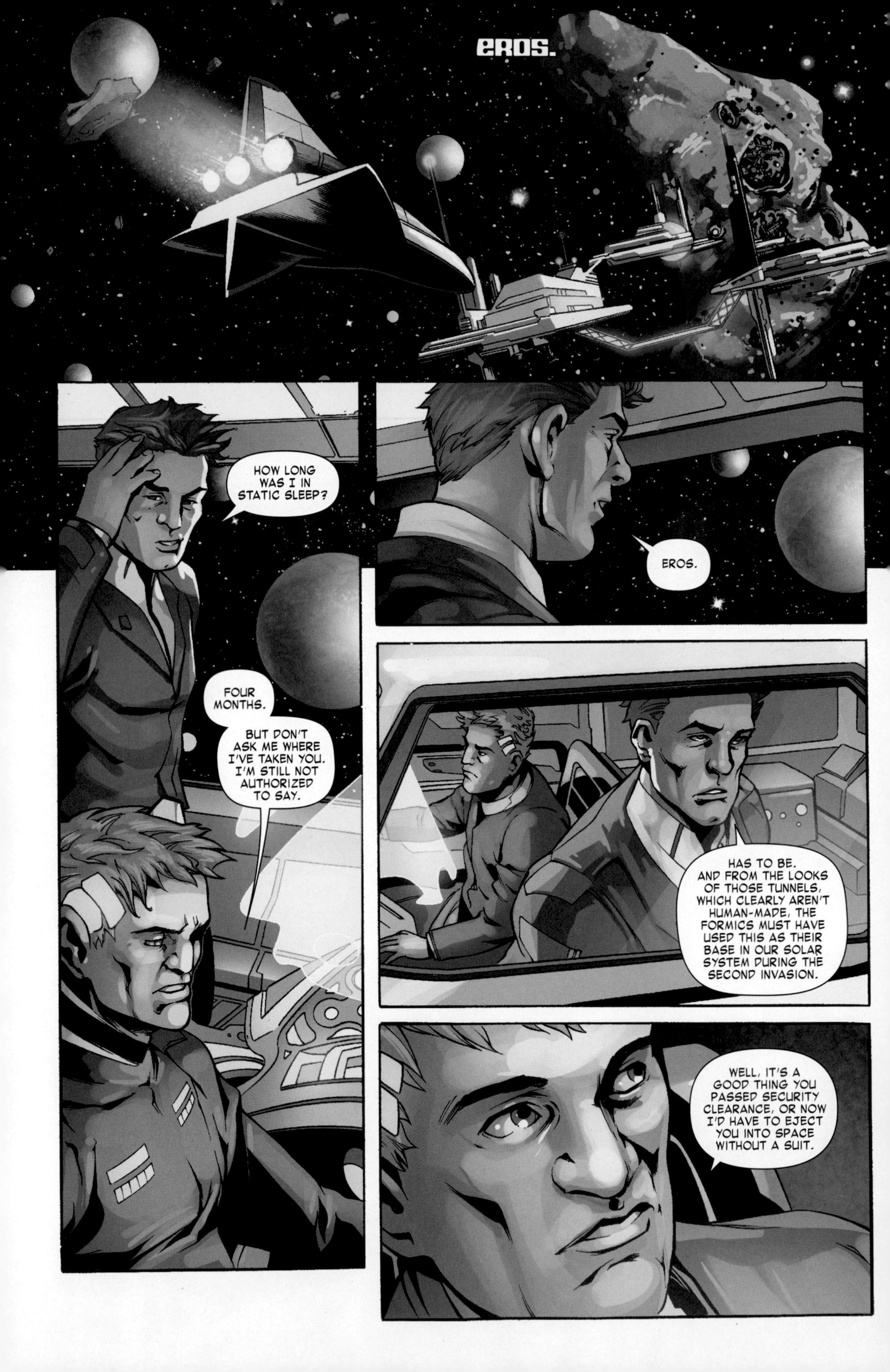
EROS.
HOW LONG WAS I IN STATIC SLEEP?
FOUR MONTHS.
BUT DON'T ASK ME WHERE I'VE TAKEN YOU. I'M STILL NOT AUTHORIZED TO SAY.
EROS.
HAS TO BE. AND FROM THE LOOKS OF THOSE TUNNELS, WHICH CLEARLY AREN'T HUMAN-MADE, THE FORMICS MUST HAVE USED THIS AS THEIR BASE IN OUR SOLAR SYSTEM DURING THE SECOND INVASION.
WELL, IT'S A GOOD THING YOU PASSED SECURITY CLEARANCE, OR NOW I'D HAVE TO EJECT YOU INTO SPACE WITHOUT A SUIT.

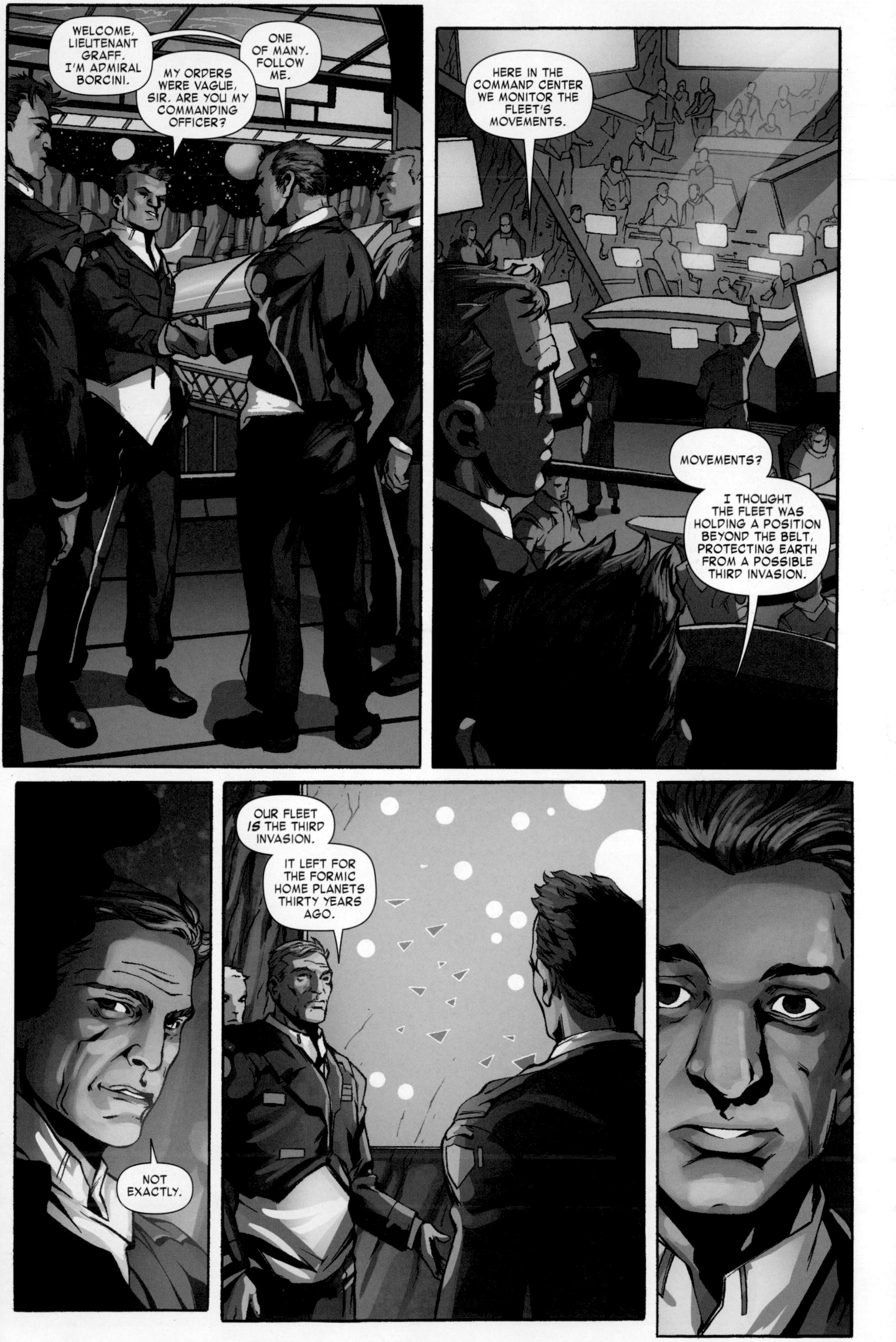
WELCOME, LIEUTENANT GRAFF. I'M ADMIRAL BORCINI.
MY ORDERS WERE VAGUE, SIR. ARE YOU MY COMMANDING OFFICER?
ONE OF MANY. FOLLOW ME.
HERE IN THE COMMAND CENTER WE MONITOR THE FLEET'S MOVEMENTS.
MOVEMENTS?
I THOUGHT THE FLEET WAS HOLDING A POSITION BEYOND THE BELT, PROTECTING EARTH FROM A POSSIBLE THIRD INVASION.
NOT EXACTLY.
OUR FLEET IS THE THIRD INVASION.
IT LEFT FOR THE FORMIC HOME PLANETS THIRTY YEARS AGO.

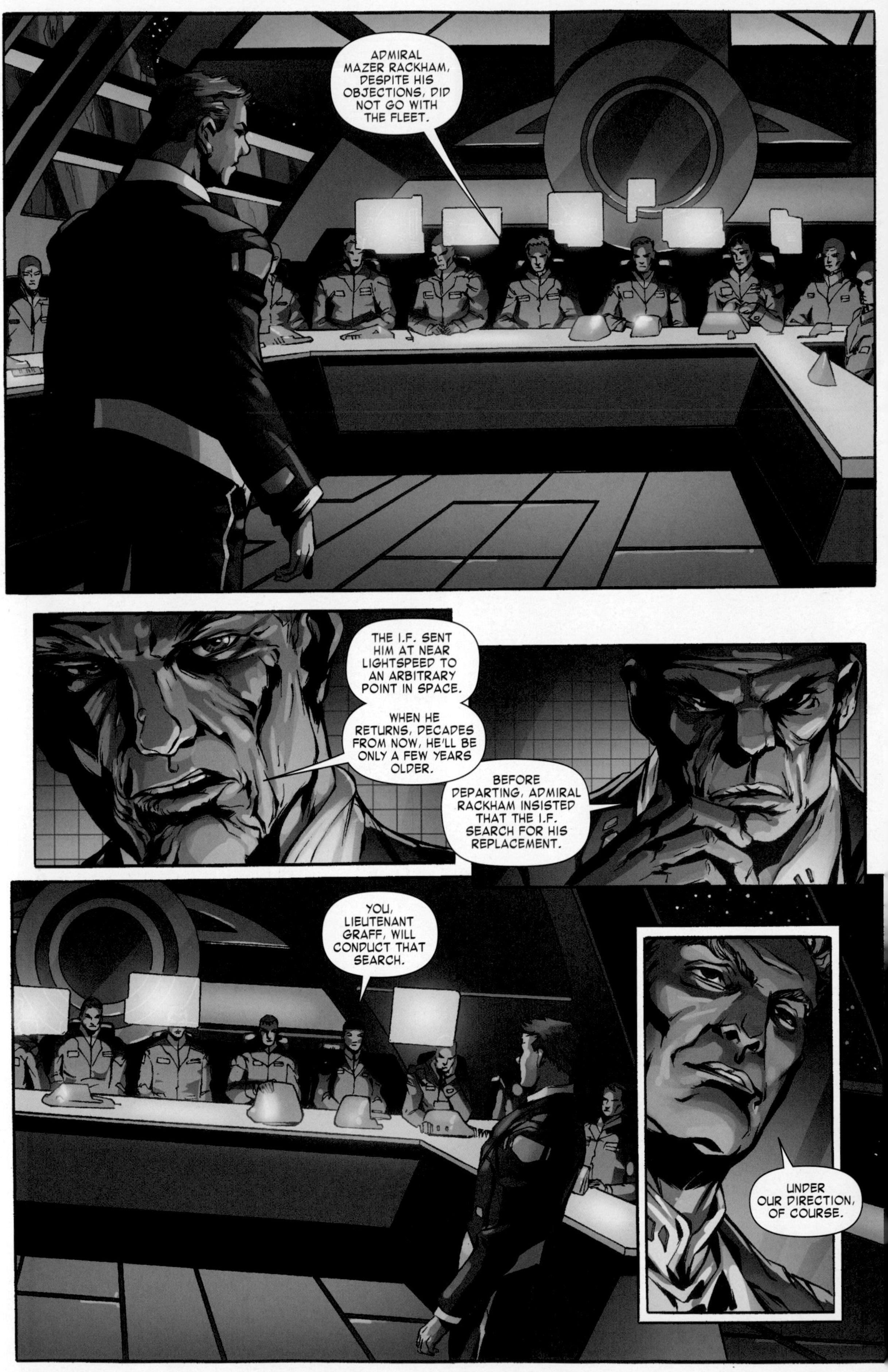
ADMIRAL MAZER RACKHAM, DESPITE HIS OBJECTIONS, DID NOT GO WITH THE FLEET.
THE I.F. SENT HIM AT NEAR LIGHTSPEED TO AN ARBITRARY POINT IN SPACE.
WHEN HE RETURNS, DECADES FROM NOW, HE'LL BE ONLY A FEW YEARS OLDER.
BEFORE DEPARTING, ADMIRAL RACKHAM INSISTED THAT THE I.F. SEARCH FOR HIS REPLACEMENT.
YOU, LIEUTENANT GRAFF, WILL CONDUCT THAT SEARCH.
UNDER OUR DIRECTION, OF COURSE.

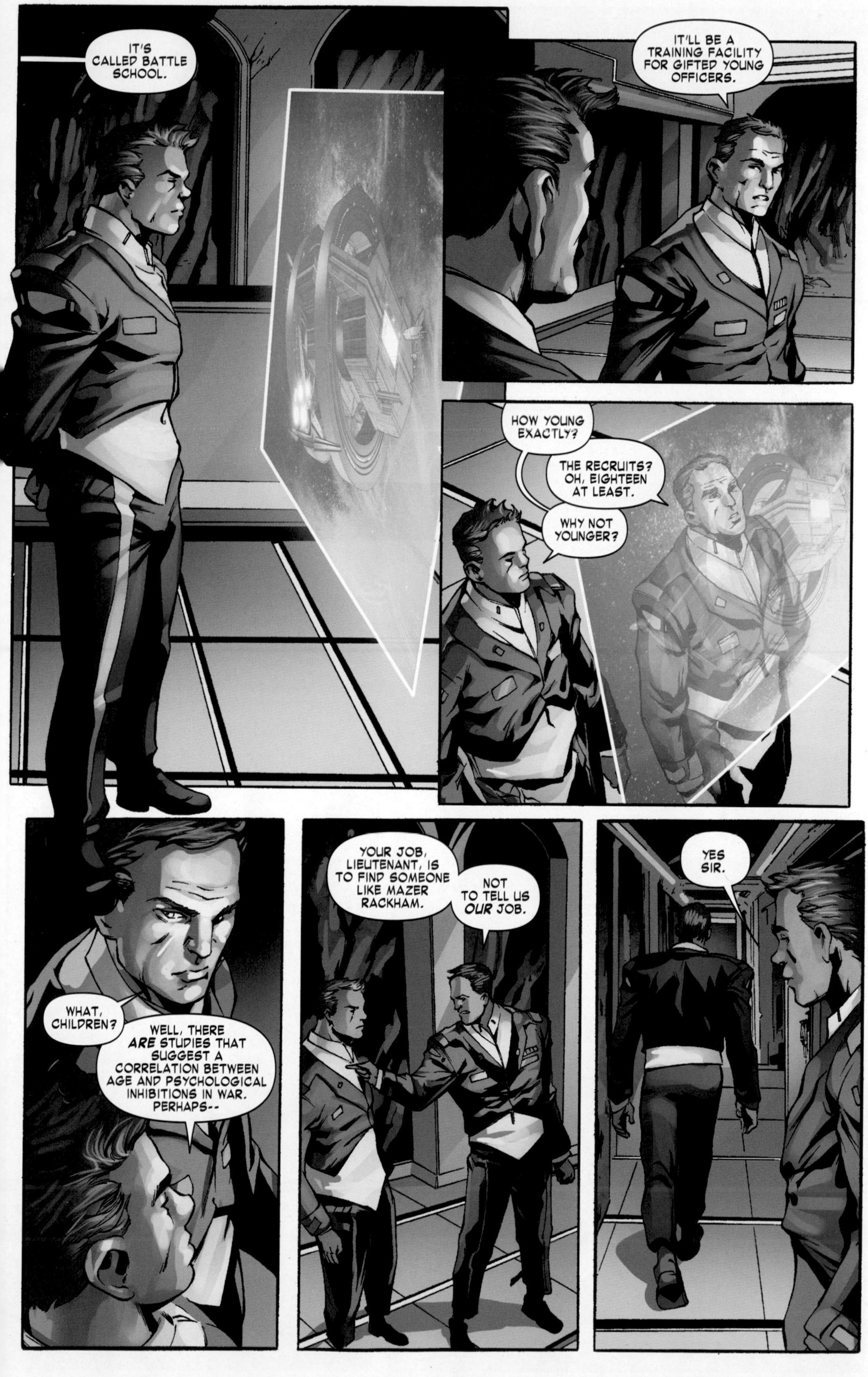
IT'S CALLED BATTLE SCHOOL.
IT'LL BE A TRAINING FACILITY FOR GIFTED YOUNG OFFICERS.
HOW YOUNG EXACTLY?
THE RECRUITS? OH, EIGHTEEN AT LEAST.
WHY NOT YOUNGER?
WHAT, CHILDREN?
WELL, THERE ARE STUDIES THAT SUGGEST A CORRELATION BETWEEN AGE AND PSYCHOLOGICAL INHIBITIONS IN WAR. PERHAPS--
YOUR JOB, LIEUTENANT, IS TO FIND SOMEONE LIKE MAZER RACKHAM.
NOT TO TELL US OUR JOB.
YES SIR.

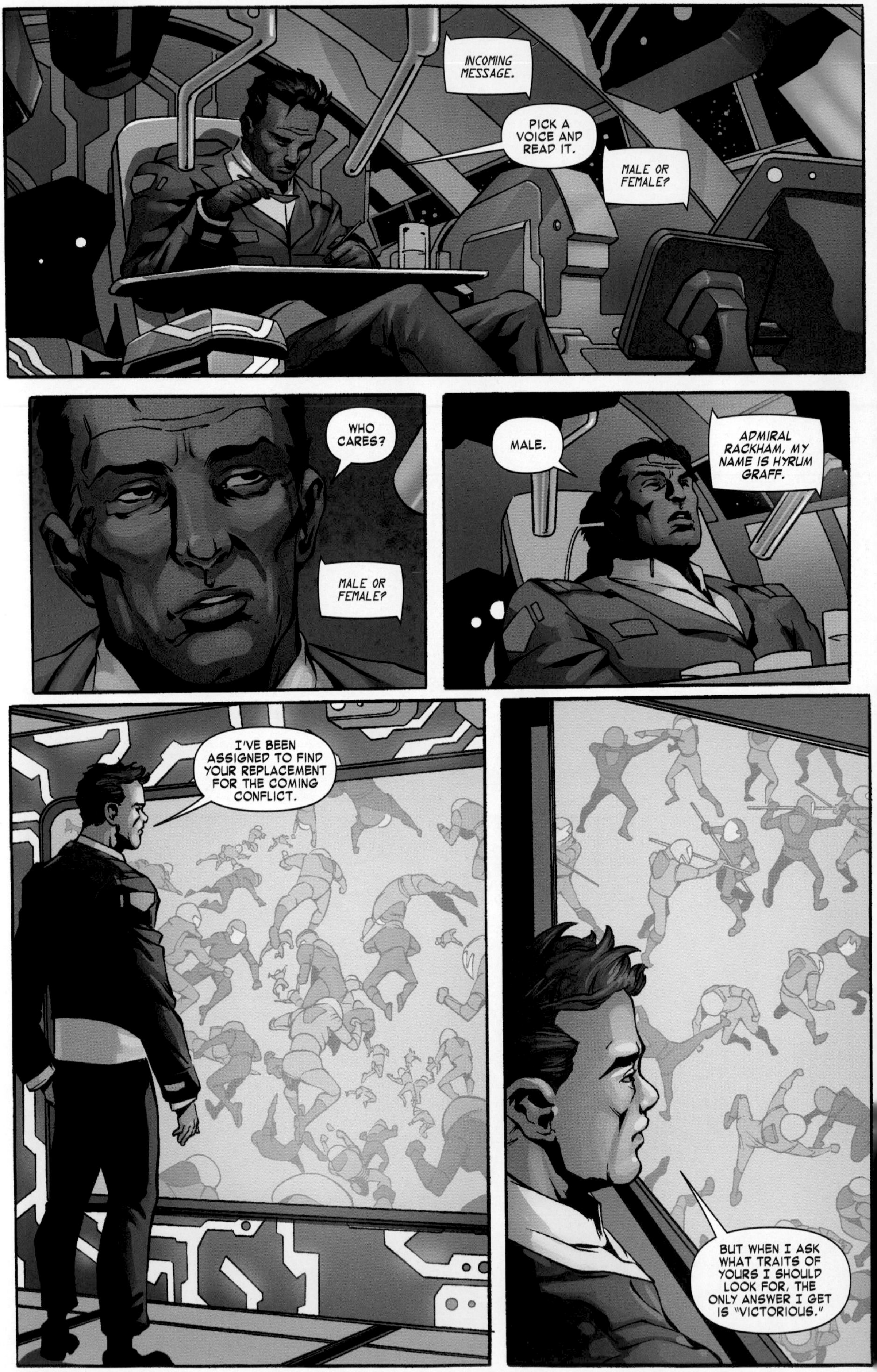
INCOMING MESSAGE.
PICK A VOICE AND READ IT.
MALE OR FEMALE?
WHO CARES?
MALE OR FEMALE?
MALE.
ADMIRAL RACKHAM, MY NAME IS HYRUM GRAFF.
I'VE BEEN ASSIGNED TO FIND YOUR REPLACEMENT FOR THE COMING CONFLICT.
BUT WHEN I ASK WHAT TRAITS OF YOURS I SHOULD LOOK FOR, THE ONLY ANSWER I GET IS "VICTORIOUS."

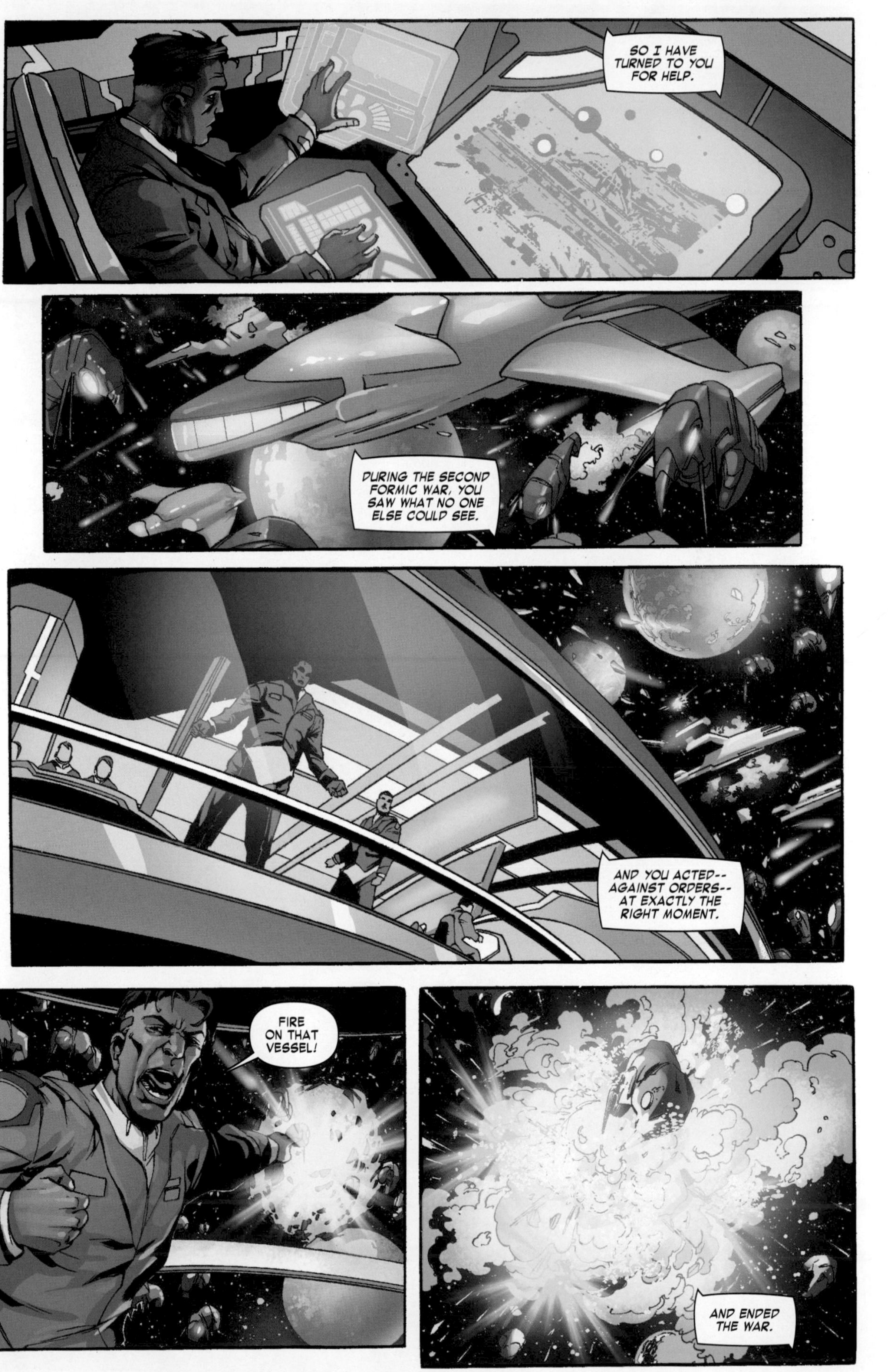
SO I HAVE TURNED TO YOU FOR HELP.
DURING THE SECOND FORMIC WAR, YOU SAW WHAT NO ONE ELSE COULD SEE.
AND YOU ACTED-- AGAINST ORDERS-- AT EXACTLY THE RIGHT MOMENT.
FIRE ON THAT VESSEL!
AND ENDED THE WAR.

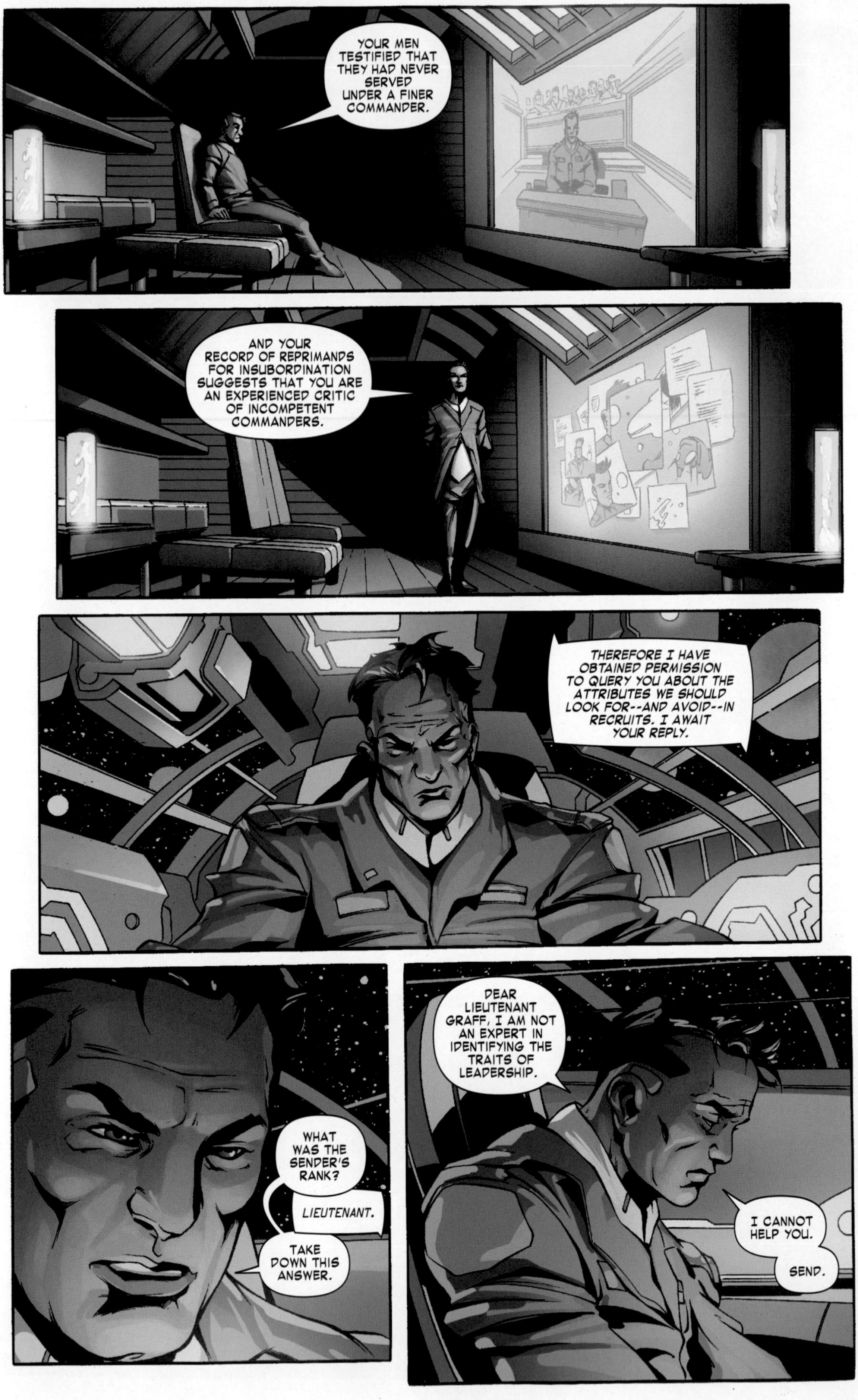
YOUR MEN TESTIFIED THAT THEY HAD NEVER SERVED UNDER A FINER COMMANDER.
AND YOUR RECORD OF REPRIMANDS FOR INSUBORDINATION SUGGESTS THAT YOU ARE AN EXPERIENCED CRITIC OF INCOMPETENT COMMANDERS.
THEREFORE I HAVE OBTAINED PERMISSION TO QUERY YOU ABOUT THE ATTRIBUTES WE SHOULD LOOK FOR--AND AVOID--IN RECRUITS. I AWAIT YOUR REPLY.
WHAT WAS THE SENDER'S RANK?
LIEUTENANT.
TAKE DOWN THIS ANSWER.
DEAR LIEUTENANT GRAFF, I AM NOT AN EXPERT IN IDENTIFYING THE TRAITS OF LEADERSHIP.
I CANNOT HELP YOU.
SEND.

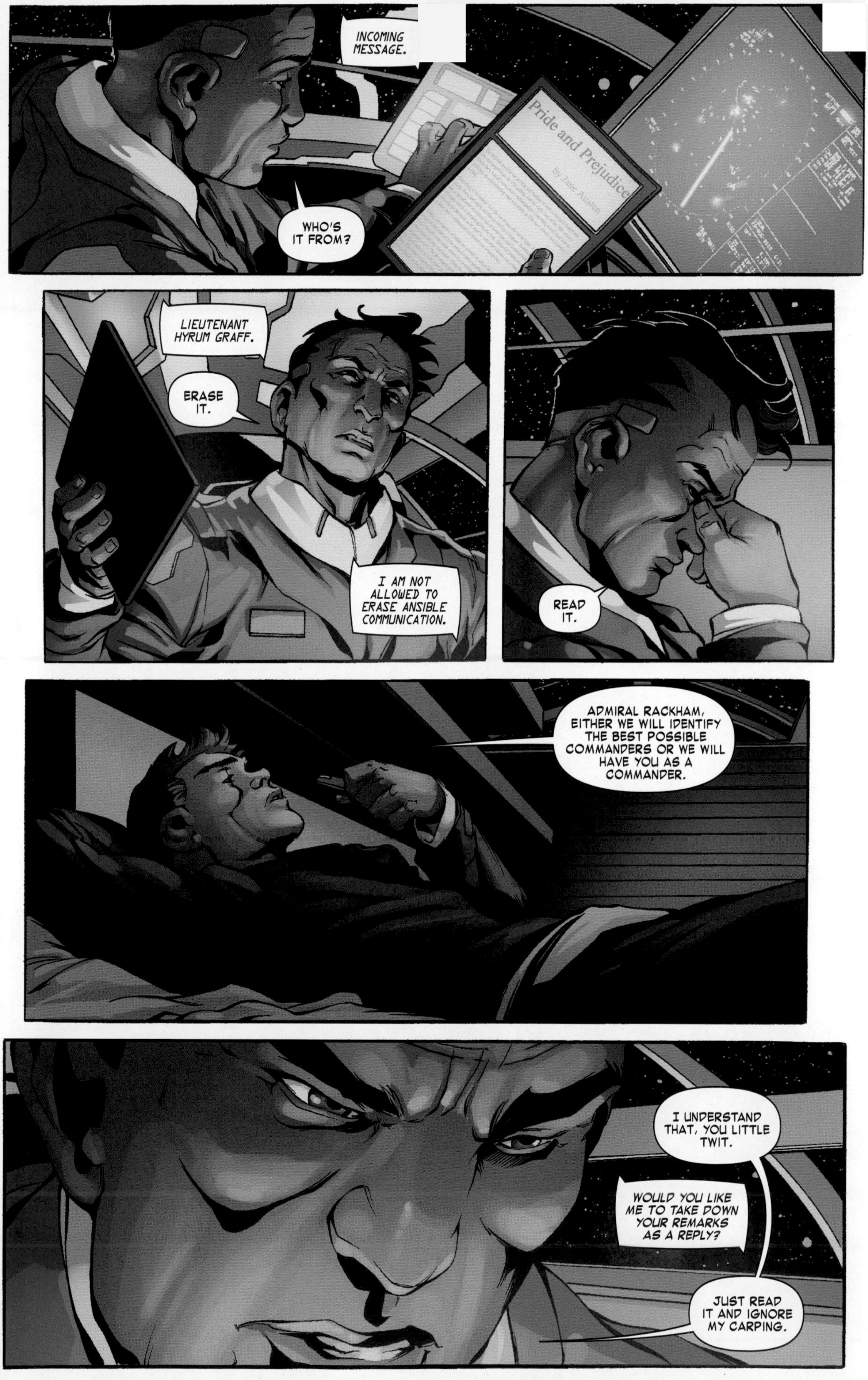
INCOMING MESSAGE.
Pride and Prejudice
by Jane Austen
WHO'S IT FROM?
LIEUTENANT HYRUM GRAFF.
ERASE IT.
I AM NOT ALLOWED TO ERASE ANSIBLE COMMUNICATION.
READ IT.
ADMIRAL RACKHAM, EITHER WE WILL IDENTIFY THE BEST POSSIBLE COMMANDERS OR WE WILL HAVE YOU AS A COMMANDER.
I UNDERSTAND THAT, YOU LITTLE TWIT.
WOULD YOU LIKE ME TO TAKE DOWN YOUR REMARKS AS A REPLY?
JUST READ IT AND IGNORE MY CARPING.

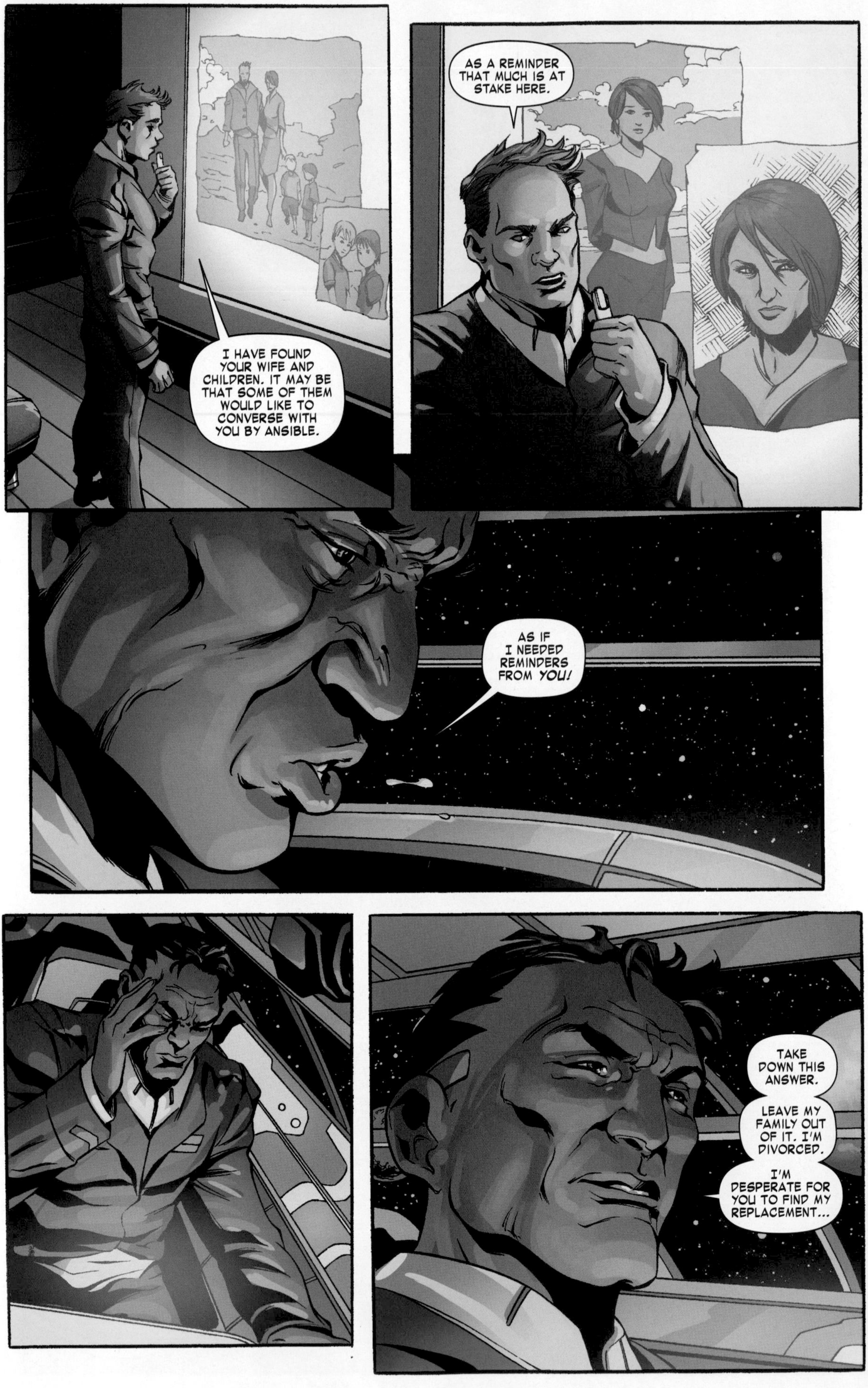
I HAVE FOUND YOUR WIFE AND CHILDREN. IT MAY BE THAT SOME OF THEM WOULD LIKE TO CONVERSE WITH YOU BY ANSIBLE.
AS A REMINDER THAT MUCH IS AT STAKE HERE.
AS IF I NEEDED REMINDERS FROM YOU!
TAKE DOWN THIS ANSWER.
LEAVE MY FAMILY OUT OF IT. I'M DIVORCED.
I'M DESPERATE FOR YOU TO FIND MY REPLACEMENT...

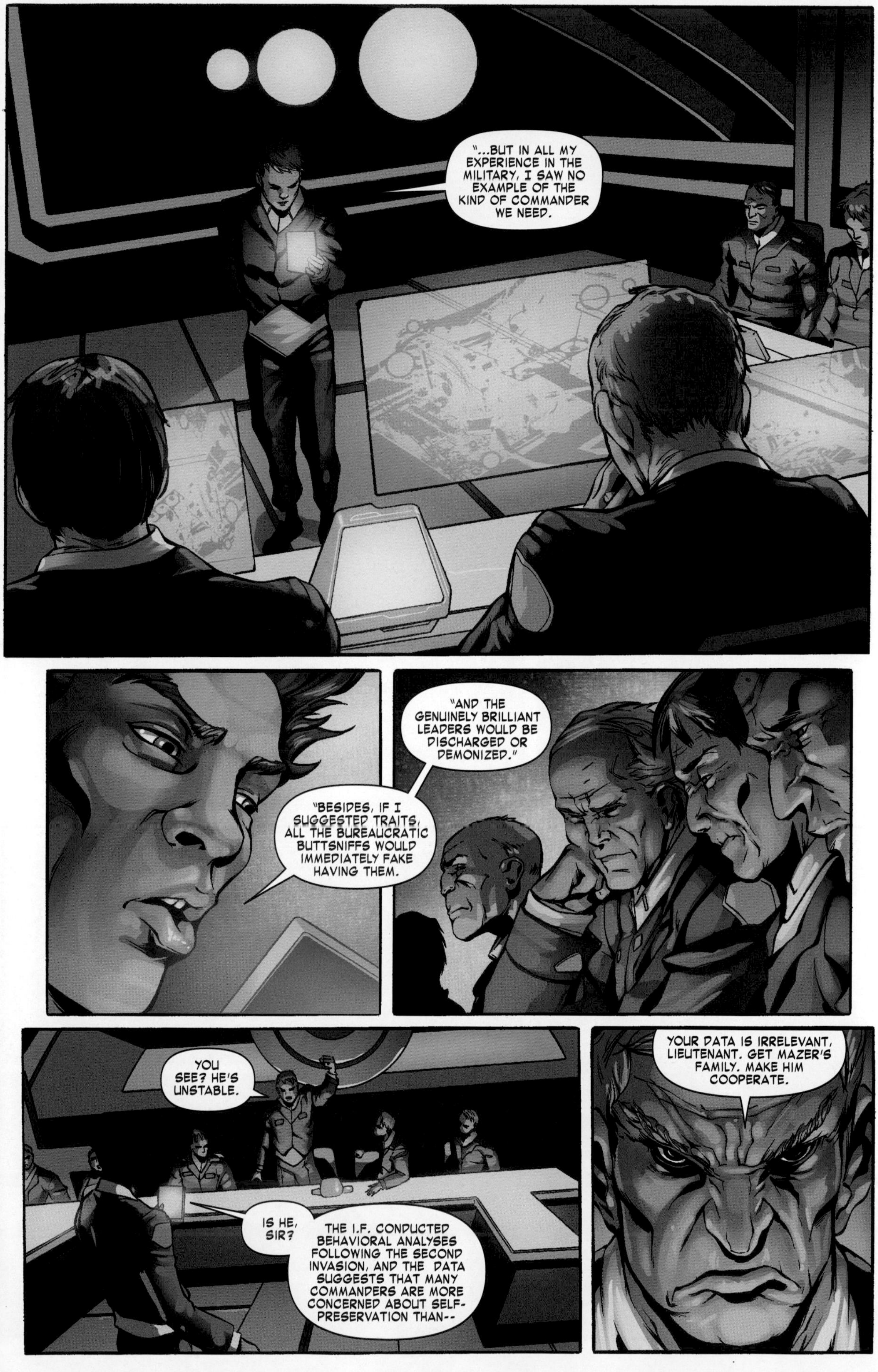
"...BUT IN ALL MY EXPERIENCE IN THE MILITARY, I SAW NO EXAMPLE OF THE KIND OF COMMANDER WE NEED.
"BESIDES, IF I SUGGESTED TRAITS, ALL THE BUREAUCRATIC BUTTSNIFFS WOULD IMMEDIATELY FAKE HAVING THEM.
"AND THE GENUINELY BRILLIANT LEADERS WOULD BE DISCHARGED OR DEMONIZED."
YOU SEE? HE'S UNSTABLE.
IS HE, SIR?
THE I.F. CONDUCTED BEHAVIORAL ANALYSES FOLLOWING THE SECOND INVASION, AND THE DATA SUGGESTS THAT MANY COMMANDERS ARE MORE CONCERNED ABOUT SELF-PRESERVATION THAN--
YOUR DATA IS IRRELEVANT, LIEUTENANT. GET MAZER'S FAMILY. MAKE HIM COOPERATE.

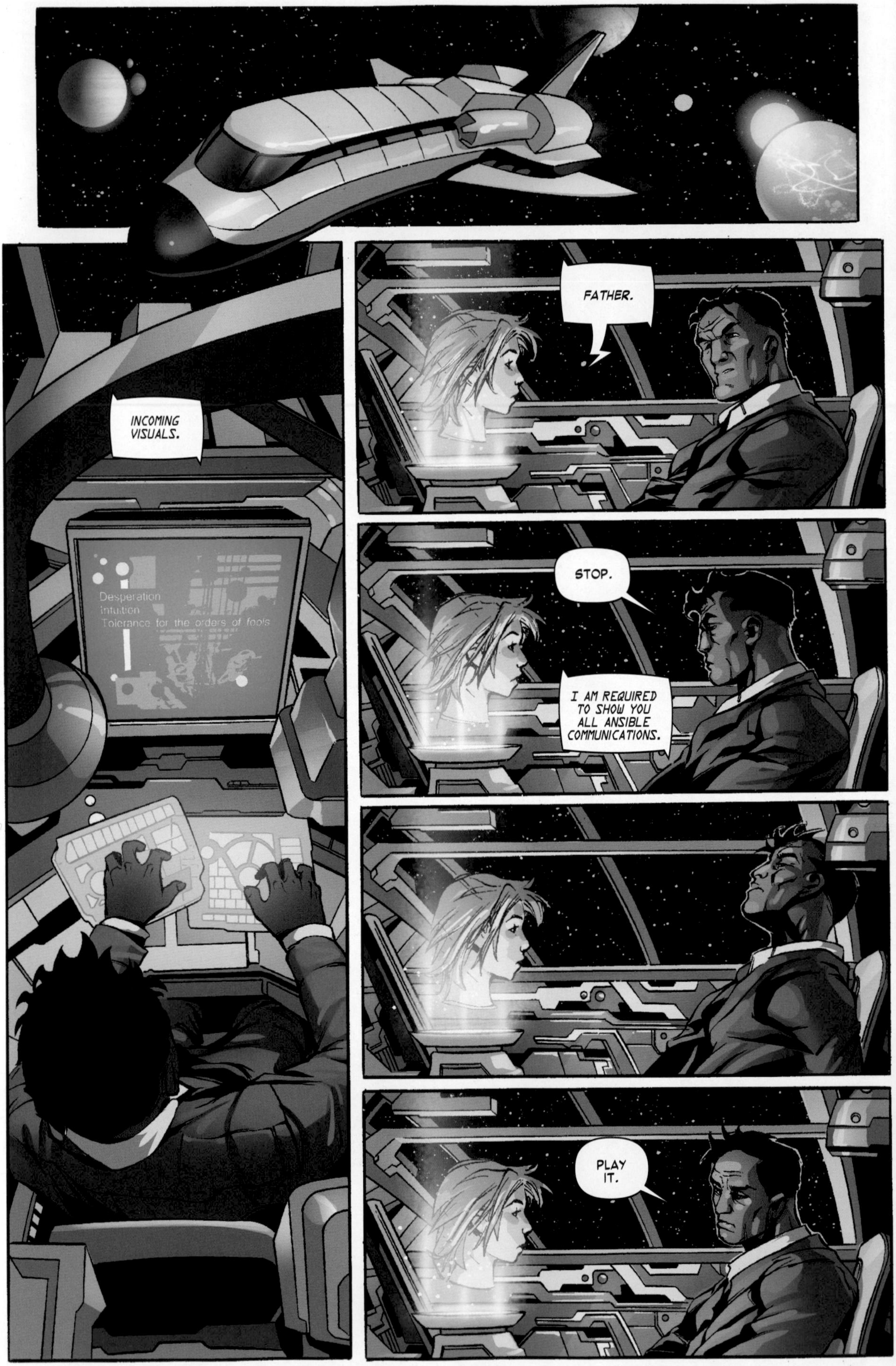
INCOMING VISUALS.
Desperation
Intuition
Tolerance for the orders of fools
FATHER.
STOP.
I AM REQUIRED TO SHOW YOU ALL ANSIBLE COMMUNICATIONS.
PLAY IT.

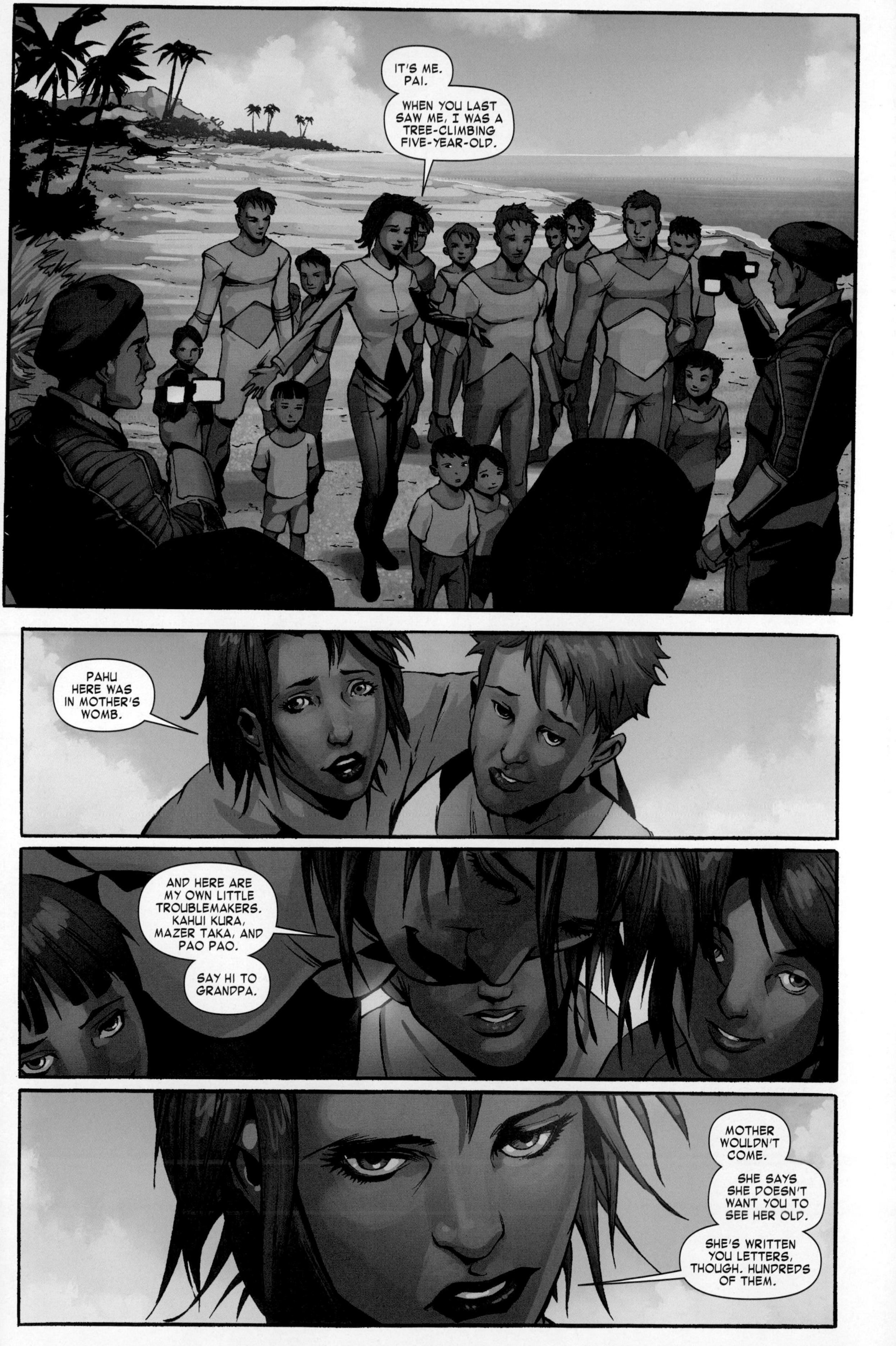
IT'S ME. PAI.
WHEN YOU LAST SAW ME, I WAS A TREE-CLIMBING FIVE-YEAR-OLD.
PAHU HERE WAS IN MOTHER'S WOMB.
AND HERE ARE MY OWN LITTLE TROUBLEMAKERS. KAHUI KURA, MAZER TAKA, AND PAO PAO.
SAY HI TO GRANDPA.
MOTHER WOULDN'T COME.
SHE SAYS SHE DOESN'T WANT YOU TO SEE HER OLD.
SHE'S WRITTEN YOU LETTERS, THOUGH. HUNDREDS OF THEM.

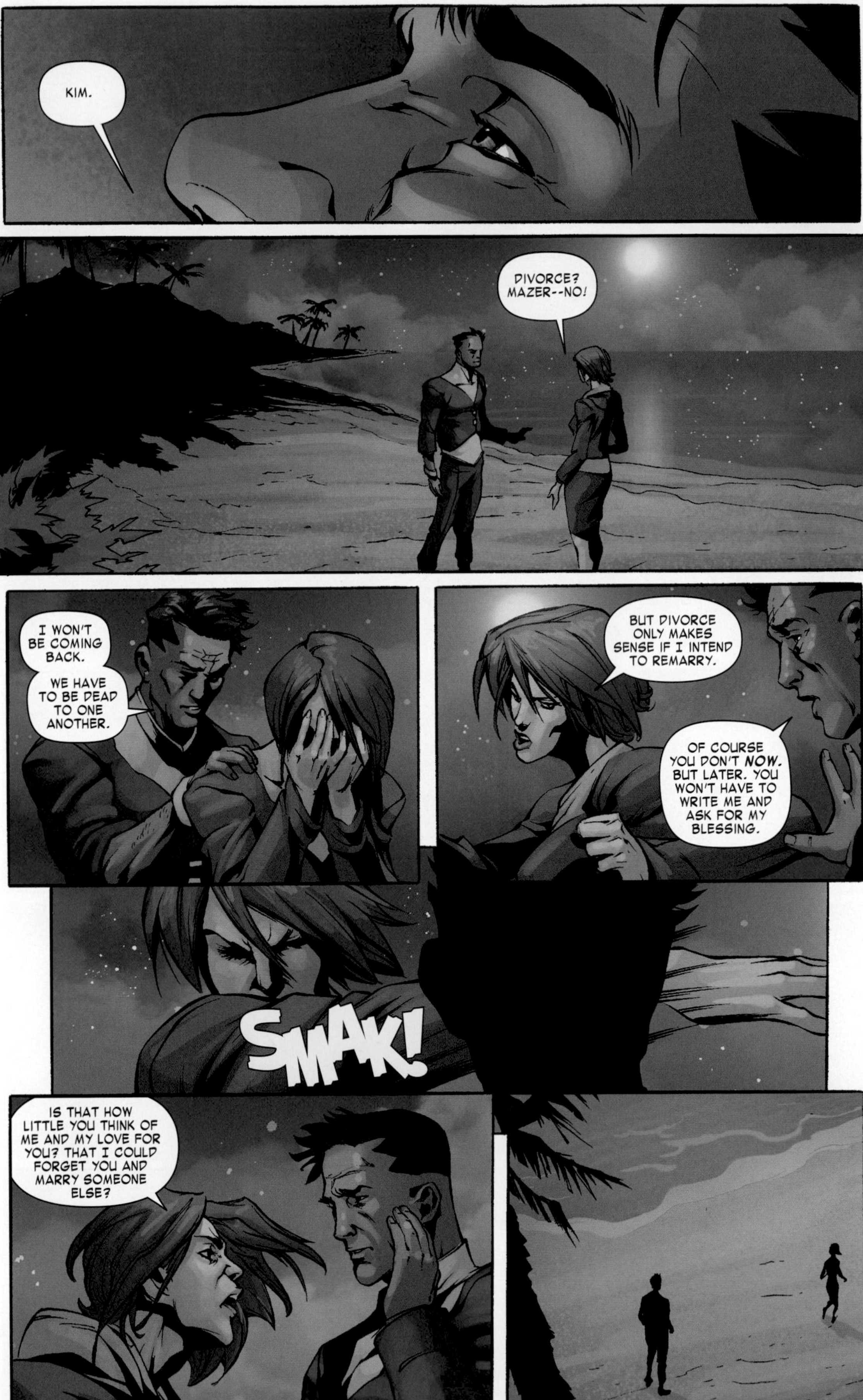
KIM.
DIVORCE? MAZER--NO!
I WON'T BE COMING BACK.
WE HAVE TO BE DEAD TO ONE ANOTHER.
BUT DIVORCE ONLY MAKES SENSE IF I INTEND TO REMARRY.
OF COURSE YOU DON'T NOW. BUT LATER. YOU WON'T HAVE TO WRITE ME AND ASK FOR MY BLESSING.
SMAK!
IS THAT HOW LITTLE YOU THINK OF ME AND MY LOVE FOR YOU? THAT I COULD FORGET YOU AND MARRY SOMEONE ELSE?

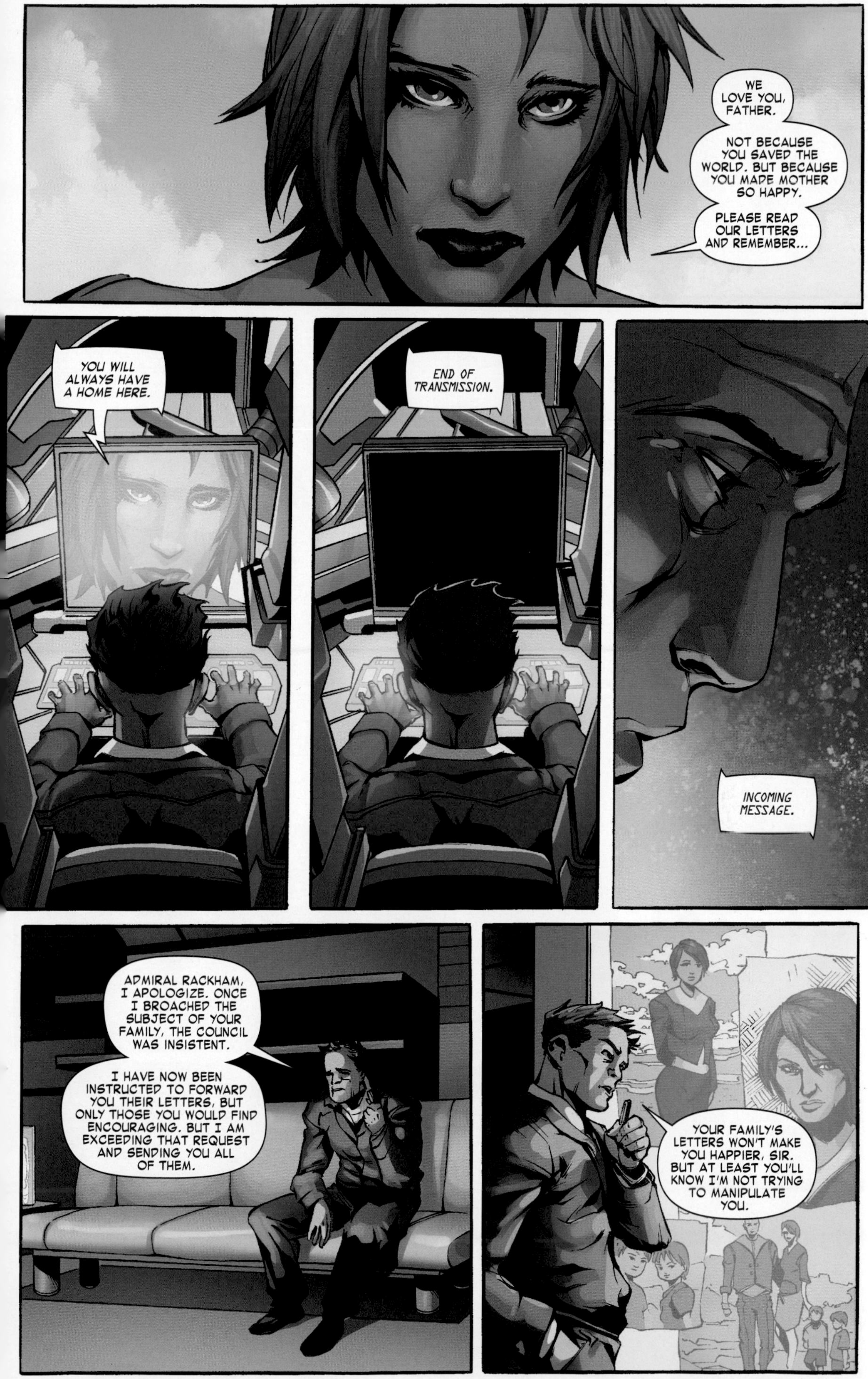

WE LOVE YOU, FATHER.
NOT BECAUSE YOU SAVED THE WORLD. BUT BECAUSE YOU MADE MOTHER SO HAPPY.
PLEASE READ OUR LETTERS AND REMEMBER...
YOU WILL ALWAYS HAVE A HOME HERE.
END OF TRANSMISSION.
INCOMING MESSAGE.
ADMIRAL RACKHAM, I APOLOGIZE. ONCE I BROACHED THE SUBJECT OF YOUR FAMILY, THE COUNCIL WAS INSISTENT.
I HAVE NOW BEEN INSTRUCTED TO FORWARD YOU THEIR LETTERS, BUT ONLY THOSE YOU WOULD FIND ENCOURAGING. BUT I AM EXCEEDING THAT REQUEST AND SENDING YOU ALL OF THEM.
YOUR FAMILY'S LETTERS WON'T MAKE YOU HAPPIER, SIR. BUT AT LEAST YOU'LL KNOW I'M NOT TRYING TO MANIPULATE YOU.

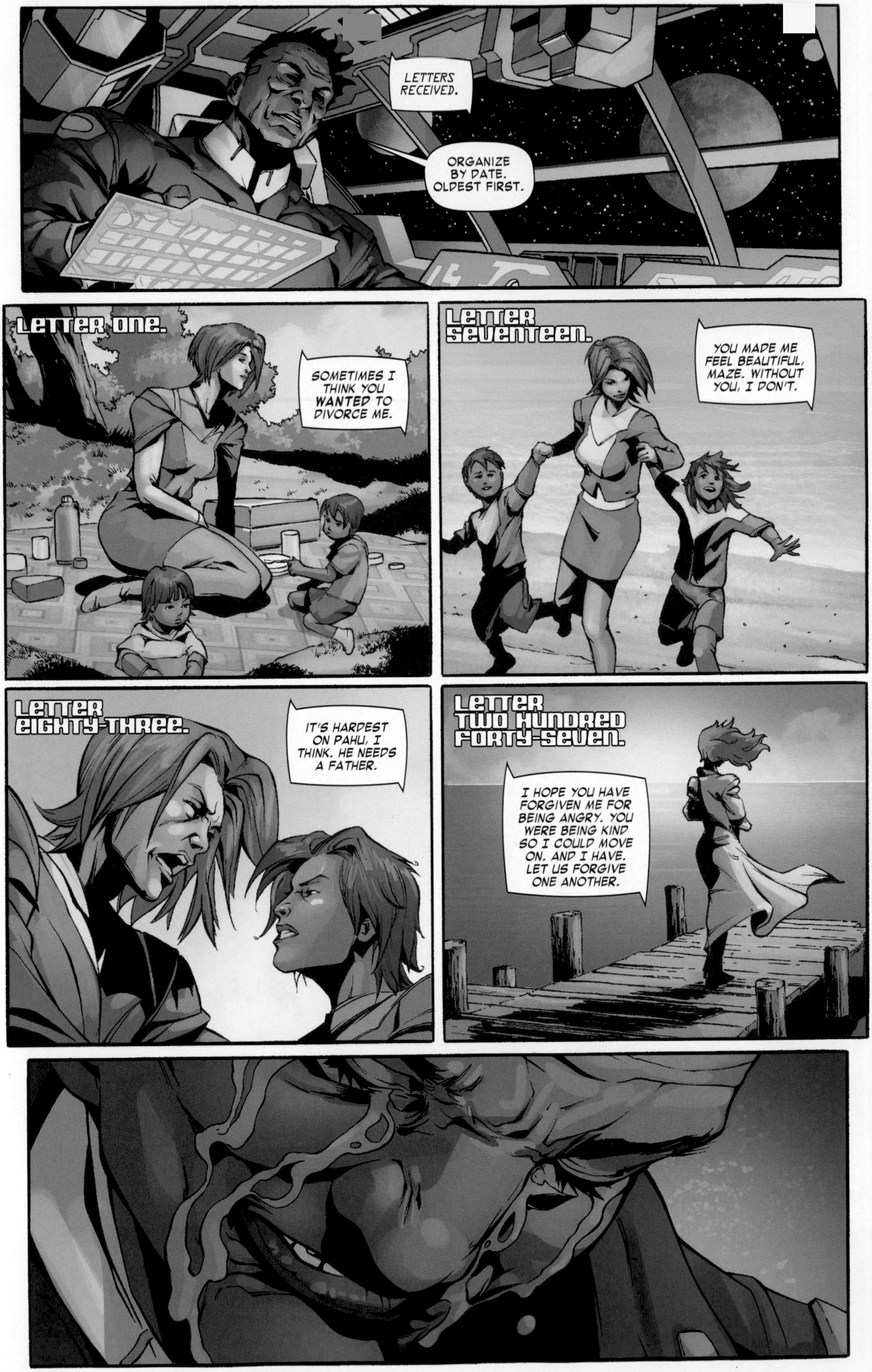
LETTERS RECEIVED.
ORGANIZE BY DATE. OLDEST FIRST.
LETTER ONE.
SOMETIMES I THINK YOU WANTED TO DIVORCE ME.
LETTER SEVENTEEN.
YOU MADE ME FEEL BEAUTIFUL, MAZE. WITHOUT YOU, I DON'T.
LETTER EIGHTY-THREE.
IT'S HARDEST ON PAHU, I THINK. HE NEEDS A FATHER.
LETTER TWO HUNDRED FORTY-SEVEN.
I HOPE YOU HAVE FORGIVEN ME FOR BEING ANGRY. YOU WERE BEING KIND SO I COULD MOVE ON. AND I HAVE. LET US FORGIVE ONE ANOTHER.

BEGIN VISUAL TRANSMISSION TO EROS.

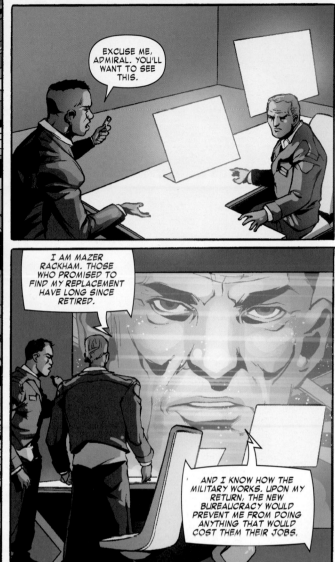

EXCUSE ME, ADMIRAL. YOU'LL WANT TO SEE THIS.

I AM MAZER RACKHAM. THOSE WHO PROMISED TO FIND MY REPLACEMENT HAVE LONG SINCE RETIRED.

AND I KNOW HOW THE MILITARY WORKS. UPON MY RETURN, THE NEW BUREAUCRACY WOULD PREVENT ME FROM DOING ANYTHING THAT WOULD COST THEM THEIR JOBS.

I WOULD BE POWERLESS.

EVERYBODY OUT!

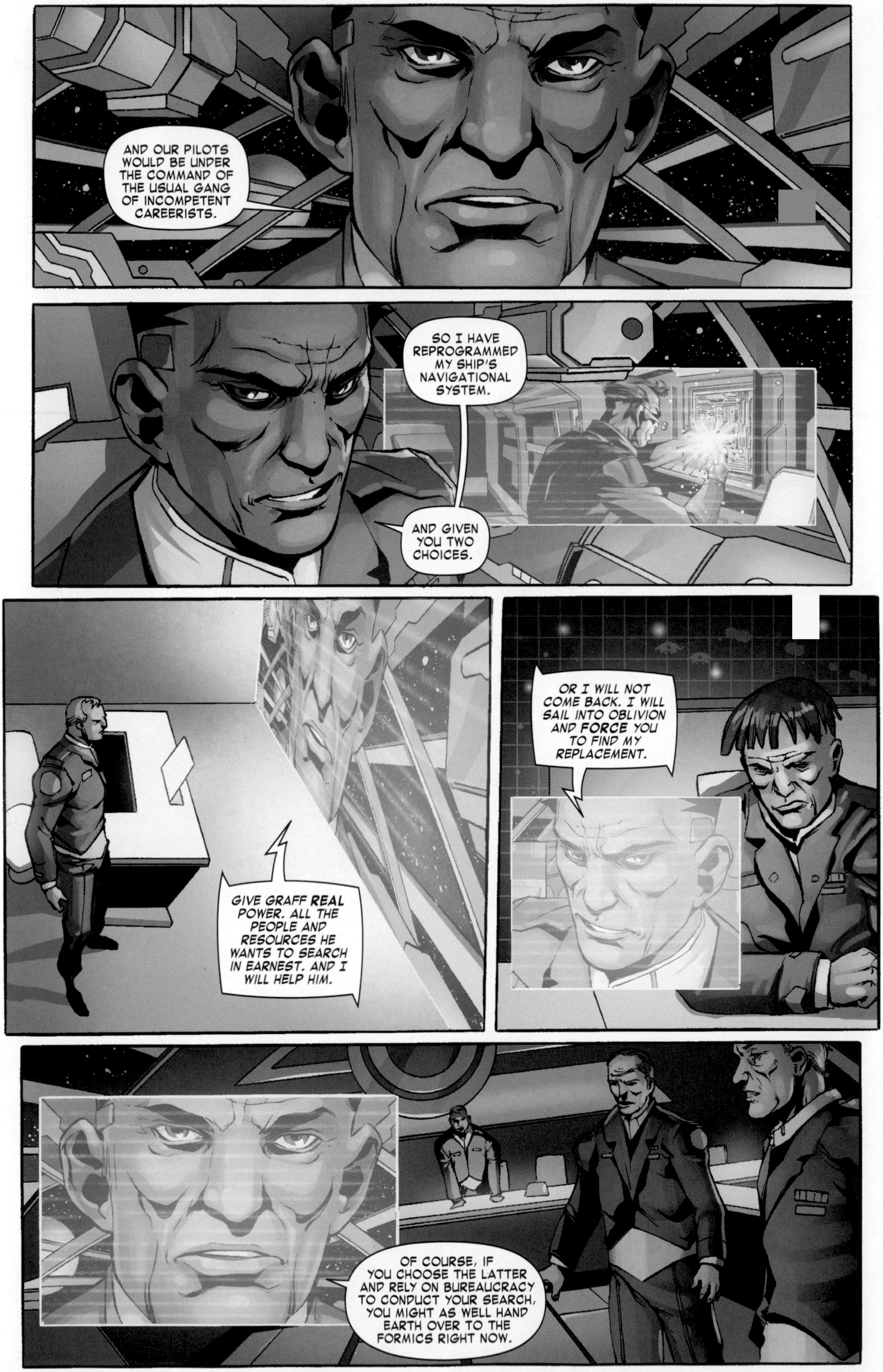
AND OUR PILOTS WOULD BE UNDER THE COMMAND OF THE USUAL GANG OF INCOMPETENT CAREERISTS.
SO I HAVE REPROGRAMMED MY SHIP'S NAVIGATIONAL SYSTEM.
AND GIVEN YOU TWO CHOICES.
GIVE GRAFF REAL POWER. ALL THE PEOPLE AND RESOURCES HE WANTS TO SEARCH IN EARNEST. AND I WILL HELP HIM.
OR I WILL NOT COME BACK. I WILL SAIL INTO OBLIVION AND FORCE YOU TO FIND MY REPLACEMENT.
OF COURSE, IF YOU CHOOSE THE LATTER AND RELY ON BUREAUCRACY TO CONDUCT YOUR SEARCH, YOU MIGHT AS WELL HAND EARTH OVER TO THE FORMICS RIGHT NOW.

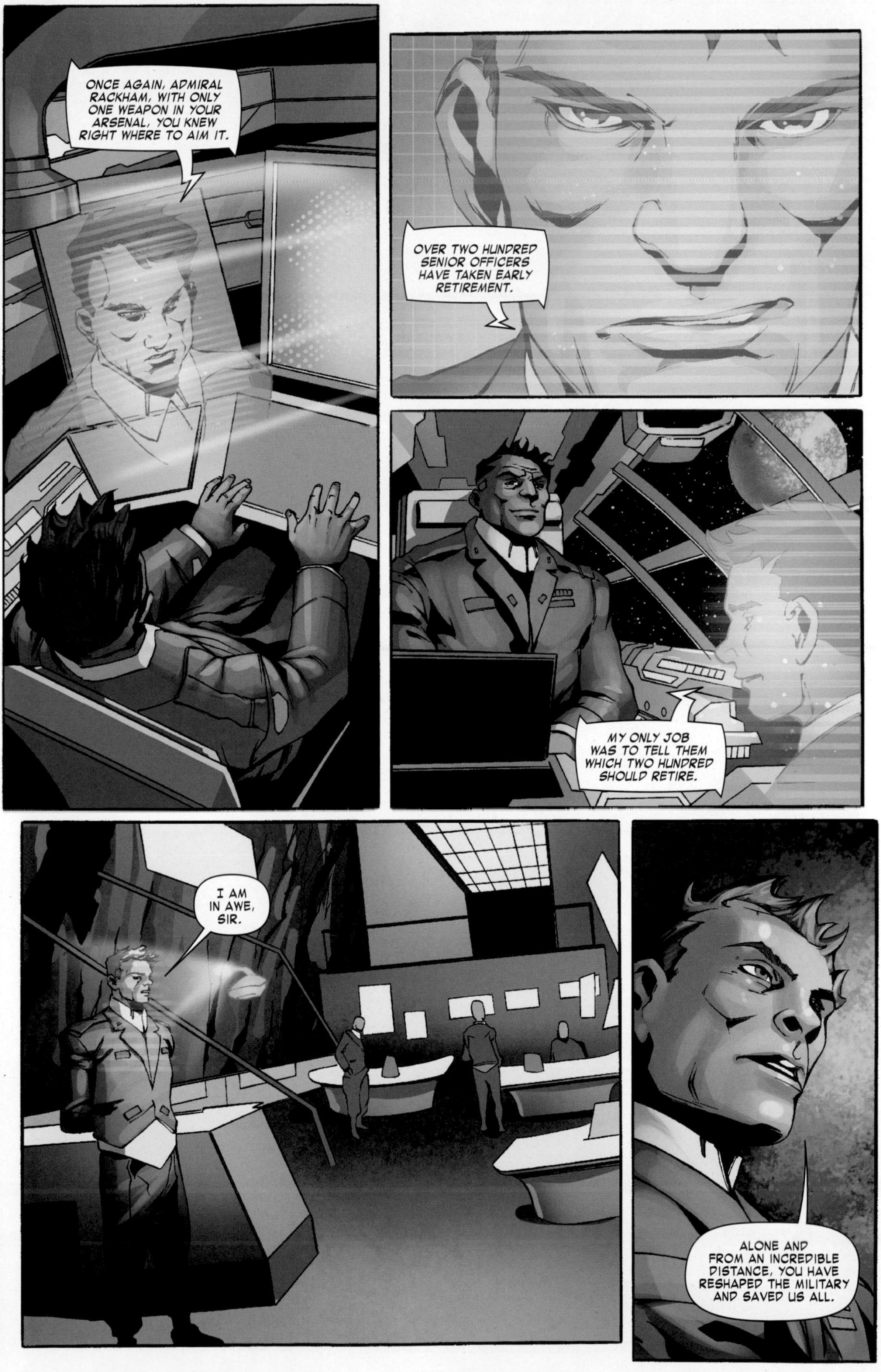
ONCE AGAIN, ADMIRAL RACKHAM, WITH ONLY ONE WEAPON IN YOUR ARSENAL, YOU KNEW RIGHT WHERE TO AIM IT.
OVER TWO HUNDRED SENIOR OFFICERS HAVE TAKEN EARLY RETIREMENT.
MY ONLY JOB WAS TO TELL THEM WHICH TWO HUNDRED SHOULD RETIRE.
I AM IN AWE, SIR.
ALONE AND FROM AN INCREDIBLE DISTANCE, YOU HAVE RESHAPED THE MILITARY AND SAVED US ALL.

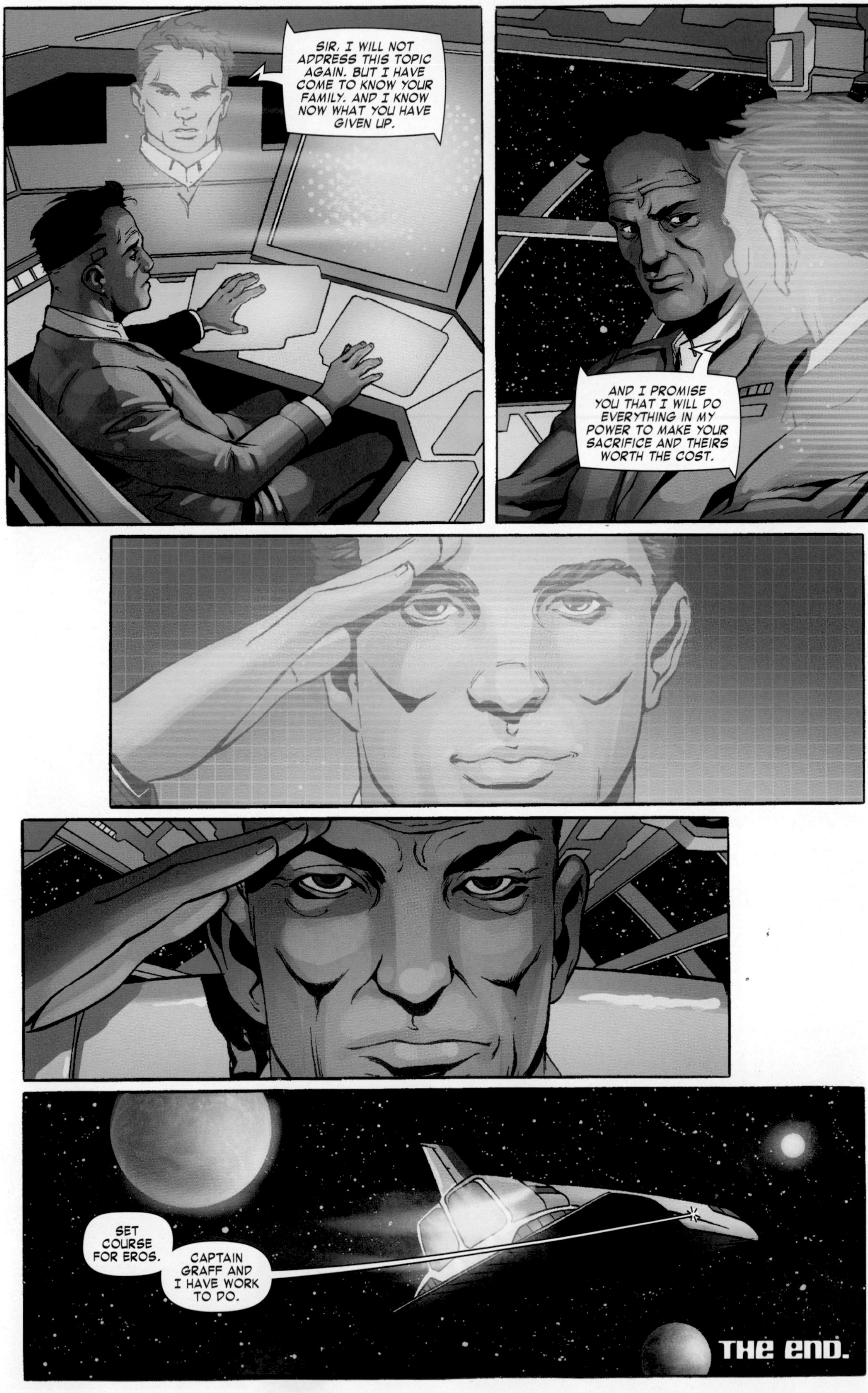
SIR, I WILL NOT ADDRESS THIS TOPIC AGAIN. BUT I HAVE COME TO KNOW YOUR FAMILY. AND I KNOW NOW WHAT YOU HAVE GIVEN UP.
AND I PROMISE YOU THAT I WILL DO EVERYTHING IN MY POWER TO MAKE YOUR SACRIFICE AND THEIRS WORTH THE COST.
SET COURSE FOR EROS.
CAPTAIN GRAFF AND I HAVE WORK TO DO.
THE END.

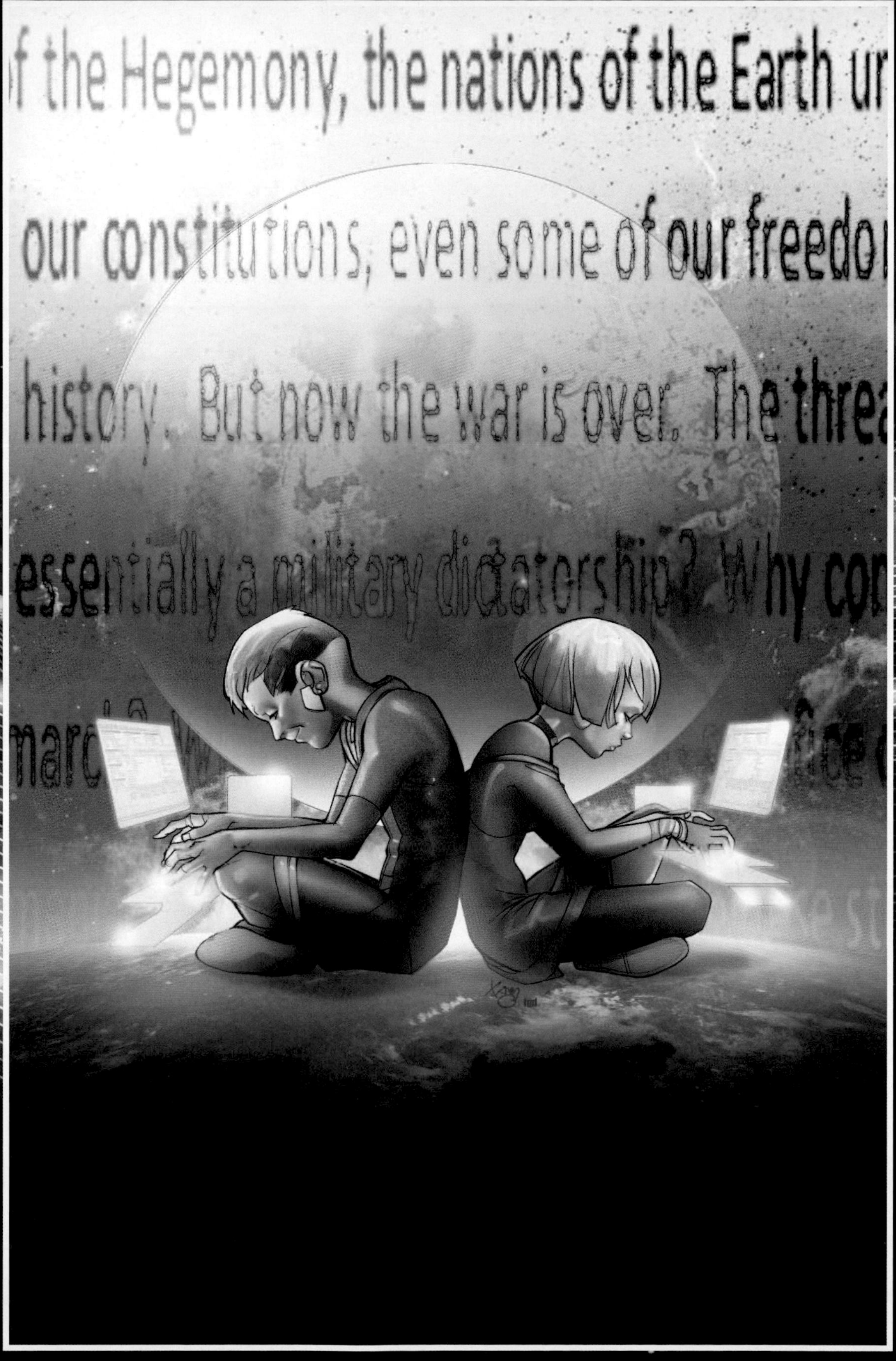
f the Hegemony, the nations of the Earth ur
our constitutions, even some of our freedo
history. But now the war is over. The threa
essentially a military dictatorship? Why con

FOR IMMEDIATE RELEASE ACROSS ALL NET CHANNELS
TITLE: Losing our inalienable rights for an unseen alien threat
AUTHOR: Demosthenes (photo not available)

EXCERPT:
By definition, any government that denies freedom to its citizens is an oppressive regime. And that is precisely what the Hegemony has become.

When the Formics attacked, every nation on Earth agreed to unite under Hegemony rule. We set aside our constitutions and our Houses of Parliament, and we accepted a single government to save us from annihilation.

But now, decades later, with no Formic invasion pending, we continue to live under a system of government that denies its citizens inalienable rights: the right to elect our officials; the right to bear as many children as we wish; the right to keep those children, even when the International Fleet wants them for Battle School. . .

FOR IMMEDIATE RELEASE ACROSS ALL NET CHANNELS
TITLE: Divided we fall
AUTHOR: Locke (photo not available)

EXCERPT:
Demosthenes argues that the Hegemony has robbed us of our freedom and stripped us of our sovereignty. But what he fails to mention is that the Hegemony has given us decades of world peace after centuries of war, oppression, and human suffering. Statistically speaking, the Hegemony has granted MORE inalienable rights, not less. Consider the citizens of war-torn Africa. Or women of the Middle East. Or any group of people who lived without true freedom prior to Hegemony rule. Are there lives not better because of unified rule?

I ask Demosthenes: Is the life we live and the freedoms we enjoy because of the Hegemony better than the alternative? Perhaps Demosthenes would rather live under Formic rule. . .

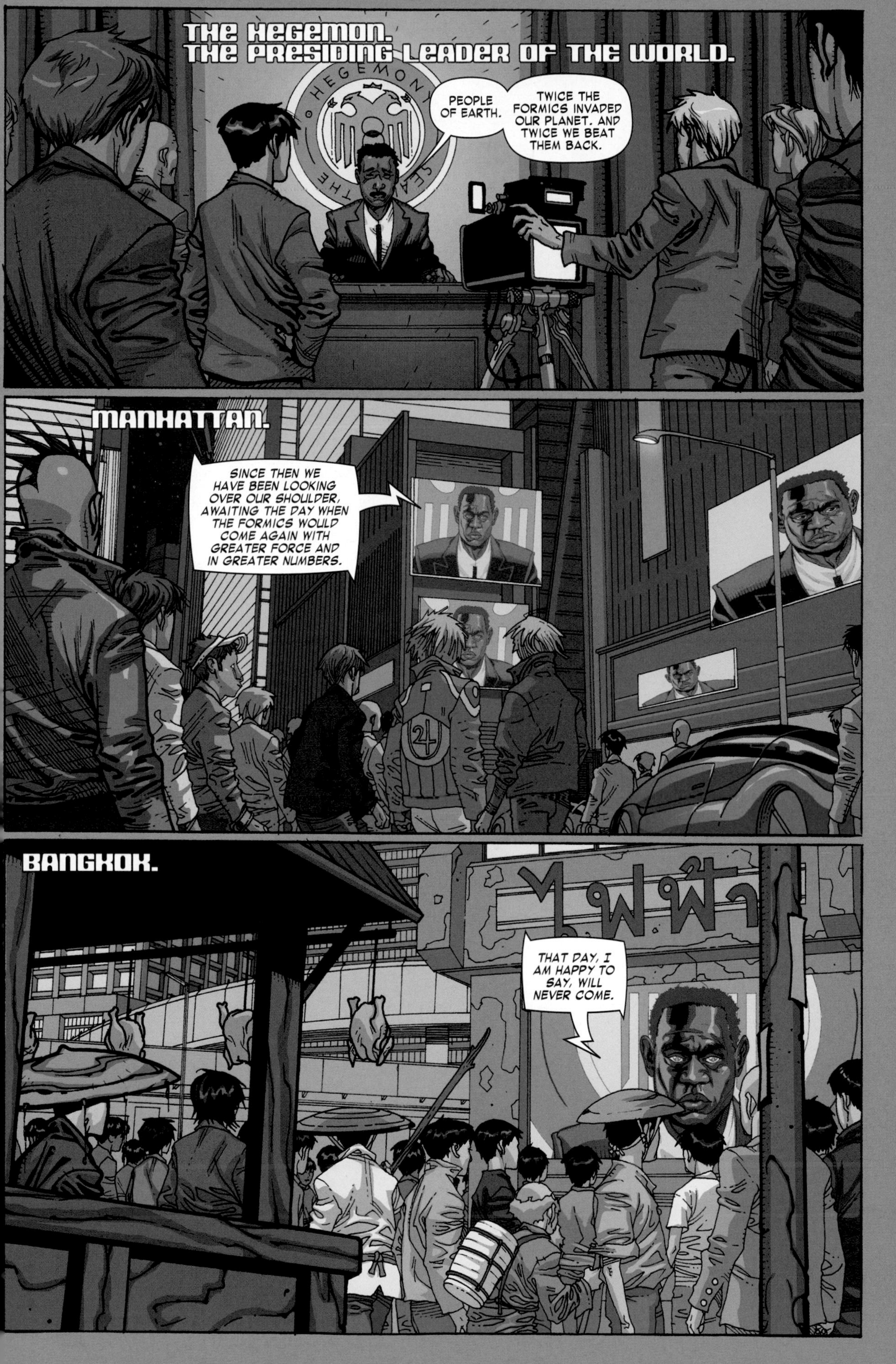
THE HEGEMON.
THE PRESIDING LEADER OF THE WORLD.
HEGEMONY
SEAT OF THE
PEOPLE OF EARTH.
TWICE THE FORMICS INVADED OUR PLANET. AND TWICE WE BEAT THEM BACK.
MANHATTAN.
SINCE THEN WE HAVE BEEN LOOKING OVER OUR SHOULDER, AWAITING THE DAY WHEN THE FORMICS WOULD COME AGAIN WITH GREATER FORCE AND IN GREATER NUMBERS.
BANGKOK.
THAT DAY, I AM HAPPY TO SAY, WILL NEVER COME.

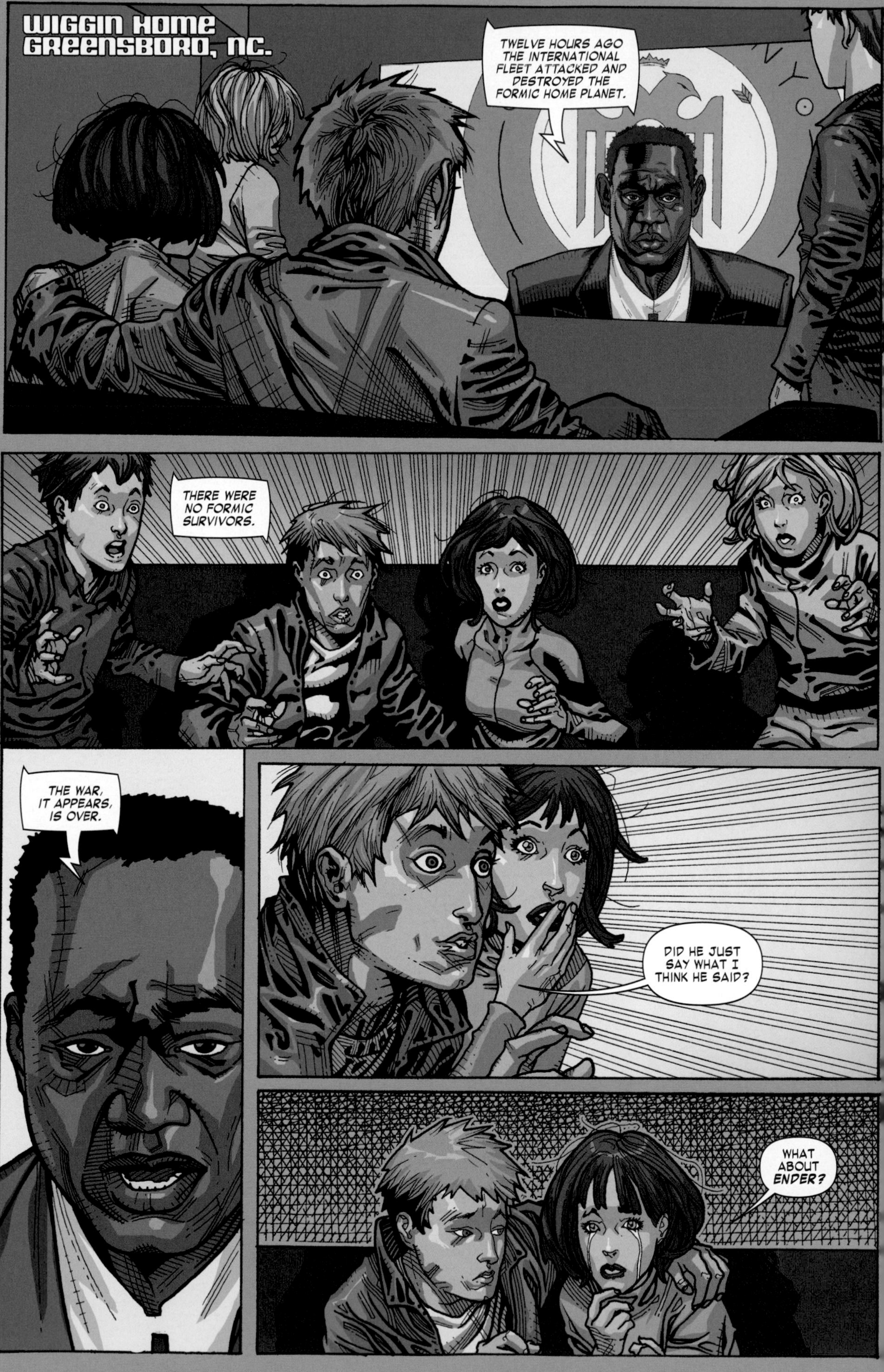
WIGGIN HOME GREENSBORO, NC.
TWELVE HOURS AGO THE INTERNATIONAL FLEET ATTACKED AND DESTROYED THE FORMIC HOME PLANET.
THERE WERE NO FORMIC SURVIVORS.
THE WAR, IT APPEARS, IS OVER.
DID HE JUST SAY WHAT I THINK HE SAID?
WHAT ABOUT ENDER?

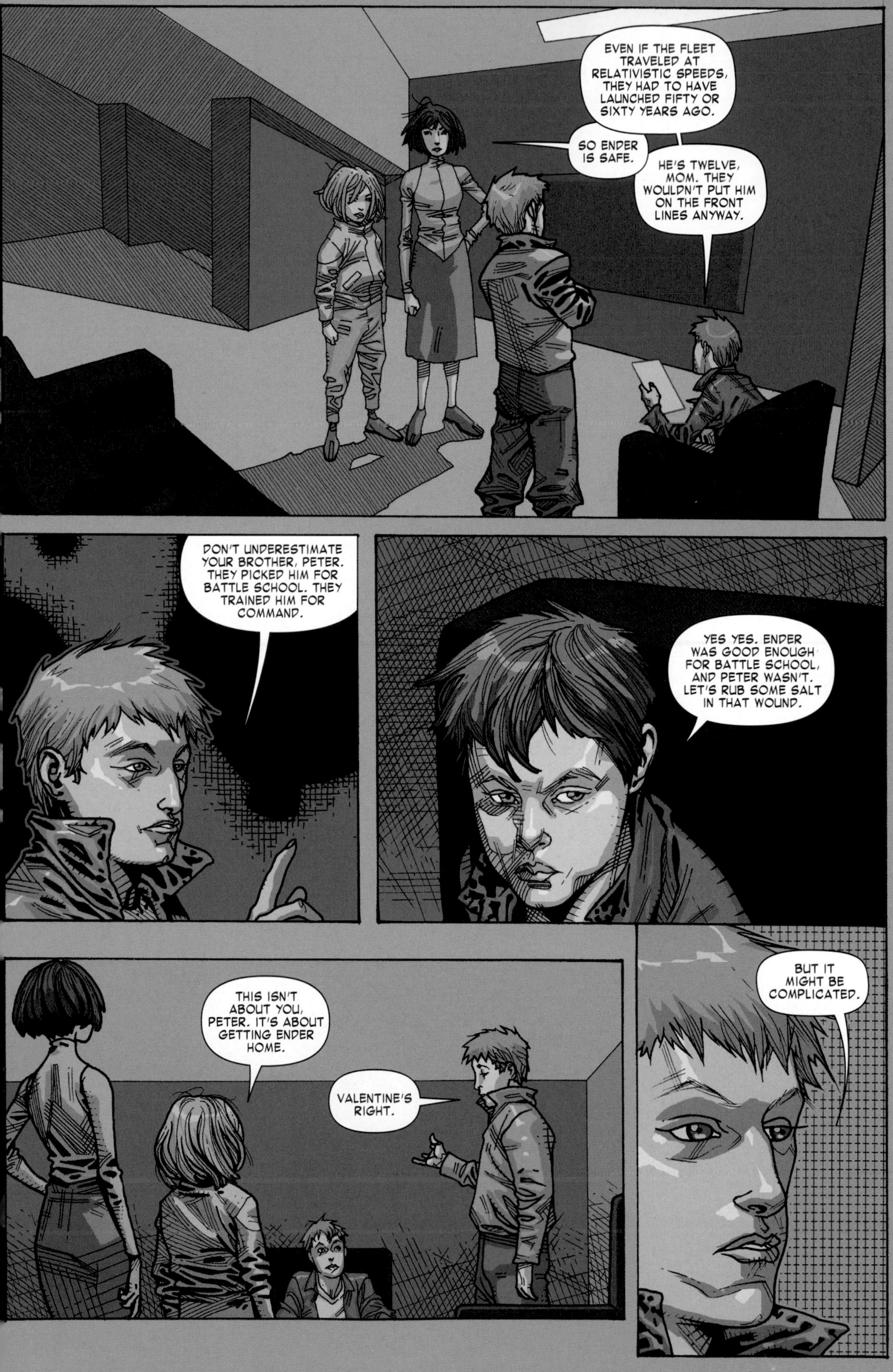
EVEN IF THE FLEET TRAVELED AT RELATIVISTIC SPEEDS, THEY HAD TO HAVE LAUNCHED FIFTY OR SIXTY YEARS AGO.
SO ENDER IS SAFE.
HE'S TWELVE, MOM. THEY WOULDN'T PUT HIM ON THE FRONT LINES ANYWAY.
DON'T UNDERESTIMATE YOUR BROTHER, PETER. THEY PICKED HIM FOR BATTLE SCHOOL. THEY TRAINED HIM FOR COMMAND.
YES YES. ENDER WAS GOOD ENOUGH FOR BATTLE SCHOOL, AND PETER WASN'T. LET'S RUB SOME SALT IN THAT WOUND.
THIS ISN'T ABOUT YOU, PETER. IT'S ABOUT GETTING ENDER HOME.
VALENTINE'S RIGHT.
BUT IT MIGHT BE COMPLICATED.

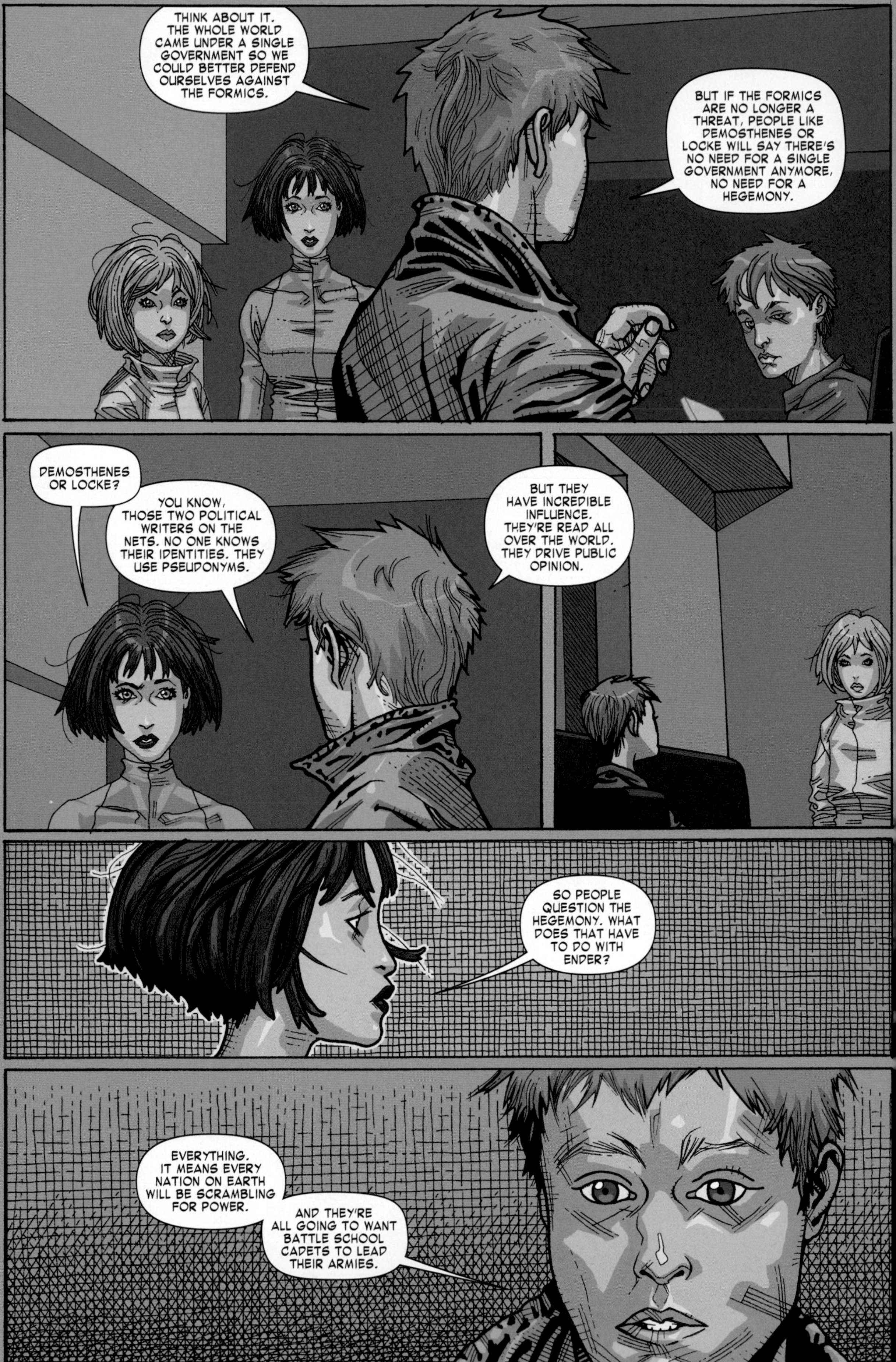
THINK ABOUT IT. THE WHOLE WORLD CAME UNDER A SINGLE GOVERNMENT SO WE COULD BETTER DEFEND OURSELVES AGAINST THE FORMICS.
BUT IF THE FORMICS ARE NO LONGER A THREAT, PEOPLE LIKE DEMOSTHENES OR LOCKE WILL SAY THERE'S NO NEED FOR A SINGLE GOVERNMENT ANYMORE, NO NEED FOR A HEGEMONY.
DEMOSTHENES OR LOCKE?
YOU KNOW, THOSE TWO POLITICAL WRITERS ON THE NETS. NO ONE KNOWS THEIR IDENTITIES. THEY USE PSEUDONYMS.
BUT THEY HAVE INCREDIBLE INFLUENCE. THEY'RE READ ALL OVER THE WORLD. THEY DRIVE PUBLIC OPINION.
SO PEOPLE QUESTION THE HEGEMONY. WHAT DOES THAT HAVE TO DO WITH ENDER?
EVERYTHING. IT MEANS EVERY NATION ON EARTH WILL BE SCRAMBLING FOR POWER.
AND THEY'RE ALL GOING TO WANT BATTLE SCHOOL CADETS TO LEAD THEIR ARMIES.

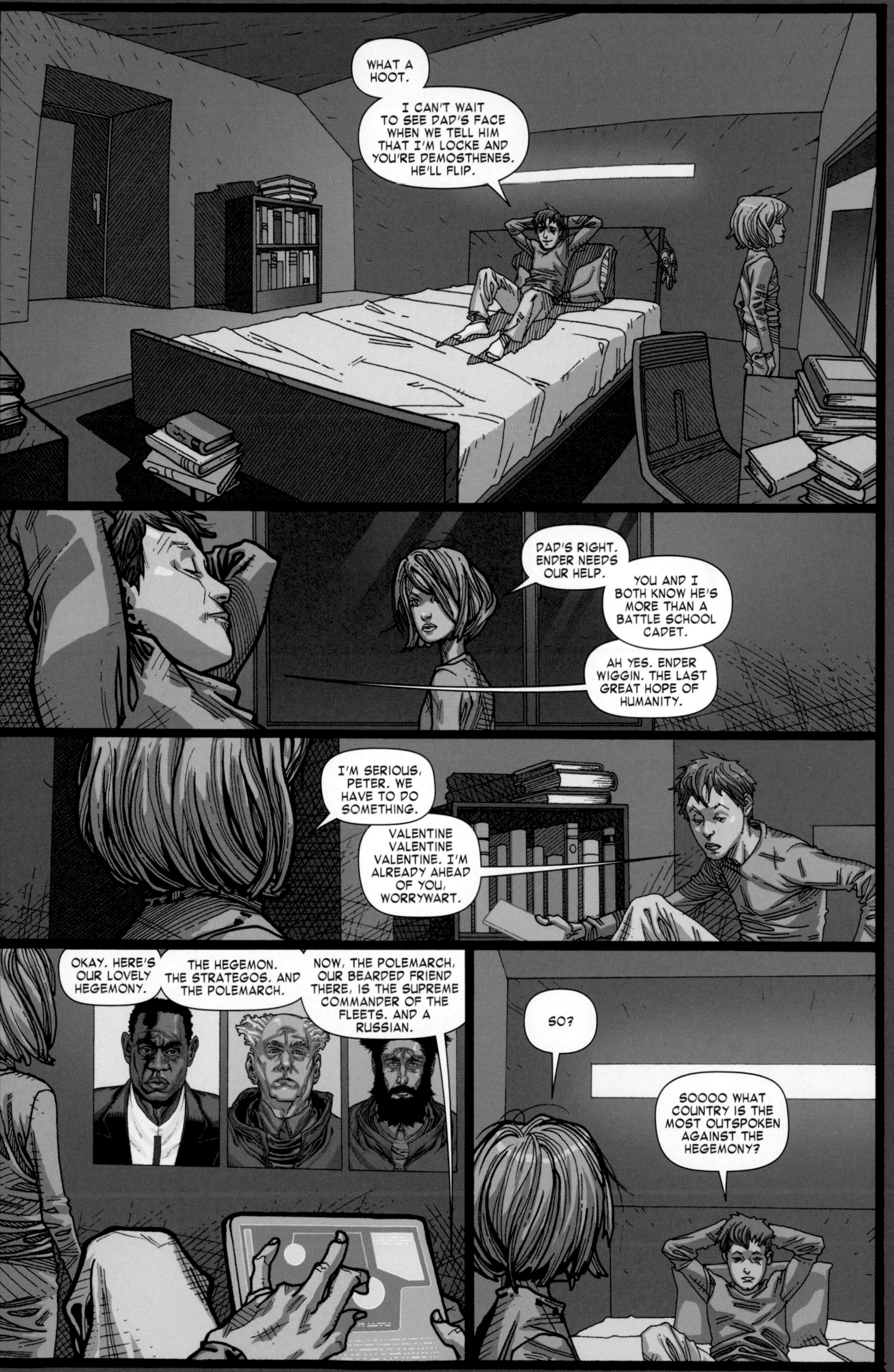
WHAT A HOOT.
I CAN'T WAIT TO SEE DAD'S FACE WHEN WE TELL HIM THAT I'M LOCKE AND YOU'RE DEMOSTHENES. HE'LL FLIP.
DAD'S RIGHT. ENDER NEEDS OUR HELP.
YOU AND I BOTH KNOW HE'S MORE THAN A BATTLE SCHOOL CADET.
AH YES. ENDER WIGGIN. THE LAST GREAT HOPE OF HUMANITY.
I'M SERIOUS, PETER. WE HAVE TO DO SOMETHING.
VALENTINE VALENTINE VALENTINE. I'M ALREADY AHEAD OF YOU, WORRYWART.
OKAY. HERE'S OUR LOVELY HEGEMONY.
THE HEGEMON. THE STRATEGOS. AND THE POLEMARCH.
NOW, THE POLEMARCH, OUR BEARDED FRIEND THERE, IS THE SUPREME COMMANDER OF THE FLEETS. AND A RUSSIAN.
SO?
SOOOO WHAT COUNTRY IS THE MOST OUTSPOKEN AGAINST THE HEGEMONY?

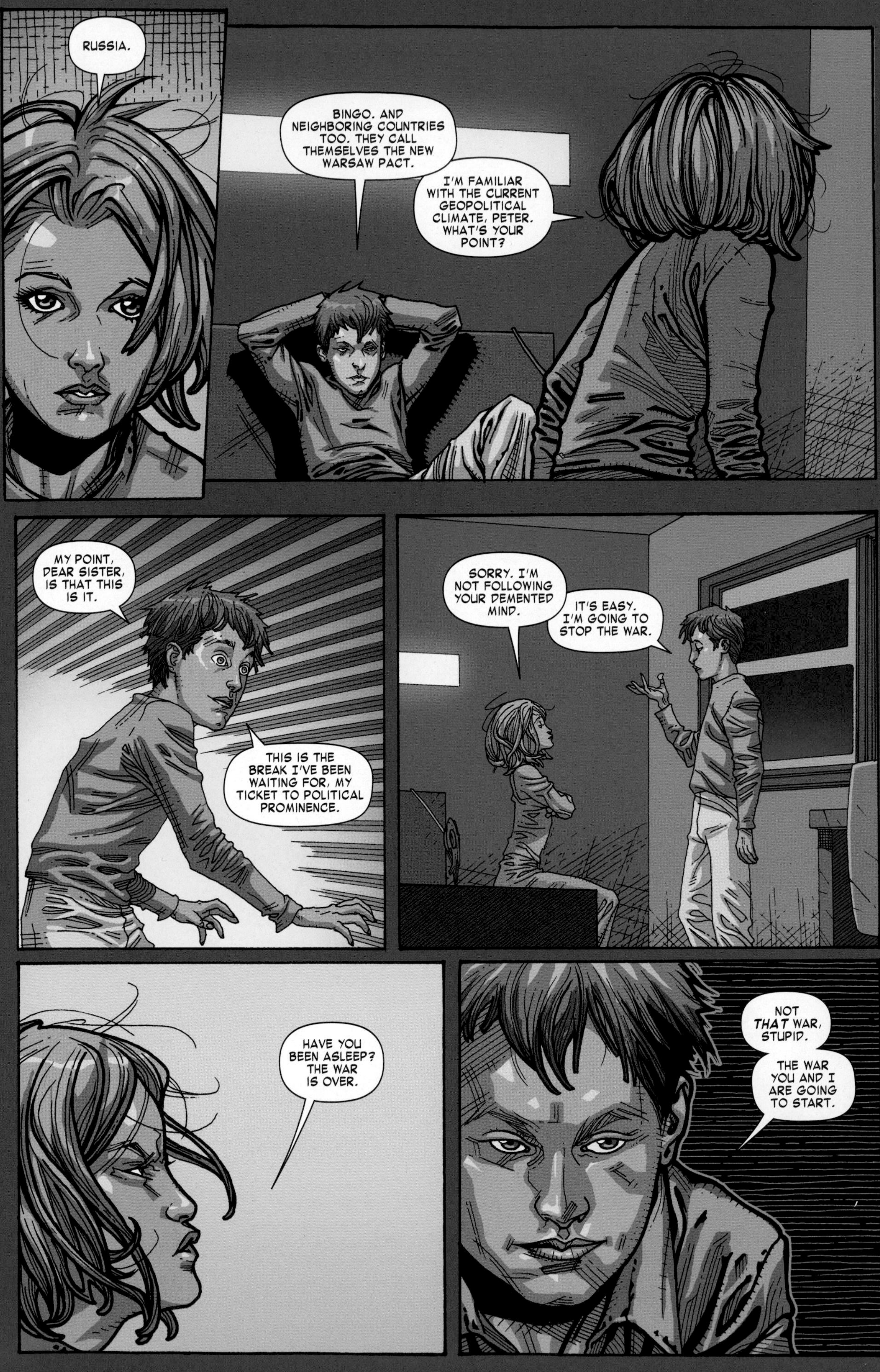
RUSSIA.
BINGO. AND NEIGHBORING COUNTRIES TOO. THEY CALL THEMSELVES THE NEW WARSAW PACT.
I'M FAMILIAR WITH THE CURRENT GEOPOLITICAL CLIMATE, PETER. WHAT'S YOUR POINT?
MY POINT, DEAR SISTER, IS THAT THIS IS IT.
THIS IS THE BREAK I'VE BEEN WAITING FOR, MY TICKET TO POLITICAL PROMINENCE.
SORRY. I'M NOT FOLLOWING YOUR DEMENTED MIND.
IT'S EASY. I'M GOING TO STOP THE WAR.
HAVE YOU BEEN ASLEEP? THE WAR IS OVER.
NOT *THAT* WAR, STUPID.
THE WAR YOU AND I ARE GOING TO START.

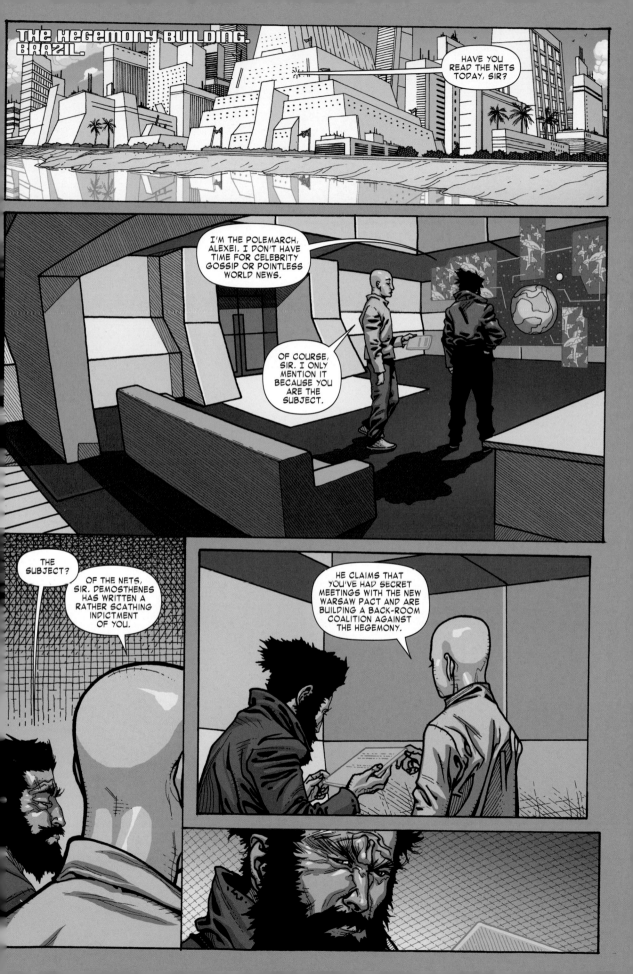

THE HEGEMONY BUILDING. BRAZIL.

HAVE YOU READ THE NETS TODAY, SIR?

I'M THE POLEMARCH, ALEXEI. I DON'T HAVE TIME FOR CELEBRITY GOSSIP OR POINTLESS WORLD NEWS.

OF COURSE, SIR. I ONLY MENTION IT BECAUSE YOU ARE THE SUBJECT.

THE SUBJECT?

OF THE NETS, SIR. DEMOSTHENES HAS WRITTEN A RATHER SCATHING INDICTMENT OF YOU.

HE CLAIMS THAT YOU'VE HAD SECRET MEETINGS WITH THE NEW WARSAW PACT AND ARE BUILDING A BACK-ROOM COALITION AGAINST THE HEGEMONY.

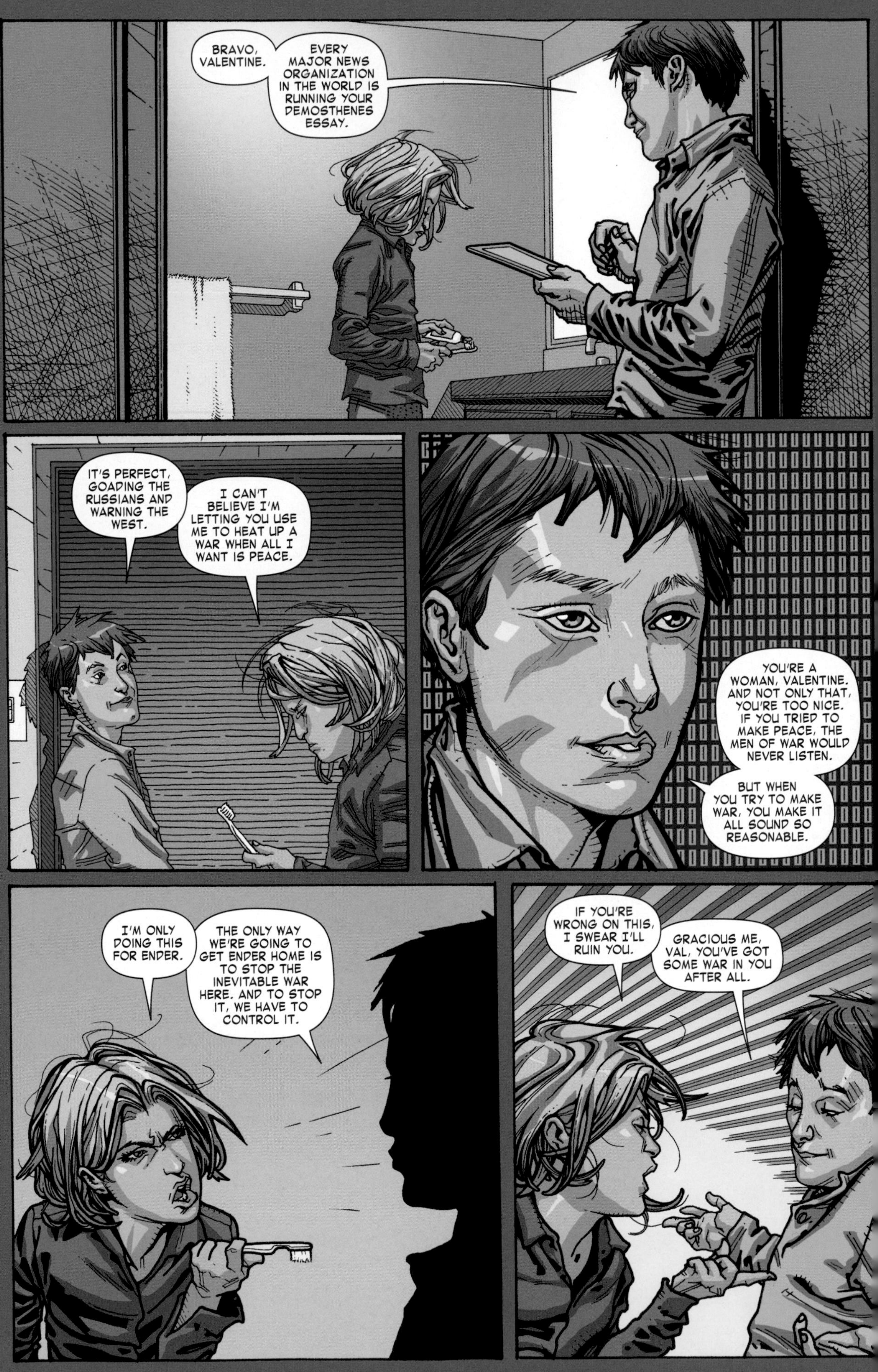
BRAVO, VALENTINE.
EVERY MAJOR NEWS ORGANIZATION IN THE WORLD IS RUNNING YOUR DEMOSTHENES ESSAY.
IT'S PERFECT, GOADING THE RUSSIANS AND WARNING THE WEST.
I CAN'T BELIEVE I'M LETTING YOU USE ME TO HEAT UP A WAR WHEN ALL I WANT IS PEACE.
YOU'RE A WOMAN, VALENTINE. AND NOT ONLY THAT, YOU'RE TOO NICE. IF YOU TRIED TO MAKE PEACE, THE MEN OF WAR WOULD NEVER LISTEN.
BUT WHEN YOU TRY TO MAKE WAR, YOU MAKE IT ALL SOUND SO REASONABLE.
I'M ONLY DOING THIS FOR ENDER.
THE ONLY WAY WE'RE GOING TO GET ENDER HOME IS TO STOP THE INEVITABLE WAR HERE. AND TO STOP IT, WE HAVE TO CONTROL IT.
IF YOU'RE WRONG ON THIS, I SWEAR I'LL RUIN YOU.
GRACIOUS ME, VAL, YOU'VE GOT SOME WAR IN YOU AFTER ALL.

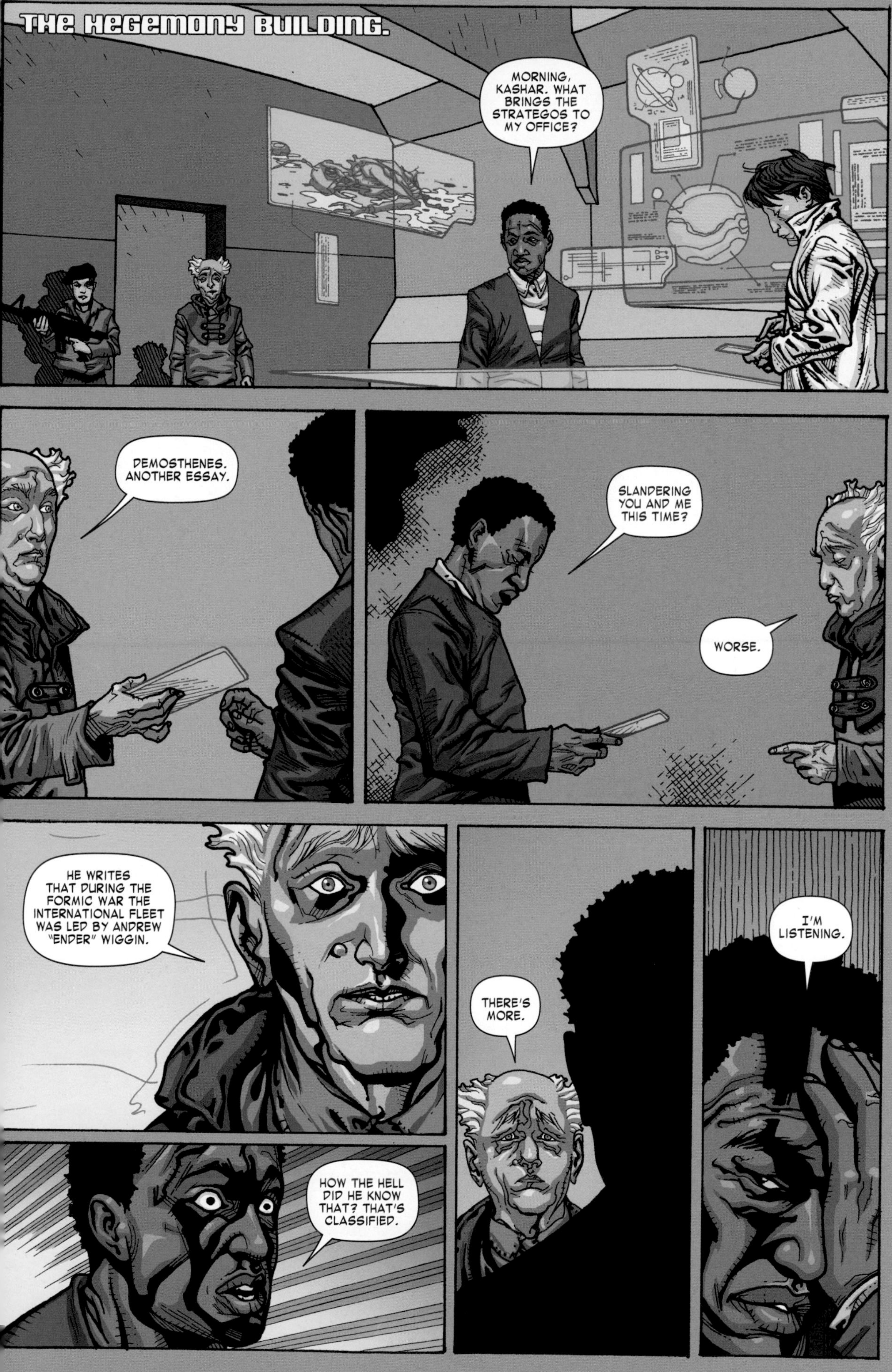
THE HEGEMONY BUILDING.
MORNING, KASHAR. WHAT BRINGS THE STRATEGOS TO MY OFFICE?
DEMOSTHENES. ANOTHER ESSAY.
SLANDERING YOU AND ME THIS TIME?
WORSE.
HE WRITES THAT DURING THE FORMIC WAR THE INTERNATIONAL FLEET WAS LED BY ANDREW "ENDER" WIGGIN.
HOW THE HELL DID HE KNOW THAT? THAT'S CLASSIFIED.
THERE'S MORE.
I'M LISTENING.

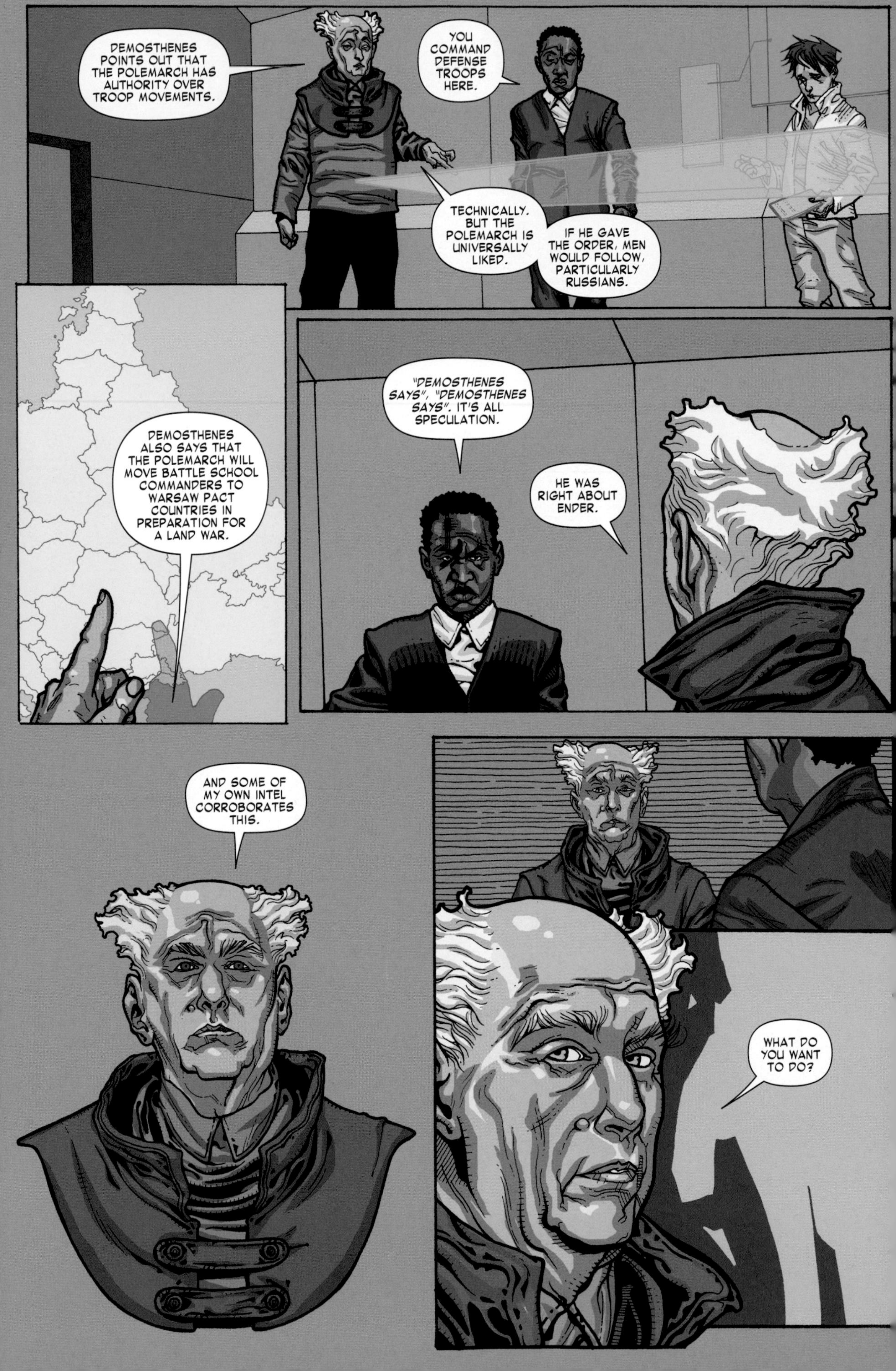
DEMOSTHENES POINTS OUT THAT THE POLEMARCH HAS AUTHORITY OVER TROOP MOVEMENTS.
YOU COMMAND DEFENSE TROOPS HERE.
TECHNICALLY. BUT THE POLEMARCH IS UNIVERSALLY LIKED.
IF HE GAVE THE ORDER, MEN WOULD FOLLOW, PARTICULARLY RUSSIANS.
DEMOSTHENES ALSO SAYS THAT THE POLEMARCH WILL MOVE BATTLE SCHOOL COMMANDERS TO WARSAW PACT COUNTRIES IN PREPARATION FOR A LAND WAR.
"DEMOSTHENES SAYS", "DEMOSTHENES SAYS". IT'S ALL SPECULATION.
HE WAS RIGHT ABOUT ENDER.
AND SOME OF MY OWN INTEL CORROBORATES THIS.
WHAT DO YOU WANT TO DO?

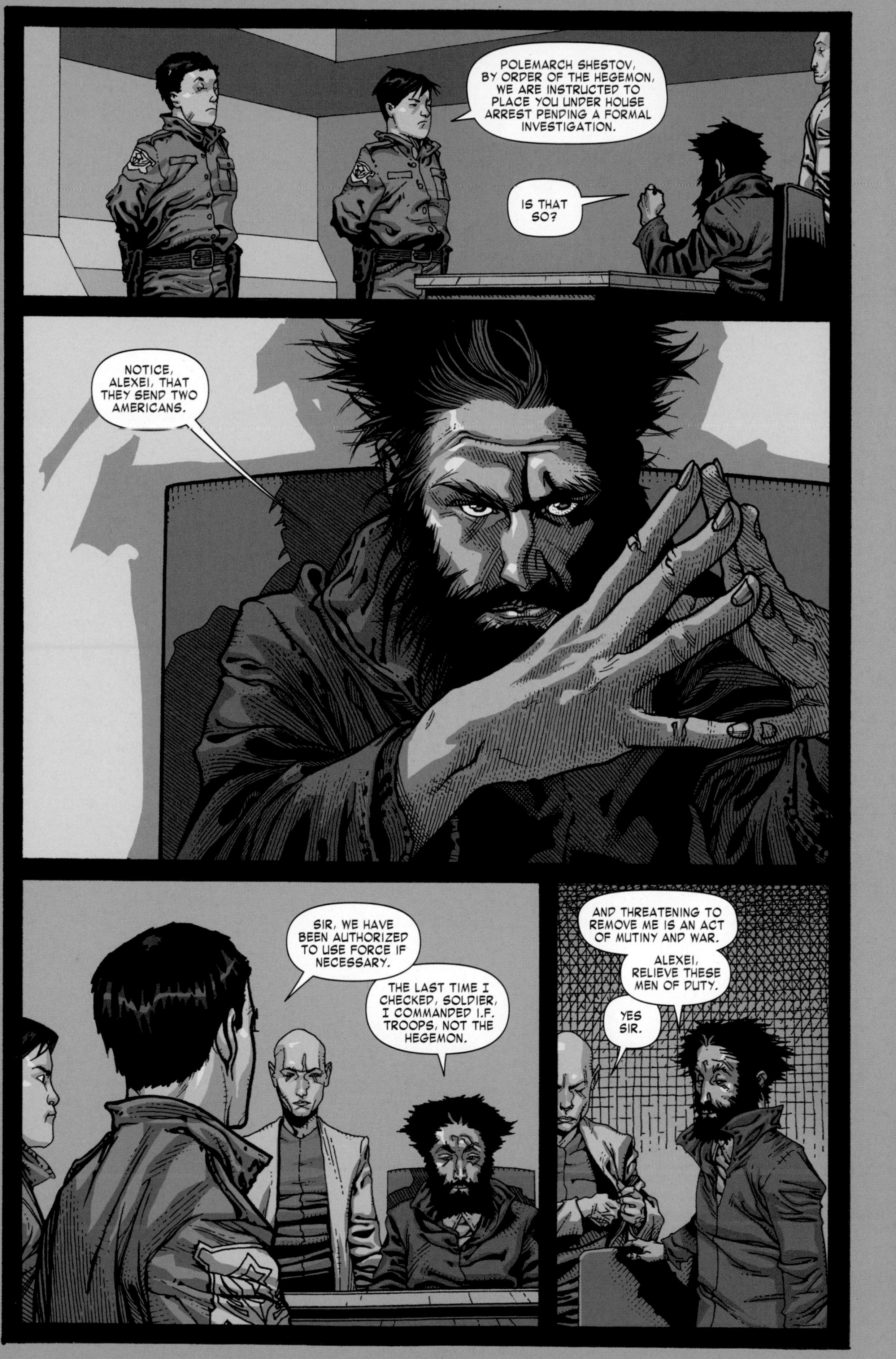
POLEMARCH SHESTOV, BY ORDER OF THE HEGEMON, WE ARE INSTRUCTED TO PLACE YOU UNDER HOUSE ARREST PENDING A FORMAL INVESTIGATION.
IS THAT SO?
NOTICE, ALEXEI, THAT THEY SEND TWO AMERICANS.
SIR, WE HAVE BEEN AUTHORIZED TO USE FORCE IF NECESSARY.
THE LAST TIME I CHECKED, SOLDIER, I COMMANDED I.F. TROOPS, NOT THE HEGEMON.
AND THREATENING TO REMOVE ME IS AN ACT OF MUTINY AND WAR.
ALEXEI, RELIEVE THESE MEN OF DUTY.
YES SIR.

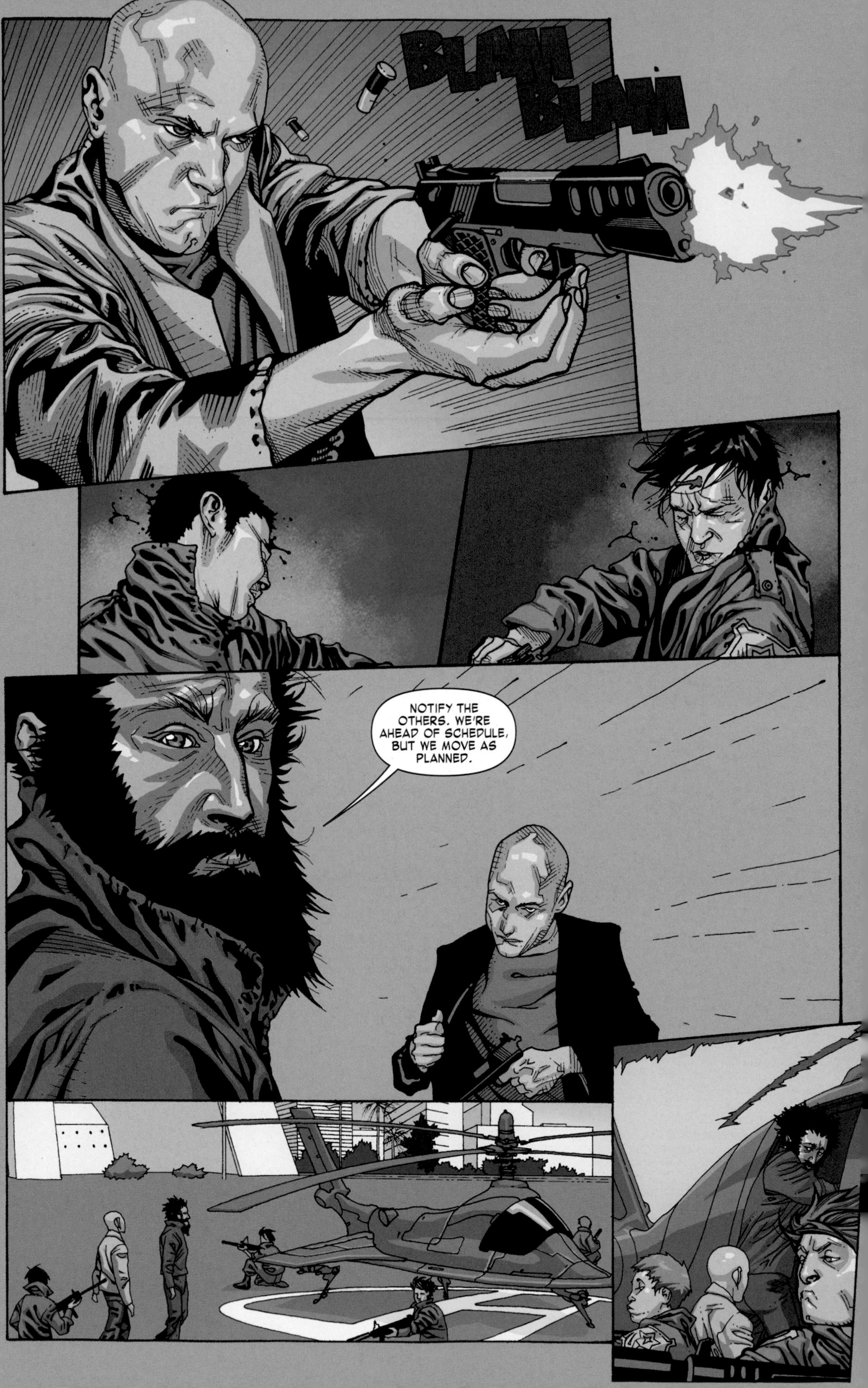
BLAM BLAM
NOTIFY THE OTHERS. WE'RE AHEAD OF SCHEDULE, BUT WE MOVE AS PLANNED.

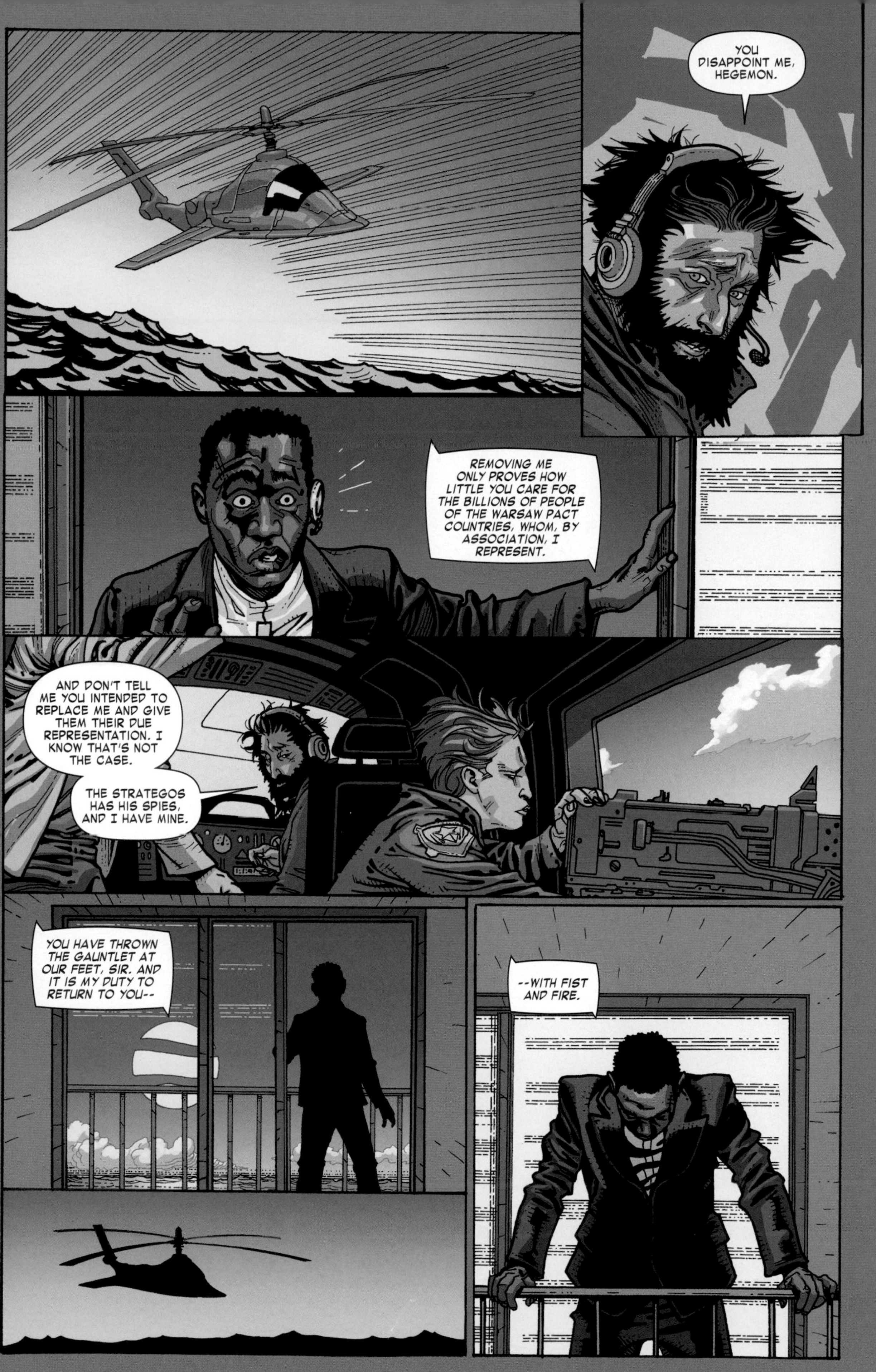
YOU DISAPPOINT ME, HEGEMON.
REMOVING ME ONLY PROVES HOW LITTLE YOU CARE FOR THE BILLIONS OF PEOPLE OF THE WARSAW PACT COUNTRIES, WHOM, BY ASSOCIATION, I REPRESENT.
AND DON'T TELL ME YOU INTENDED TO REPLACE ME AND GIVE THEM THEIR DUE REPRESENTATION. I KNOW THAT'S NOT THE CASE.
THE STRATEGOS HAS HIS SPIES, AND I HAVE MINE.
YOU HAVE THROWN THE GAUNTLET AT OUR FEET, SIR. AND IT IS MY DUTY TO RETURN TO YOU--
--WITH FIST AND FIRE.

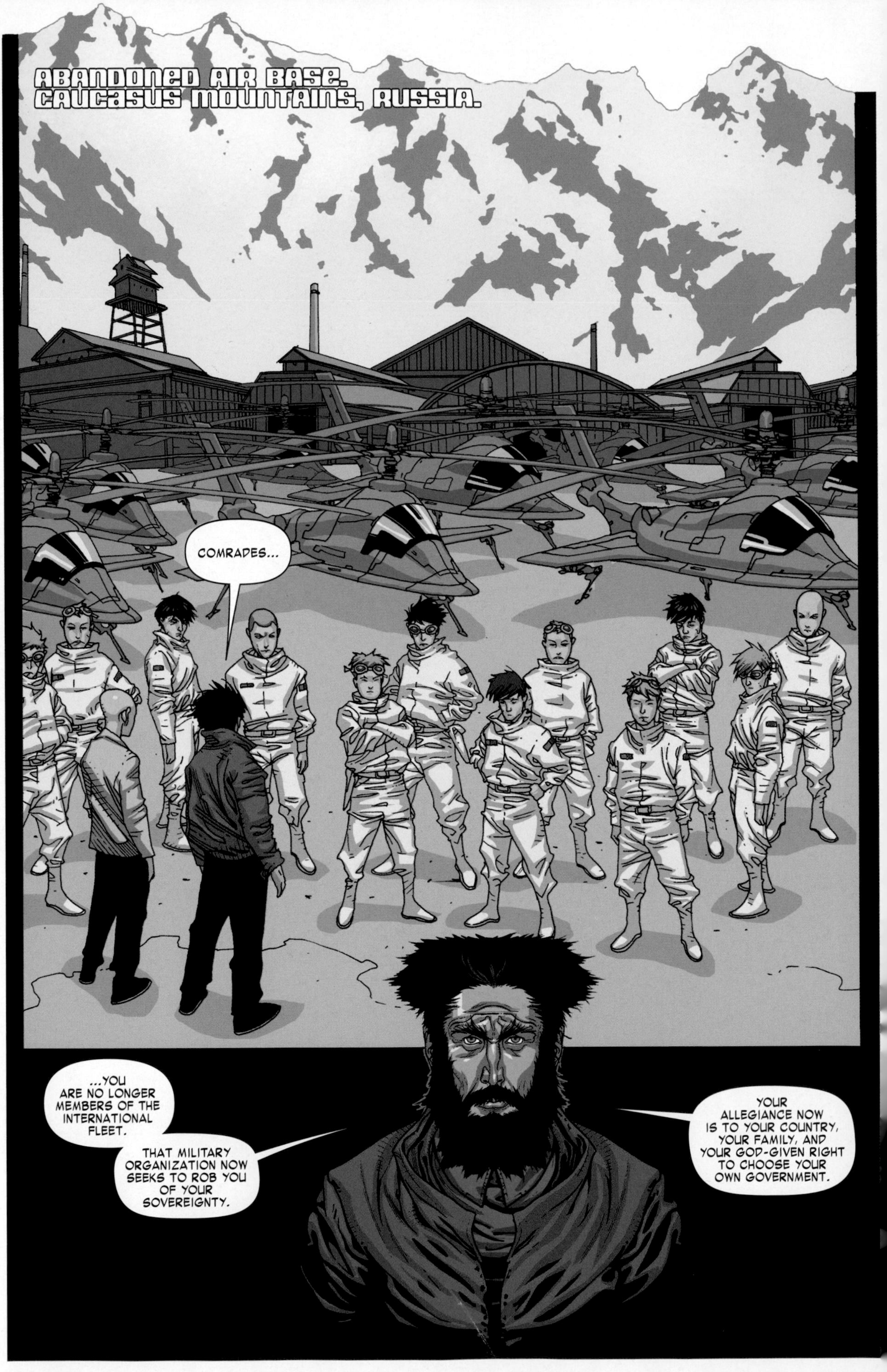
ABANDONED AIR BASE.
CAUCASUS MOUNTAINS, RUSSIA.
COMRADES...
...YOU ARE NO LONGER MEMBERS OF THE INTERNATIONAL FLEET.
THAT MILITARY ORGANIZATION NOW SEEKS TO ROB YOU OF YOUR SOVEREIGNTY.
YOUR ALLEGIANCE NOW IS TO YOUR COUNTRY, YOUR FAMILY, AND YOUR GOD-GIVEN RIGHT TO CHOOSE YOUR OWN GOVERNMENT.

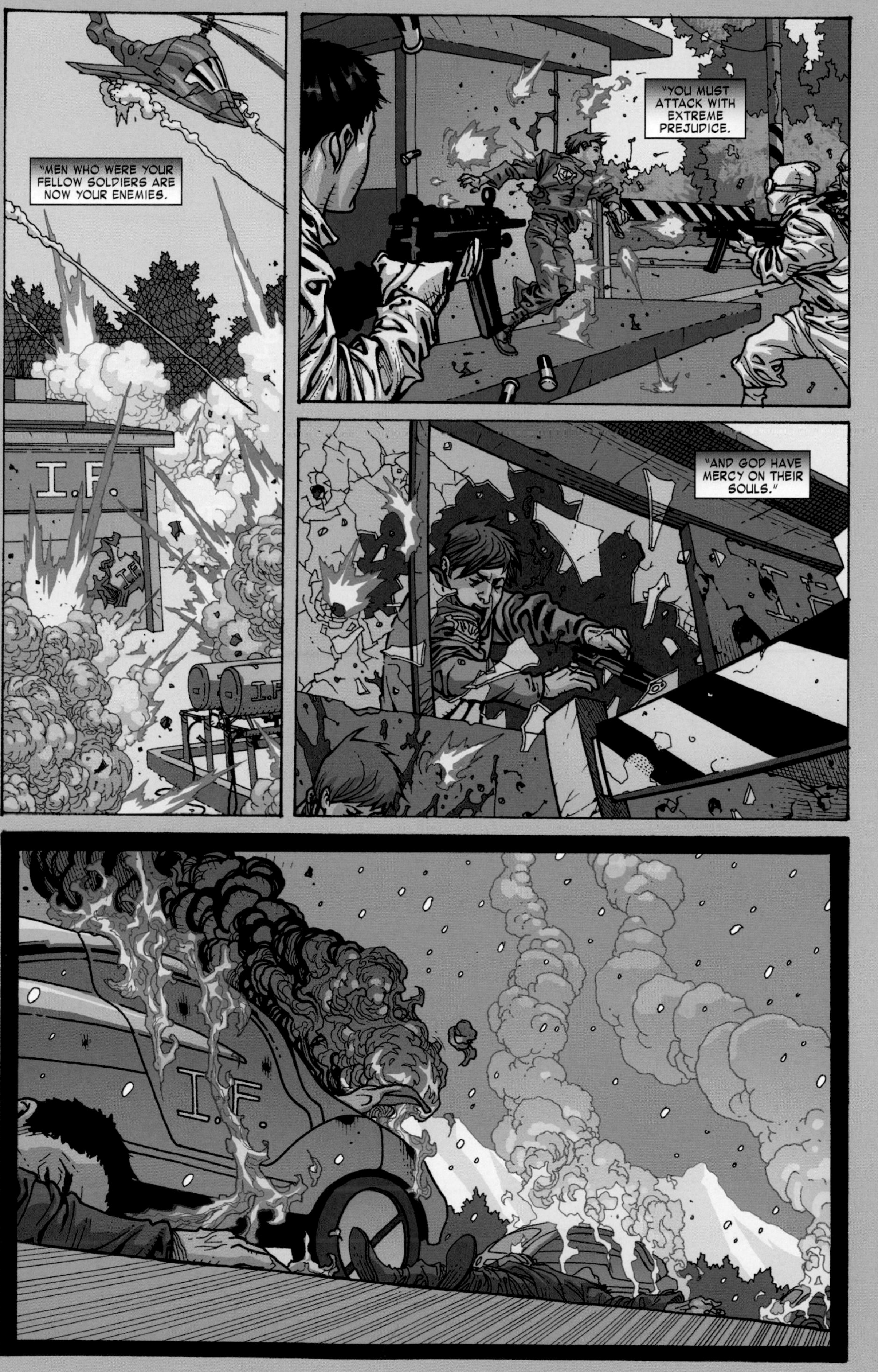
"MEN WHO WERE YOUR FELLOW SOLDIERS ARE NOW YOUR ENEMIES.
"YOU MUST ATTACK WITH EXTREME PREJUDICE.
"AND GOD HAVE MERCY ON THEIR SOULS."
I.F.
I.F.
I.F

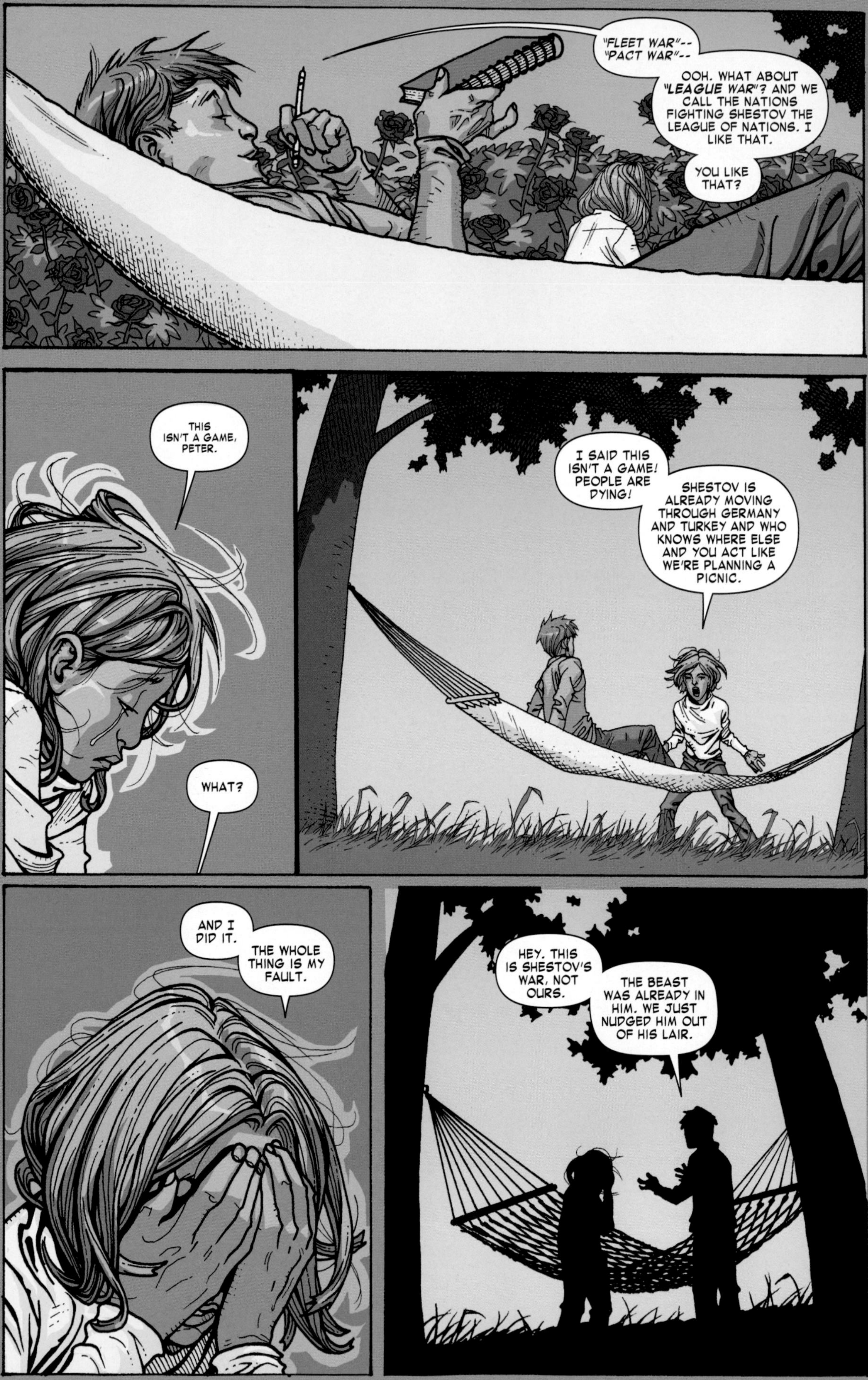
"FLEET WAR"-- "PACT WAR"--
OOH. WHAT ABOUT "LEAGUE WAR"? AND WE CALL THE NATIONS FIGHTING SHESTOV THE LEAGUE OF NATIONS. I LIKE THAT.
YOU LIKE THAT?
THIS ISN'T A GAME, PETER.
WHAT?
I SAID THIS ISN'T A GAME! PEOPLE ARE DYING!
SHESTOV IS ALREADY MOVING THROUGH GERMANY AND TURKEY AND WHO KNOWS WHERE ELSE AND YOU ACT LIKE WE'RE PLANNING A PICNIC.
AND I DID IT.
THE WHOLE THING IS MY FAULT.
HEY. THIS IS SHESTOV'S WAR, NOT OURS.
THE BEAST WAS ALREADY IN HIM. WE JUST NUDGED HIM OUT OF HIS LAIR.

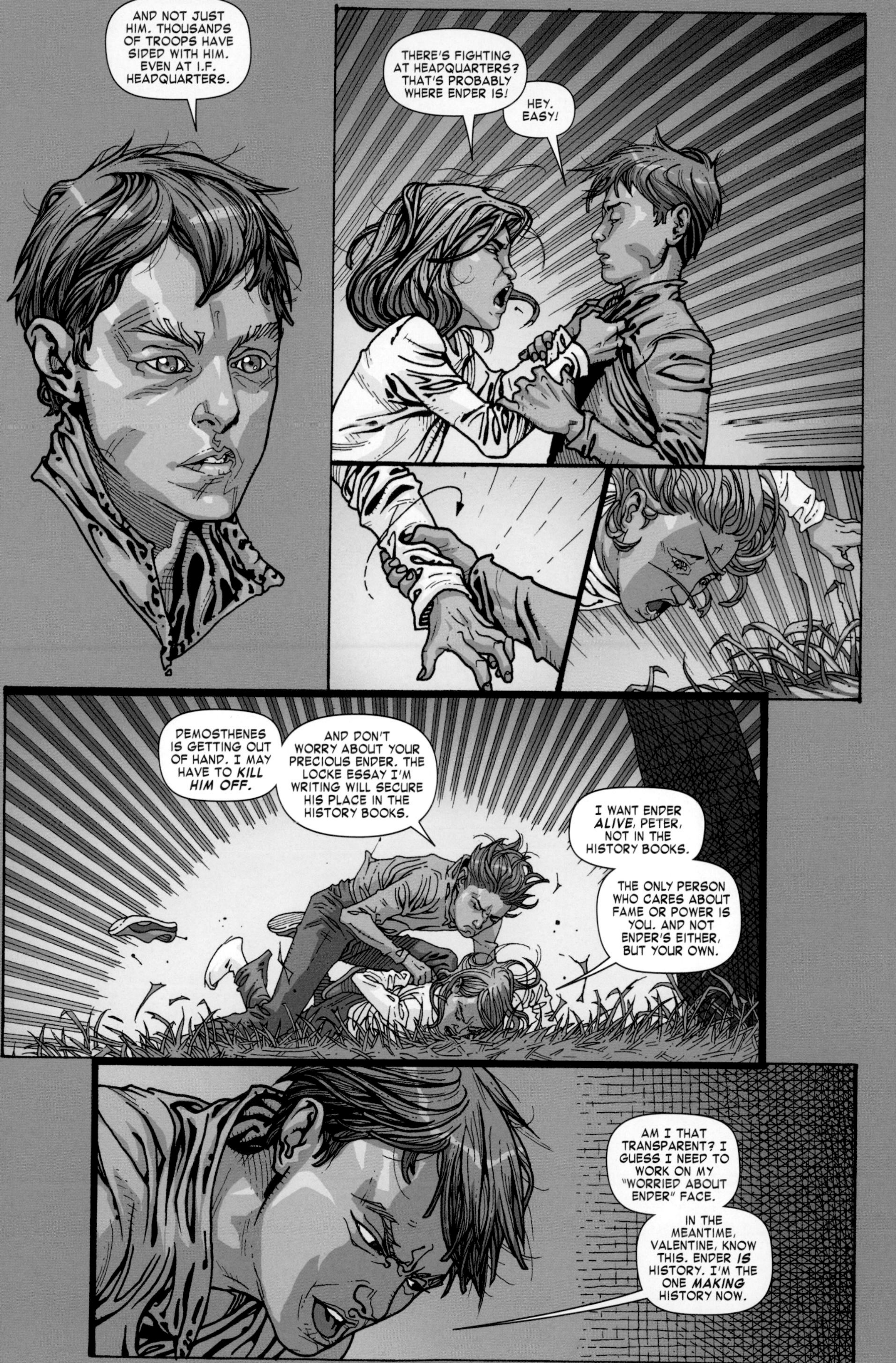
AND NOT JUST HIM. THOUSANDS OF TROOPS HAVE SIDED WITH HIM. EVEN AT I.F. HEADQUARTERS.
THERE'S FIGHTING AT HEADQUARTERS? THAT'S PROBABLY WHERE ENDER IS!
HEY. EASY!
DEMOSTHENES IS GETTING OUT OF HAND. I MAY HAVE TO KILL HIM OFF.
AND DON'T WORRY ABOUT YOUR PRECIOUS ENDER. THE LOCKE ESSAY I'M WRITING WILL SECURE HIS PLACE IN THE HISTORY BOOKS.
I WANT ENDER ALIVE, PETER, NOT IN THE HISTORY BOOKS.
THE ONLY PERSON WHO CARES ABOUT FAME OR POWER IS YOU. AND NOT ENDER'S EITHER, BUT YOUR OWN.
AM I THAT TRANSPARENT? I GUESS I NEED TO WORK ON MY "WORRIED ABOUT ENDER" FACE.
IN THE MEANTIME, VALENTINE, KNOW THIS. ENDER IS HISTORY. I'M THE ONE MAKING HISTORY NOW.

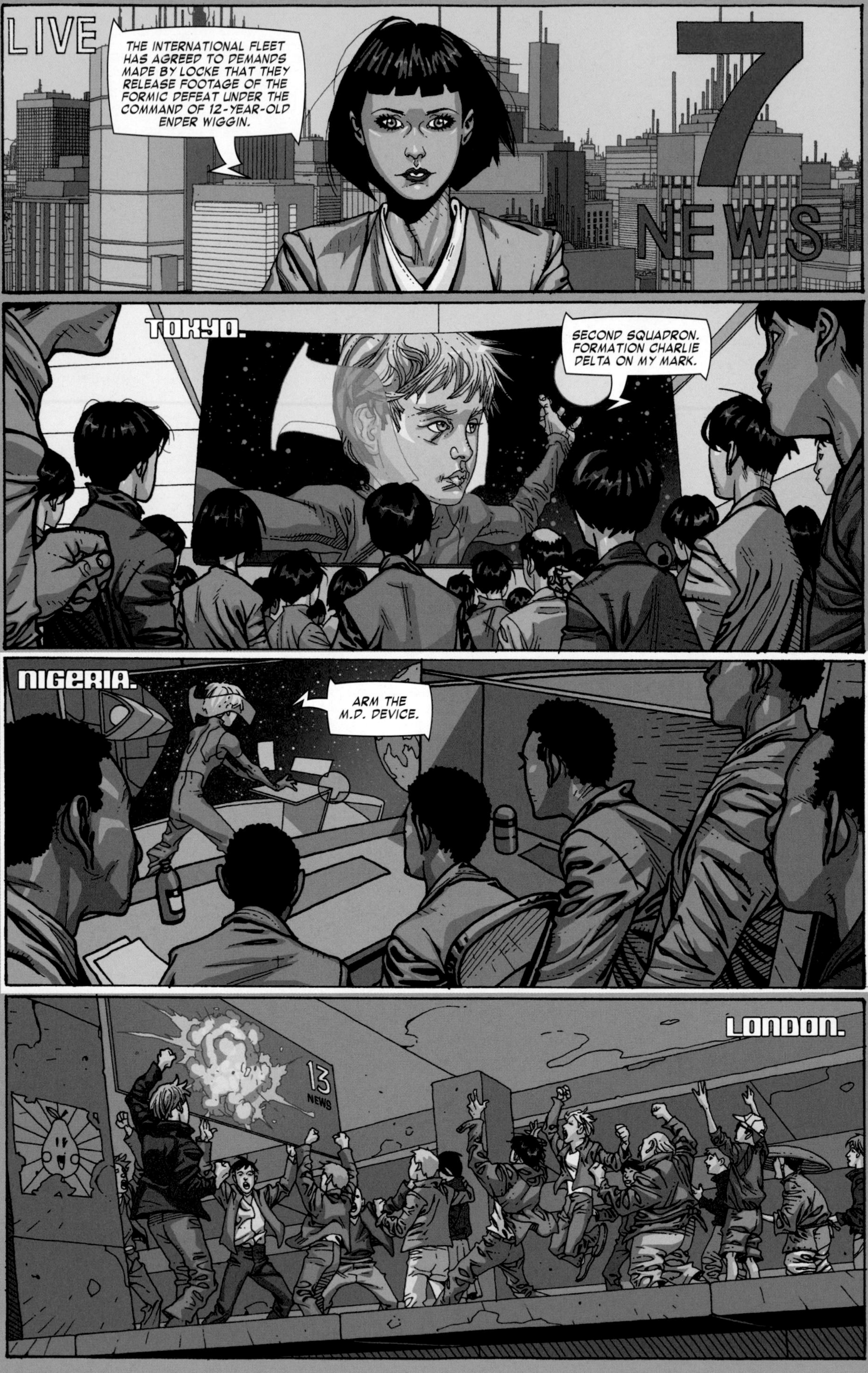
LIVE
THE INTERNATIONAL FLEET HAS AGREED TO DEMANDS MADE BY LOCKE THAT THEY RELEASE FOOTAGE OF THE FORMIC DEFEAT UNDER THE COMMAND OF 12-YEAR-OLD ENDER WIGGIN.
7
NEWS
TOKYO.
SECOND SQUADRON. FORMATION CHARLIE DELTA ON MY MARK.
NIGERIA.
ARM THE M.D. DEVICE.
LONDON.
13
NEWS

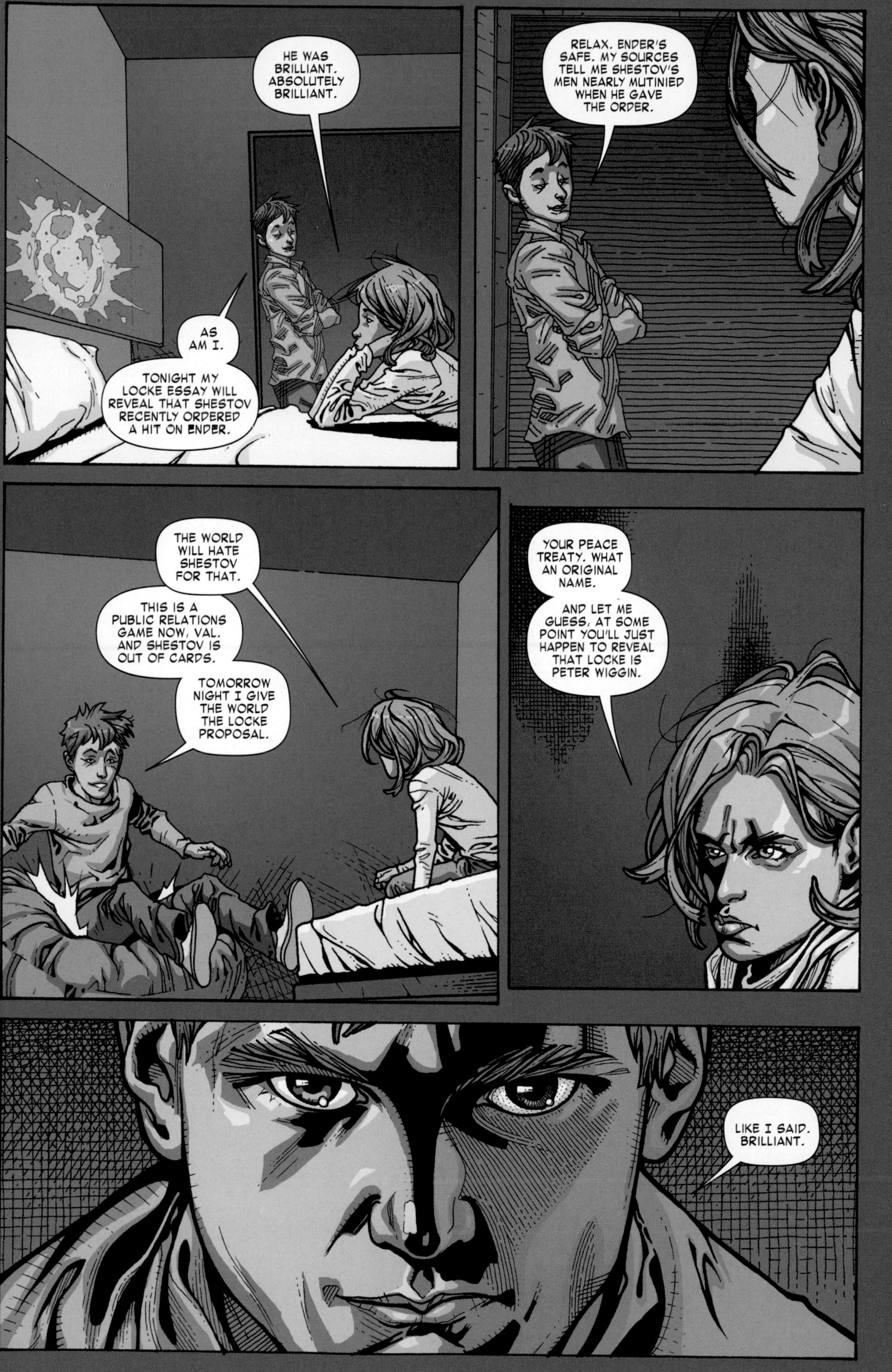
HE WAS BRILLIANT. ABSOLUTELY BRILLIANT.
AS AM I.
TONIGHT MY LOCKE ESSAY WILL REVEAL THAT SHESTOV RECENTLY ORDERED A HIT ON ENDER.
RELAX. ENDER'S SAFE. MY SOURCES TELL ME SHESTOV'S MEN NEARLY MUTINIED WHEN HE GAVE THE ORDER.
THE WORLD WILL HATE SHESTOV FOR THAT.
THIS IS A PUBLIC RELATIONS GAME NOW, VAL. AND SHESTOV IS OUT OF CARDS.
TOMORROW NIGHT I GIVE THE WORLD THE LOCKE PROPOSAL.
YOUR PEACE TREATY. WHAT AN ORIGINAL NAME.
AND LET ME GUESS, AT SOME POINT YOU'LL JUST HAPPEN TO REVEAL THAT LOCKE IS PETER WIGGIN.
LIKE I SAID. BRILLIANT.

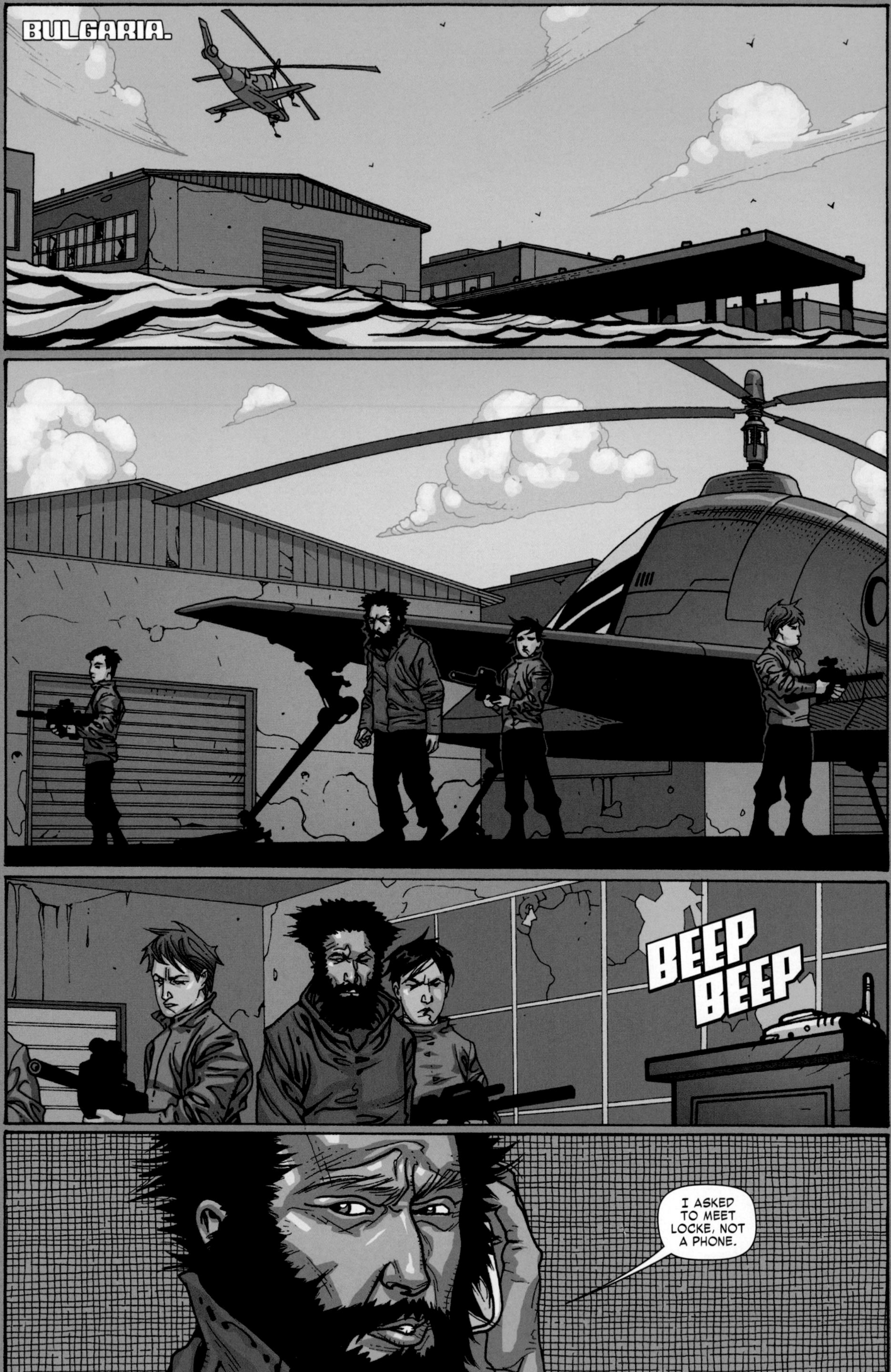
BULGARIA.
BEEP BEEP
I ASKED TO MEET LOCKE, NOT A PHONE.

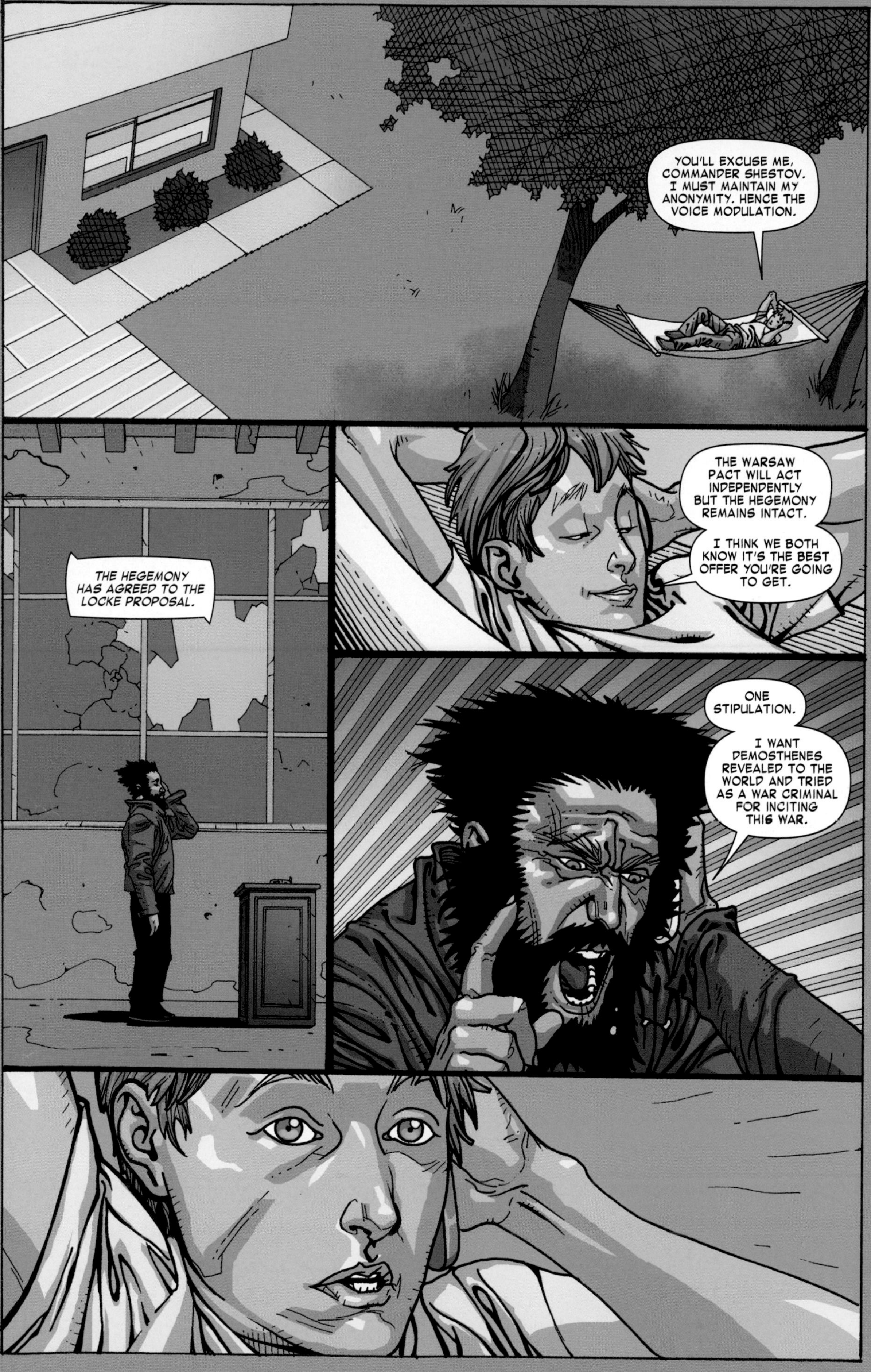
YOU'LL EXCUSE ME, COMMANDER SHESTOV. I MUST MAINTAIN MY ANONYMITY. HENCE THE VOICE MODULATION.
THE HEGEMONY HAS AGREED TO THE LOCKE PROPOSAL.
THE WARSAW PACT WILL ACT INDEPENDENTLY BUT THE HEGEMONY REMAINS INTACT.
I THINK WE BOTH KNOW IT'S THE BEST OFFER YOU'RE GOING TO GET.
ONE STIPULATION.
I WANT DEMOSTHENES REVEALED TO THE WORLD AND TRIED AS A WAR CRIMINAL FOR INCITING THIS WAR.

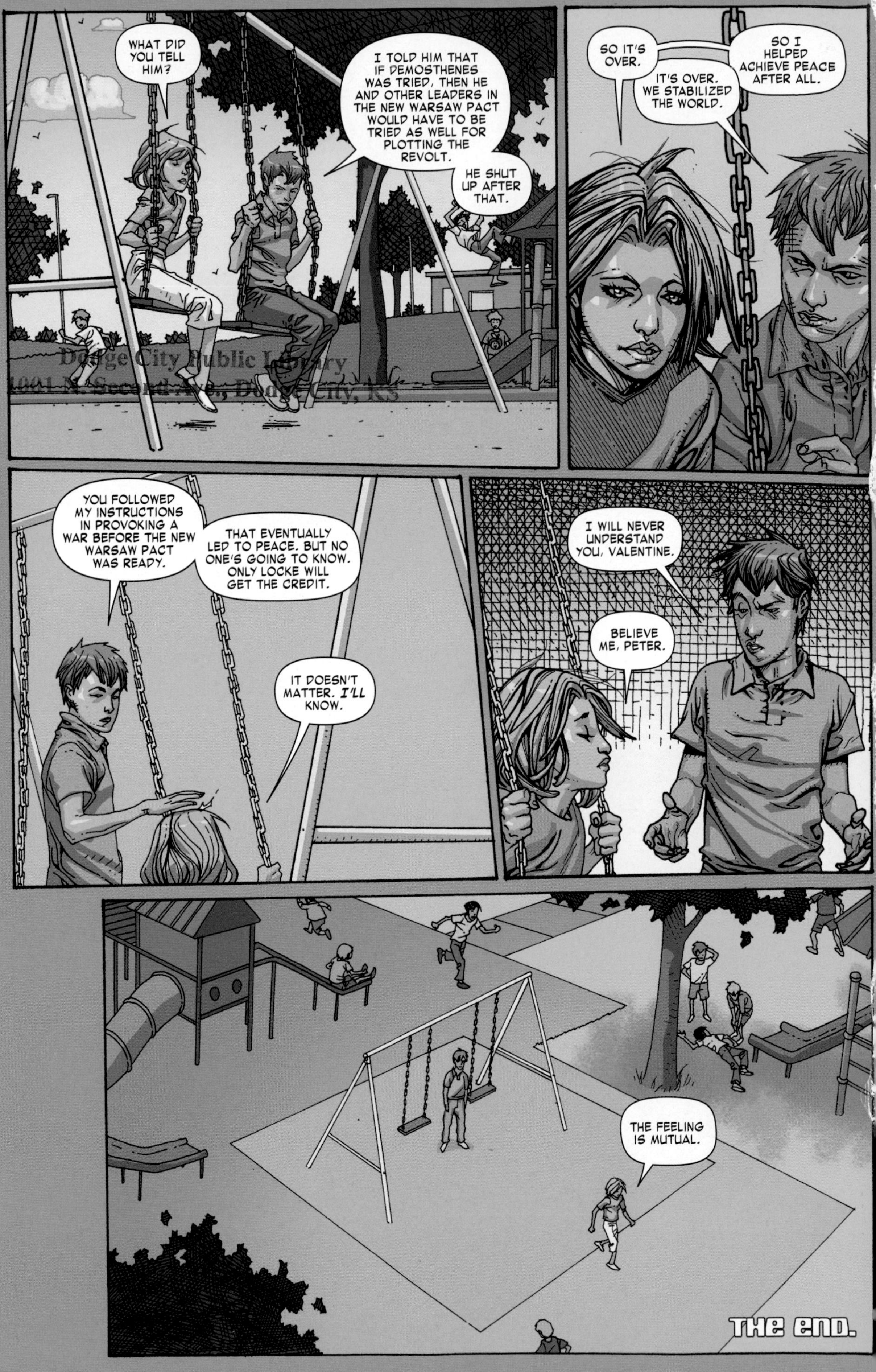
WHAT DID YOU TELL HIM?
I TOLD HIM THAT IF DEMOSTHENES WAS TRIED, THEN HE AND OTHER LEADERS IN THE NEW WARSAW PACT WOULD HAVE TO BE TRIED AS WELL FOR PLOTTING THE REVOLT.
HE SHUT UP AFTER THAT.
SO IT'S OVER.
SO I HELPED ACHIEVE PEACE AFTER ALL.
IT'S OVER. WE STABILIZED THE WORLD.
YOU FOLLOWED MY INSTRUCTIONS IN PROVOKING A WAR BEFORE THE NEW WARSAW PACT WAS READY.
THAT EVENTUALLY LED TO PEACE. BUT NO ONE'S GOING TO KNOW. ONLY LOCKE WILL GET THE CREDIT.
IT DOESN'T MATTER. *I'LL* KNOW.
I WILL NEVER UNDERSTAND YOU, VALENTINE.
BELIEVE ME, PETER.
THE FEELING IS MUTUAL.
THE END.